REFLECTIONS OF AN HONEST SKEPTIC

An Unorthodox Approach to Genesis

MICHAEL MALINA

DEVORA PUBLISHING
NEW YORK◆JERUSALEM◆LONDON

Reflections of an Honest Skeptic:
An Unorthodox Approach to Genesis
Published by Devora Publishing Company
Text Copyright © 2011 by Michael Malina

COVER DESIGN: Moshe Meyron
TYPESETTING: Koren Publishing Services
EDITORIAL AND PRODUCTION DIRECTOR: Daniella Barak
EDITOR: Meshulam Gotlieb

Soft Cover ISBN: 978-1-936068-06-7

First Edition. Printed in Israel.

Distributed by:
Urim Publications
POB 52287
Jerusalem 91521, Israel
Tel: 02.679.7633
Fax: 02.679.7634
urim_pub@netvision.net.il

Lambda Publishers, Inc.
527 Empire Blvd.
Brooklyn, NY 11225, USA
Tel: 718.972.5449
Fax: 718.972.6307
mh@ejudaica.com
www.UrimPublications.com

To Anita,
my wife, partner, and best friend

There lives more faith in honest doubt
Believe me, than in half the creeds

Alfred Lord Tennyson

CONTENTS

ACKNOWLEDGMENTS

To list all those who should be acknowledged for anything of value in this book would require more words than space allows. But I must mention a few of them. My grandfathers, Morris Malina and Jacob Kutlowitz, instilled in me a love for Judaism and Jewish learning that is the true genesis of everything between these covers. My parents, William and Jean Malina, continued that process and provided me and my brother with a genuinely Jewish home in which the tradition could flourish. My brother Robert, who at this stage of our lives has become more observant than I, remains a constant example of how one can be a good Jew, a good family man, and a good person all wrapped in one.

I owe an enormous debt to my teachers. Rabbi Samuel J. Chill started my Jewish education. My colleagues at law, Julius Berman and Myron Kirschbaum, taught me more than anyone could expect to learn in the course of informal discussions over the years. My friends, Joshua Greenberg and Milton Schubin (who regretfully died before this book was completed), have encouraged my Jewish study and consistently provided me with perspectives very different than those available from others. Rabbi Reuven Grodner, a dear and cherished friend, taught me the important lesson that being observant does not necessarily make one religious and that being religious means being God-aware – a state of being which it is hoped observance can help foster. Rabbi Lewis Warshauer, with whom I have had the privilege to study over the past few years, brings a breadth of knowledge of all human affairs to bear on his equally deep understanding of the Jewish tradition. He is able to impart these insights in a pleasant yet stimulating manner. Would that the Jewish community had more teachers like him. My brother-in-law, Michael Bohnen, is one of the true leaders of modern American Jewry and a scholar of the first rank. His insights and perspectives inform much of what is in this book. I have been particularly fortunate in the past few years to be able to learn from one of our generation's giants of Jewish theology, Rabbi Neil Gillman. His friendship and insight have enabled me to begin to understand some of the difficult issues that have troubled me throughout my lifelong effort to grasp what it means to be Jewish. I am eternally in his debt. I also have to thank my editor, Meshulam Gotlieb, who has added immeasurably to whatever quality this book may have. He is a Jewish scholar of remarkable erudition and has been a joy to work with. Special thanks are also due to Miriam Heller Lidji. While I am deeply indebted to these wonderful people for whatever value these thoughts may have, any errors are mine and mine alone.

Finally, and most importantly, I have to thank my family. My children, Rachel, Stuart, and Joel, have been the joys of my life, as are my daughters-in-law, Nancy Malina and Marty Malina, and my six wonderful grandchildren, Olivia, William, Sara, Zev, Ben, and Hallie. My beloved wife Anita, to whom this book is dedicated, has been a constant source of encouragement in this endeavor. She has tolerated more time at the computer keyboard than any human being should be expected to endure. Her constant friendship and love are what has kept me going. I fear I do not deserve her.

PREFACE

Like many American Jews of my generation, I was raised with both a deep commitment to the Jewish tradition and a paradoxical propensity for skepticism about its premises. As a result, while this book contains my reflections on the Written Torah, I am still highly skeptical about the Jewish tradition's fundamental axiom that the Pentateuch's actual words are of divine origin. On the one hand, I am certain that the Written Torah is the ultimate source of all things genuinely Jewish; but, on the other hand, I find it difficult to accept the traditional postulate that God dictated it to Moses verbatim and that the entire body of the Oral Torah accompanying it is also of divine origin. Since my paradoxical approach to reflecting upon the Torah stems from my upbringing, it is appropriate to set forth my personal history in this preface; for tellingly it is the history of a life lived in proximity to – though not entirely in accord with – the Orthodox Judaism I experienced and was taught in my childhood.

As a child, I had the good fortune to attend a unique Talmud Torah, which was operated by an Orthodox synagogue, the Kingsway Jewish Center, in Brooklyn, New York. Far more rigorous than a typical American Hebrew school of the 1940s (and certainly more so than the afternoon or Sunday schools of today), this school provided classes Monday through Thursday afternoon, required us to attend Shabbat morning services, and included an additional three-hour class on Sunday morning. During the years before my bar mitzvah I was exposed to Jewish religious customs and ceremonies, the Hebrew language, the prayer book (in its unexpurgated Orthodox version), and the text of the *Chumash* (Pentateuch), together with Rashi's commentary. After my bar mitzvah, the extraordinary zeal for Jewish learning of my first teacher, Rabbi Samuel J. Chill, enabled me to continue my Jewish studies until I graduated from high school. It was at the Kingsway Jewish Center Talmud Torah that I acquired the foundation for my lifelong quest to understand my Jewish heritage and the essence of Judaism.

While my family attended an Orthodox synagogue – *mechitzah* (that is, a physical partition between men and women) and all – mine was not in any genuine sense an observant Orthodox family. All four of my immigrant grandparents were traditionally observant, but my parents (both American born), while highly respectful of a tradition they dearly cherished, were not. Shabbat was not observed to traditional standards, even though we attended synagogue weekly. The house was kosher, but outside the house we ate "kosher style" (having no compunction about eating meat from kosher animals that were not ritually slaughtered). The holidays were celebrated to varying degrees. For the eight days of Pesach, our home was as kosher as an Orthodox rabbi's, and both Rosh Hashanah and Yom Kippur were strictly observed. On the other hand, my father never built a sukkah, nor did we fast on Tisha b'Av. Nonetheless, in contrast to most other Jews in Brooklyn of the 1940s and '50s, we were relatively observant.

At college, I cannot say that I spent much time worrying about things Jewish. Jewish studies as a formal discipline in secular universities had not yet been invented, and there was no Jewish content at all in the course program I undertook during four years at Harvard College and another three at Harvard Law School.[1] Only when I returned to New York to practice law was my intellectual interest in the tradition piqued again. One of my "classmates" at the law firm I joined in 1960 (and remained with for forty years until my retirement) was (and is today) a remarkable attorney, Julius Berman. Julie also happened to be an Orthodox rabbi and a prized pupil of the reigning Modern Orthodox authority of the day, Rabbi Joseph B. Soloveitchik. It was Julie Berman who reawakened my interest in the intellectual side of Judaism. In my discussions with him – and in the course of weekly classes in Mishnah that he arranged for a number of the Jewish lawyers at the firm – I began to learn in depth about *Halacha* (Jewish law) and the Jewish way from a highly educated, modern American who also happened to be a *talmid chacham* (Torah scholar). That started a course of intensive reading in the field which has continued to this day – reading which included, among many others, the works of Rabbi Soloveitchik; the books of Rabbi Neil Gilman, my rebbe and a major Conservative theologian; the literary oeuvre of Rabbi Mordechai Kaplan, creator of Reconstructionist Judaism; the works of Rabbi Abraham Joshua Heschel, the most prominent Conservative Jewish philosopher and theologian of the 1950s and '60s; and, more recently, the somewhat eclectic but always interesting writings of David Weiss Halivni, a leading contemporary Talmudist.

While I consider myself a religious (that is, a God-aware) person, I have never been able to "convert", if you will, to traditional Orthodoxy.[2] To reiterate and expand upon what I stated

1. One of my regrets is that I did not take the opportunity to study with Professor Harry Austryn Wolfson, who was at Harvard when I was there.
2. The word "convert" with its emphasis on belief over intellect is especially appropriate. In reading James Kugel's recent books *How to Read the Bible* (Free Press, 2007) and *The Bible as It Was* (Harvard UP, 1997), I realized that Kugel maintains a belief in the divine inspiration of the text and practices Orthodox Judaism while noting all of the scholarly reasons why it is hard to do so intellectually. In all honesty, I

above, I do not believe in the divine origin of every word of the Torah text (even though I am persuaded that in some sense it was divinely inspired); nor do I believe that each and every one of the *mitzvot* (commandments) has divine sanction (although I observe many of them and, indeed, feel commanded to do so). Within a traditional context, this lack of belief has dire consequences. The final chapter of the Babylonian Talmud's Tractate *Sanhedrin* (known as *Perek Chelek*) states categorically that all Israel has a portion in the World to Come – a very consoling notion. But it goes on to condition that statement with the warning that there are some Jews who forfeit their right to the afterlife – including those who do not believe that every one of the six hundred and thirteen mitzvot traditionally found in the Written Torah has a divine origin. I, unhappily, like many of my fellow American Jews, fall into this category.

Within a modern American context, however, this position has one happy consequence; it enables me to ask the hard questions that need to be asked about our tradition. As I reflect in this book upon the Written Torah, in general, and the book of *Bereshit*, in particular, I shall raise difficult questions about the Bible and our tradition. Sometimes I find satisfactory answers and sometimes I am left with my questions unanswered. As always, the wisdom achieved through questioning is the most important part of the journey. I hope you enjoy these reflections of an honest skeptic.

cannot do the same. Apparently, there is a difference between scholarship's truth and faith's truth.

BERESHIT

First Principles: God, Torah, and Israel

The Torah begins with God – more particularly with God's creation of the cosmos: "In the beginning, God created heaven and earth" (1:1).[1] While that may be an obvious place for Judaism's core text to begin, the fact that the Torah commences by emphasizing God's role is significant because it places the deity firmly at the center of the Torah's narrative and the Jewish experience. The Torah, as its story unfolds, has two foci: God and His people, Israel. These two concepts are the pillars upon which Judaism stands, and I categorically reject modern attempts to create "ethnic", "secular", or "humanistic" versions of Judaism because, by definition, Judaism is about Jews' relationship with God.[2]

---

1. This is the traditional translation into English of the King James Bible. More recent – and I believe more accurate – translations read the text as "in the beginning of God's creation". All other biblical translations in this book are taken from the *Tanakh: A New Translation of The Holy Scriptures According to the Traditional Hebrew Text* (Philadelphia/Jerusalem: The Jewish Publication Society, 1985). This version translates the first verse as "when God began to create heaven and earth".

2. While sociologists may, from their perspective, categorize certain approaches to Judaism using these terms, I assert that without God in the center, no ideology or world outlook can legitimately claim to represent the Jewish religion or, indeed, the Jewish idea.

While I do not claim to be a theologian – and this is certainly not a theological treatise – I think it necessary at the outset to stress that the deity referred to throughout the Torah is a personality, not merely a force of or in nature. The God of the Torah is aware of what happens in the world of men and women and He influences its affairs;[3] indeed, a brief glance at the Torah might lead one to conclude that everything that happens in our world is pursuant to a divine plan. Whether God as described by the Torah transcends the world – existing outside of time and space, utterly "other" to us – or whether He is immanent, functioning in the sublunary world and apprehensible to humanity,[4] the Torah clearly teaches that He is shockingly real, not just some abstract metaphysical or naturalistic concept, and that his relationship with humanity is intensely personal.

In Judaism the Torah is the core text, and everything we know about God is ultimately derived from it. It follows, of course, that the modern predilection of many religious thinkers to critically question the Torah's authenticity (or, more precisely, its veracity) calls into question the very authority of our tradition. I was taught from childhood that the Written Torah (that is, the five books of Moses) contains God's very words that were revealed to Moses who wrote them down verbatim. Modern biblical scholarship disputes this premise, pointing to substantial evidence that the five books derive from numerous, separate sources which were gathered together centuries after Moses' death[5] by a "redactor".[6]

3. I use the pronoun "He" to refer to God solely as a linguistic convenience – to avoid either "It" (which lacks personhood) or "He/She" (which is awkward in the extreme). I certainly understand that God has no gender, and the reader should not take my use of the masculine personal pronoun to suggest otherwise.
4. There are, as we shall see, elements of both philosophical positions in the picture of God drawn by the biblical text.
5. This assumes that Moses in fact existed, which some scholars seriously question.
6. I am taken with Franz Rosenzweig's idea that the "R" source posited by the supporters of the so-called documentary hypothesis should stand, not for "redactor", but rather for *Rabbeinu* (our rabbi or our teacher), suggesting that however the text was put together historically, it derives in its entirety from the Jewish tradition and, ultimately, from God – a point of view that is also espoused by Louis Jacobs

I find the documentary hypothesis – that the Pentateuch is the product of one or more people editing a number of separate texts into a single whole– persuasive;[7] however, I also recognize that the very foundation of Judaism stands (and, I believe, depends) upon the notion that the biblical text we have was in some manner divinely revealed or, at the very least, is a seminal work embodying the Jewish people's understanding of its special relationship with God. In other words, even if we view the Written Torah as the product of early Jewish thinkers who pondered the relationship between God and humanity, in general, and between God and Israel, in particular, the starting point of any discussion of Judaism remains this God-centered text which is the wellspring from which every other Jewish idea derives.[8] Thus, it is entirely appropriate for the Torah to begin by declaring that everything in the world was created by God, for this theocentric focus is the foundation of our relationship with God and the beginning of our quest to find Him.

and in a somewhat different formulation by Abraham Joshua Heschel, who teaches that the entire Torah is a *midrash* (expansive and imaginative exegesis, in this case) on the indescribable revelatory event which took place at Mount Sinai. See Jacobs, *God, Torah, Israel: Traditionalism Without Fundamentalism* (HUC Press, 1990) 33; Heschel, *God in Search of Man* (Jewish Publication Society, 1965) 185.

7. Nonetheless, in this book I generally do not try to identify which material derives from which source. Rather, I treat the received text as a single entity for purposes of trying to understand it. Such an approach to the text is reminiscent of Umberto Cassuto's work. Cassuto (professor of Bible at Hebrew University) accepted both the observation of source-criticism – that the textual difficulties required explanation – and the non-Mosaic authorship of the Pentateuch; however, he felt these textual difficulties would be better explained by approaching the Pentateuch as a uniform work.

8. Note that in the next section, in the context of discussing the Jewish people's chosenness, I more boldly argue that God must have revealed Himself to the Jewish people at Mount Sinai or, at the very least, that the people felt that they had received a revelation. For the Sinai event is the foundation of the covenantal relationship between God and Israel, and the tradition is built on the notion that the revelatory act had content that is to be found in the Written Torah. Even if this claim is not historically accurate, the Bible's human authors clearly felt that the "event" was of signal importance to the story they were telling.

Israel and the Nations – Universalism vs. Parochialism

One of the most difficult Jewish concepts for moderns to accept is the notion of *bechirah* (chosenness), the belief that although God is Creator of the entire world, He chose a particular family, the descendants of Abraham, Isaac, and Jacob, as His chosen nation. Rashi's commentary on the Torah's very first verse pointedly introduces us to this fundamental (and seemingly irresolvable) paradox between Judaism's universality and its parochialism. The Torah commences with a sublime statement of universality: the one and only God creates the entire cosmos, particularly all of humanity, and therefore every human being shares a common origin and deserves to receive an equal portion of the world.[9] However, Rashi (1:1) – the most authentic of Torah commentators – tells us that the reason the Torah opens with this verse is *not* to teach a message of universal equality but rather to emphasize the very opposite: Israel's uniqueness, especially its entitlement to *Eretz Yisrael* (the Land of Israel). In Rashi's words, the reason that the Torah begins with the creation story and not with the first commandment given to the Jewish people is to teach us that "He [God] created [the entire world] and gave it to whoever was right in his eyes".[10] In other words, for Rashi the essential message of the Torah's opening chapters is that God, as the Creator, is free to choose the Jewish people and give it whatever He deems fit. Rashi thus converts a verse preaching universalism into one legitimating national parochialism.

Rashi's argument notwithstanding, this putatively chauvinist approach disturbs many contemporary Jews, so much so that the Reconstructionist Movement has eliminated the entire concept

---

9. I am reminded of the famous Mishnaic admonition to witnesses in capital cases that the risk of a mistake is unacceptable, since the loss of a single life is equivalent to the loss of the entire world. In one of the final scenes in the film *Schindler's List*, the Holocaust survivors Schindler saved from destruction present him with a watch engraved with this quotation.
10. This, for Rashi, explains why the Torah (primarily a book of mitzvot) begins with the story of creation.

of chosenness from its prayer book.[11] While I am sympathetic to some of the philosophical and rationalist underpinnings of the Reconstructionist view,[12] I continue to maintain that, for Judaism to have any validity, the Jews must have been chosen; and this chosenness must have expressed itself in the Sinaitic revelation (where, according to tradition, the written text of the Torah was received). Whether we conclude that the text was dictated verbatim by God or that it reflects not God's words given at Sinai[13] but man's understanding (informed, of course, by the culture of the times) of what was divinely revealed,[14] I maintain that the mo-

11. I have a fundamental problem accepting the theology of Rabbi Mordecai Kaplan and of the Reconstructionist Movement that follows his teachings, among other reasons because of their elimination of bechirah.

12. In particular, I have sympathy for the notion that the Written Torah, according to all the historical evidence we have available to us, was not dictated word for word by God to Moses and, indeed, is not totally of divine origin, but rather essentially a human invention. This notwithstanding, I cannot accept the Reconstructionist view negating chosenness. To be fair to the Reconstructionist point of view, the movement's founder, Mordecai Kaplan, did not believe in the existence of a metaphysical God; instead he defined the deity as a force within human beings for good. Hence, he quite logically viewed the Torah as a man-made construct, lacking a divine origin. If one accepts that approach, it would appear to follow that adopting the notion of chosenness is an act of national self-aggrandizement. I do not go so far as Kaplan. I cannot accept any conception of God that is not metaphysical. In my opinion, to define God as Kaplan does is to eliminate any meaningful conception of God and to reduce Judaism to a form of ethical humanism decorated with ethnically Jewish ritual – if you will, Kant with *tallit* (ritual prayer shawl) and *tefillin* (phylacteries). For me, the Written Torah, at the very least, gives us a picture of what the Jewish community thought it was receiving when a very real God revealed Himself at Sinai. From my perspective, bechirah – in the sense of the Jews having been chosen to receive the Torah at Sinai– becomes critically necessary. For further insight into Kaplan's theology, see *Questions Jews Ask: Reconstructionist Answers* (Reconstructionist Press, 1966). For Kaplan's understanding of the Torah's authority and the role of dogma, see especially pages 158–59.

13. Some significant modern Jewish philosophers, Buber and Rosenzweig in particular, understand the Sinaitic revelation to have been wordless, arguing that God did not (indeed, does not) speak in words. For them, the revelatory event was some sort of an existential theophany in which God made himself known (or perhaps was sensed) by the Israelite nation. This, of course, is not the traditional view.

14. Above, on a purely historical basis, I posited the possibility of the Torah as a totally human invention. This hypothesis indeed allows for the Jewish people's relationship with God; but it does not provide a basis for the sense of chosenness necessary to

ment of revelation was crucial. It is that revelation which forms the basis for the covenantal Israel-God relationship that I believe is at the heart of Judaism. The revelation of the Torah to the Jewish people both confirmed and created its chosenness. And absent the revelation of Torah to the Jews (and not others), the Jewish tradition becomes merely a cultural pastiche of Chanukah latkes (potato pancakes), chocolate *matzah* (unleavened bread eaten on Passover), klezmer music, and overprotective mothers.

While I can well appreciate the contemporary desire to avoid the inference of cultural or ethnic superiority that the concept of chosenness appears to some to imply, I maintain that one can be chosen without being superior – or, indeed, without even feeling so. Put another way, one can believe that the Jews were chosen by the deity to bring the Torah to the world and that other nations or individuals may have been chosen for other exalted purposes. Such an outlook does not, to my way of thinking, imply that Jews are better or more deserving people (although it does imply that the Torah's message is unique in some way). On the contrary, all of *Tanakh* (the twenty-four books of the Hebrew Bible) records in painful detail Israel's consistent failure to live up to its end of its covenant with God – which at least to me belies any notion that the Bible inherently assumes the ethnic superiority or intrinsically moral nature of the Jewish people.

To be sure, the *Tanakh* is a parochial book. It sets forth the self-understanding of one culture and, understandably, focuses upon the Jewish people.[15] It is, for the most part, the story of God's relationship with His people, the Jewish people. But no objective reader could conclude that the book's view of Israel is skewed in its favor. Virtually from the beginning of Jewish existence (Abram's call to leave Mesopotamia for Canaan), we see the

---

create a covenantal relationship and thus validate the very essence of Judaism. I accordingly do not accept it. At the very least the Written Torah reflects what the Jewish people perceived was the essence of God's continuing revelation to it.

15. By the same token, one could say that the *Iliad* is centered upon the Greeks and the Koran is centered upon the Arabs. This is hardly grounds for criticism.

Jewish people through glasses that are far from rose-colored. The patriarchs, matriarchs, prophets, generals, judges, and kings are presented to the reader warts and all. Jews are commanded to be a kingdom of priests – holy and a light unto the nations (*Vayikra* 19), but the Bible shows them, for the most part, to be utter failures in this regard.

This notwithstanding, the task of bringing God to the world remains, and God has entrusted this mission to the Jewish people. God is the Master of the Universe, but He has chosen one small nation to disseminate his message of goodness and truth. The same tradition that gives us Isaiah, Zechariah, and other prophets who foresee a universal messianic age when everyone will recognize God also stresses the unique character of the Jewish people and its special place in the divine scheme of things. For this reason, Rashi's commentary on the opening verse of *Tanakh* is crucial for it limns the issue of Israel's unique calling in bold relief within the very context of God's creation of the cosmos.[16]

Two Different Versions of the Creation Story

The first two chapters of *Bereshit* contain two disparate, sometimes contradictory, creation stories. The most significant difference between them is in how they account for humankind's creation. To sum it up briefly, the first version provides a bare-boned description of the seven "days" of creation. It begins by describing how God separated various elements from one another: light from darkness, earth from sky, upper waters from lower waters, and land from sea. Then it relates how God created the heavenly bodies and the living organisms: the sun and the moon, the stars and the planets, plants and birds, and sea animals and land animals. Finally, as the pinnacle of creation, God created humankind, "And God created man...male and female He created them" (1:27),[17] and

16. Why God chose one small clan to spread his message is the subject for another essay.
17. This creation of man as male and female leads some commentators to posit the creation of a hermaphroditic or androgynous being with two bodies (male and

on the seventh day [the *Shabbat*] He rested. The second version dispenses with a day-by-day account. Instead it places the creation of the primordial man and woman, Adam and Eve, at the center of the story and even changes the order of creation so that both plants and animals are created after Adam.[18] In this latter version God's creation of the various other elements of the cosmos goes virtually unmentioned,[19] as does His resting on the Sabbath.

One of the perennial cosmological questions that has engaged philosophers is whether the world (or, more appropriately, the cosmos) was created out of pre-existing matter or out of nothing, *ex nihilo*. A literal reading of the Torah's first creation story makes it quite clear that in this text the cosmos was *not created ex nihilo*, and the second version focusing on humankind's creation does not take a clear stand on the issue. Perhaps it defers to the first version's approach. No matter how later Jewish thinkers – most notably Maimonides – may have interpreted the biblical account, we cannot escape the fact that the text explicitly tells us that when God began to create "heaven and earth" (1:1), *something* was already there. The earth was in a state of *tohu vavohu* (translated in the New JPS version as "unformed and void", suggesting some sort of unformed matter); there was darkness and God's spirit wafted over the water (1:2).[20] To be sure, one could

female) connected like Siamese twins. See *Bereshit Rabbah* (henceforth, BR) 8:1. I will explore this idea further when I discuss the second account of Adam and Eve's creation.

18. Note that both the classical rabbinic *Midrash* (a corpus containing aggadic or halachic expositions of the underlying significance of the biblical text) and Rashi address and resolve, to their satisfaction, these apparent chronological inconsistencies. Rabbi Dr. J.H. Hertz provides a useful English-language summary of these approaches along with his own insights in his commentary on *Bereshit* 2:4–3 (*The Pentateuch and Haftorahs: Hebrew Text and English Translation and Commentary* [Soncino Press: London, 1987]). I find these efforts at reconciliation utterly unconvincing.

19. Curiously, *Bereshit* 2:5 rather than recording the creation of plant life reports in the negative, "no grasses of the field had yet sprouted" when Adam was created.

20. Indeed, even Rashi (1:1) notes that the Torah does not intend to teach the order of creation. He even goes so far as to say that "anyone who claims that heaven and earth were created first should be ashamed of himself, for the text explicitly states

easily explain that the Torah's account does not really begin at the beginning, and that these forms of matter existed only because God had created them *ex nihilo* before the biblical story begins. Be that as it may, the existence of some matter before the creation story begins clearly implies that this text is principally about God's ordering of matter, not his creation of it.[21]

Whether one chooses to focus upon the messages contained in the first or second versions, both posit God's "creation" of the cosmos and, in particular, of the plant and animal life on Earth. Today these aspects of the creation story have socio-political as well as religious importance. Both the creationists and the evolutionists present the so-called "creationism-evolution" controversy as an either-or proposition. On the one hand, the creationists tell us that if one accepts the enormous amount of scientific evidence supporting the theory of evolution, then one must jettison the notion that God created the cosmos (and, in particular, each species of plant and animal life), as set forth in *Bereshit*. On the other hand, the evolutionists (or at least many of them) suggest that the Genesis creation story is untenable once Darwin's insight is accepted as scientifically sound. I do not see the contradiction. The Torah's story does not purport to explain *how* God went about creating the cosmos and our world, other than by insisting upon His use of words as the primary motive force[22] and by focusing upon His practice of separating pre-existing elements to create the world as we know it. That God created each animal species "male and female" does not preclude the possibility that the mechanism

---

that the waters were already in existence before the creation of heaven and earth, as it is written, 'And the spirit of God wafted over the face of the waters'". While Rashi is not taking a stand on whether creation was *ex nihilo* or not, he is clearly arguing that this text proves that something existed before heaven and earth.

21. This insight has great significance in light of the Holiness Code enumerated in the Torah's midsection (the book of *Vayikra*, see especially 19:1). Therein, God commands Israel to be holy because He is holy. As I read that commandment, it requires us to order our lives to avoid chaos as a way of emulating God's ordering matter as He created the cosmos.

22. For instance, "And God said, 'Let there be light'" (1:3).

God used to create these species was Darwinian natural selection. While the process of mutation central to Darwinian evolution could not have taken place in six twenty-four hour days, Judaism has a long tradition of viewing each day of creation as an otherwise undefined unit of time, and not as a twenty-four hour period.[23] Thus, we can, without jettisoning the Torah text, explain that the species mentioned in the Bible were created over time by virtue of mutation.

Having accepted the logic of Darwinian evolution, however, I do find it difficult to explain how humanity evolved into several races following the flood (described in 6:9–9:28). For even if we were to conclude that several races evolved from Adam and Eve during the six days of creation, all of humanity following the flood descended from one man, Noah. The Torah explicitly claims that the various human races descended from him (*Bereshit* 10), and evolutionists would contend that in the time given, Noah's descendants could not have mutated from the one race they presumably belonged to into various races.[24]

Both the first and second creation stories are hard to square with the heliocentric solar system we take for granted today – not to mention with the notion that our solar system comprises but a very small part of the universe. The first version seems to posit a Ptolemaic structure in which the Earth is at the center and the heavens spread out above it; the second version, while it can be read as allowing a heliocentric structure, places humankind at the center of the cosmos. Either way, the text's perspective clearly puts humanity at the center of everything, which is belied both physically and, I suppose, philosophically by our knowledge of cosmological physics. Particularly with respect to the first version,

---

23. The classical rabbinic Midrash, BR 19:8, whose traditions date to more than fifteen hundred years before Darwin's birth, already explained that the term "day" need not be taken literally, as a verse from *Psalms* teaches us that one day from God's perspective is a thousand years.

24. It is, of course, possible that Noah's sons married women of different antediluvian races, which would account for different races in their progeny.

I have trouble making sense of the notion of the *rakia* (firmament) other than on the assumption that the Earth stands in the center of a Ptolemaic universe with the sun, planets, and stars revolving around it. According to the Torah, God created the firmament as some sort of a physical barrier (like a sheet of metal) between the separated upper waters and lower waters. I can understand that concept if we assume that the Earth is at the center of things and that the sky is literally above it. But it is difficult for me to conceptualize the sky as a physical barrier in the context of modern cosmology, in which the Earth is moving around the Sun in a solar system that itself is but a minute part of the universe of stars. In short, the conclusion appears to me to be inescapable that the creation stories set forth in the Torah are not physically accurate. Nor do I think that they were intended to be.

If, as I believe is appropriate, we view the creation stories homiletically – as intended to teach us that the one God formed and placed us in an ordered cosmos by a process of separation– Earth's and humanity's marginal place in the universe takes on much less significance.[25] Put differently, the Torah does not necessarily intend to present us with a detailed account of precisely what happened, but rather is designed to convey how we should understand our place in a cosmos created by the one and only divine source.[26] Viewed this way, the Torah's opening verses teach us that God's separation of Earth and humankind from the rest

---

25. Since the facts related in the second creation story are not entirely compatible with those told in the first, reading the two versions homiletically seems to be the only rational way to approach the text. If we do not do so, it follows that we must admit that the two versions are in dispute over how exactly the world was created. No less an authority than Maimonides sanctions such a non-literal approach when he declares: "The account given in Scripture of the creation is not, as is generally believed, intended to be in all its parts literal" (cited by Rabbi Hertz, *Pentateuch and Haftorahs*, 194).

26. The *how* of creation – the so-called *Ma'aseh Bereshit* – forms the core of kabbalist mysticism which, as I understand it, bears very little resemblance to what we read in the Torah itself. For an explanation of the kabbalistic mode of interpretation, see Gershom Scholem, "The Meaning of the Torah in Jewish Mysticism," *On the Kabbalah and Its Symbolism* (Schocken: New York, 1969) 33, 36.

of the cosmos underscores the unique importance of humanity in the entire scheme of things.[27] And that, after all, is what Judaism teaches – that the life of even a single human being is of ultimate significance.

The Creation of Humanity

It is the creation of humanity that I find most interesting. Having created the physical world, the heavenly bodies, the plants, and the entire animal kingdom in the first version of the creation story, God then announces His intention to create a being in His own image: "Let us make man in Our image, after Our likeness" (1:26).[28] As the verse relates, the resulting "man" was male and female: "And God created man in His image…male and female He created them" (1:27). Reading this verse, we must conclude that either God created two distinct human beings, a man and a woman, or, as suggested by some midrashists (exponents of midrash, the classic rabbinic method of exposing the underlying significance of the biblical text), He created a single creature with both male and female or masculine and feminine aspects.[29]

27. I think it highly significant that no less an Orthodox authority than Rav Joseph Soloveitchik essentially reads *Bereshit* homiletically when he posits in *The Lonely Man of Faith* that through the two divergent accounts of Adam and Eve's creation the Torah is teaching us something about the dual nature of humankind (where majestic man, who successfully dominates the world, and the lonely man of faith coexist in an uncomfortable dialectical relationship).

28. The classical commentators (who posit as a fundamental principle of Jewish faith that there is only one God) dismiss the text's reference to God's announcement that "we" should make a man in "our" image either as God talking to Himself using the royal "we" or as God consulting with His heavenly entourage of angels (BR 8:3). The point of this text almost seems to be that especially in the creation story, it is dangerous (and incorrect) to take the text literally. The creation story is not meant to be a dry, historical statement of fact, but rather a homiletic discourse.

29. BR 8:1. I think this idea has particular importance in understanding the nature of God. If we follow Maimonides' classic approach to this issue, God is pure spirit, incorporeal, and genderless. But the Jewish mystical tradition takes a different approach suggesting that God possesses aspects of *both* the masculine and the feminine in His/Her nature. If that is the case, what human being could be more in God's image than one that is both male and female?

Just what does it mean that mankind is made in God's image, and what does it mean if this image is composed of both male and female components?

Taking the text at face value, having been created in God's image would mean that both Adam's body and his appearance quite literally reflect God's. This, of course, would be a radically anthropomorphic interpretation and, thus, was not popular among classic Jewish theologians who posit God's incorporeality.[30] Abandoning the literal reading we can adopt a metaphorical one: human beings possess fundamental traits that enable them to function as living embodiments of God (that is to say, they can act like Him).[31] Traditionally, this sort of thinking has led to the conclusion that man – like God – has the ability to recognize right from wrong and to exercise free will – qualities which separate men and women from the rest of the animal kingdom.[32]

The second creation story, appearing right after God rests and initiates the first Shabbat, focuses entirely on the creation of Adam and then Eve. Significantly, in this second version the order of creation is changed and the way in which Adam's female counterpart comes into being is different. Here the separation of light from darkness, earth from sky, upper waters from lower

30. Dr. Benjamin Sommer of the Jewish Theological Seminary of America demonstrates in *The Bodies of God and the World of Ancient Israel* (Cambridge, 2009), that there is a great deal of such anthropomorphism in the Torah text and that the authors of many of these passages plainly believed that God indeed has a body.

31. My teacher, Rabbi Neil Gillman, points out that it is impossible for human beings to know what God is like; accordingly, he notes, our images of God are metaphoric and derive from our understanding of our own human nature. The idea that we can speak of God only in metaphor has a long and noble tradition in Jewish theology. The first section of Maimonides' *Guide for the Perplexed*, for example, is devoted almost entirely to a discussion of the various anthropomorphic metaphors used throughout *Tanakh*. Explaining this particular instance, Maimonides declares that the Torah speaks using human terms so that we can understand it.

32. How this understanding of humanity fits in with the Garden of Eden story where Adam and Eve are forbidden to eat from the Tree of Knowledge of Good and Evil is discussed below in the section on the Garden of Eden. If humanity already had the ability to distinguish between good and evil, it is difficult to understand why eating from the tree was forbidden.

waters, and land from sea go virtually (or, perhaps, completely) unmentioned;[33] and both plant and animal life come into being only after Adam is created. Indeed, the animals arrive *after* Adam's creation, as God tries to provide him with companionship. The newly created man names each of the animals as they parade before him, but the beasts do not do the trick, and God has to create woman to be man's helpmate. This He does by fashioning her from a part of Adam's body, traditionally understood to be his rib. At this juncture, the Torah takes the opportunity to indulge in a beautiful, poetic metaphor which it places in Adam's mouth: "bone of my bones and flesh of my flesh, this one shall be called Woman for from man she was taken" (2:23). Finally, in a third-person narrative voice, the Torah concludes this section by teaching that for this reason "a man leaves his father and mother and clings to his wife, so that they become one flesh" (2:24).

The explicit notion of woman being fashioned from man's body in the second version of the creation of humanity gives rise to some interesting midrashic speculation, especially in light of the Torah's earlier affirmation that man was created "male and female". As noted above, the midrash on the first version suggests that the first human being was both male and female. This human being was either hermaphroditic or, perhaps, more correctly androgynous. Weaving together the two versions of humankind's creation, the midrash is able to explain that the male and female bodies were originally joined like Siamese twins, and, in order to create Eve, God merely had to separate the female part from the male.[34] Thus, Adam's praise of Eve as "bone of my bones" in the second version fits in nicely with the gender-equal majesty of "man" having been created "male and female" in the first version. More importantly for modern sensibilities, this interpretation provides an answer – indeed, a refutation – to the age-old claim

---

33. Depending upon how 2:4 is understood.
34. In keeping with this approach, the ArtScroll Chumash translates the word traditionally rendered as "rib", as "side".

that woman is inferior to man because she was formed from his rib. By conflating the two versions, humanity can definitively be said to have been created "male and female".

The homiletic lesson of this account is apparent. The ideal family unit is composed of one man and one woman. To be sure, the Torah permits a man to take more than one wife – and such luminaries as Abraham, Jacob, Moses,[35] and David actually do so. But the conclusion is inescapable that the ideal remains one man married to one woman.[36] What I find interesting is that, in light of this ideal, the Torah is nonetheless quite lenient when it comes to permitting a man to divorce his wife, thereby permitting her to remarry. If a couple reflects a unity so powerful that we are told they are of one flesh, I would expect a far greater reticence to letting them break their marital bonds and concordantly more obstacles placed in the path of a man wishing to divorce his wife.[37] I would certainly not expect a legal system that clearly favors the man in matters of divorce. Perhaps the Torah recognizes the gulf we must often confront between the ideal and the pragmatic. In a way, that is one of the messages conveyed by Rav Soloveitchik in his book *Halachic Man*. His point, as I understand it, is that Halacha is an ideal system that the Jew strives to translate into the reality of everyday living; but there is always a gap between the ideal and the doable. In many respects, the legal system derived from the Torah recognizes this gap. Reflecting this awareness, the Rabbis refrained from enacting rabbinic decrees that the community could not (or perhaps even would not) accept.

---

35. My assumption that Moses had two wives is based on the Torah's reference in *Bamidbar* 12:1 to the Cushite woman that Moses married. While some midrashists (*ad locum*) stretch the text to argue that this woman is really Zipporah, Moses' Midianite wife, a simple reading of the text indicates that it reflects a tradition that Moses had another wife.
36. This is not a commentary on the twenty-first century issue of homosexual marriage, which the Torah does not even contemplate as a possibility.
37. The Midrash does note that the heavenly altar cries when a man divorces the wife of his youth; however, the Rabbis permit him to do so with relatively little ado.

Shabbat

Unlike the second creation story, which views the creation of humankind as the climax, the first narration reaches its pinnacle on the seventh day with God's rest and the first Shabbat. This is interesting in light of how Shabbat is perceived later in the Torah. For one would expect that all human beings would celebrate a rest day commemorating the singular creation of the one world by the one and only God. Yet the Torah clearly limits mandatory Sabbath observance to Israel. I wonder why Shabbat is not included (like murder and incest) among the few rules universally applicable to everyone. To be sure, Shabbat has become over thousands of years a signal mark of Jewish identity, but if its purpose is to remind us that one God created everything, parochial observance seems to be contraindicated. Perhaps God commanded the Jews, in particular, to observe this universal day to remind them on a weekly basis that, despite their special covenant with God and their special historical calling, all humanity shares a common origin.[38]

The Garden of Eden and the Forbidden Fruit

In the second creation story the Torah states that God planted a garden for Adam (and later Eve) in a place called Eden, and it goes to some length to tell us that this garden was located near four rivers: Tigris, Euphrates, Pishon and Gihon (2:8–14). The Euphrates and the Tigris are Mesopotamia's two principal waterways, but cartographers have not identified the other two, so they are probably entirely fictitious. I suppose the Torah refers to the Euphrates and the Tigris to assure the reader that the place indeed exists. Perhaps this geographical information is even offered as a subtle

---

38. Significantly, the Torah also assigns a different parochial reason for Shabbat observance. As the version of the Decalogue set forth in *Devarim* makes plain, Shabbat also serves to remind the Jewish people – and it alone – of God's miraculous role in the exodus from Egypt. Notably, in the *kiddush* (literally, sanctification; a ceremony sanctifying the Shabbat) recited every Friday night over the wine, the passage from *Bereshit* is recited and Shabbat is referred to as commemorating both God's creation of the world and His redemption of the Jewish people from Egypt.

invitation to humanity to try and locate this earthly (or perhaps unearthly) paradise, notwithstanding the sword-wielding cherubim God appointed to guard it from human intrusion (2:24).

The abundant edible vegetation in the garden suggests that God originally intended human beings to be vegetarians and farmers.[39] Indeed, the text explicitly states that Adam was placed in the garden in order to till and tend it (2:15).[40] In the Garden's center stand the two famous (or infamous) trees: the Tree of Life (whose fruit when eaten provides the eater with eternal life according to 2:22)[41] and the Tree of the Knowledge of Good and Evil (whose fruit was forbidden to Adam and Eve on pain of death). The consequences of eating from these two trees raise an interesting theological question. On the one hand, God forbids human beings from eating the fruit of the Tree of Knowledge on pain of death; but, on the other hand, the fruit of the Tree of Life (which is permitted to be eaten) seems to offer immortality. Why would God forbid the fruit of the Tree of Knowledge when the fruit of the Tree of Life was freely available to humanity to provide an antidote to the promised punishment of death? Perhaps the Torah is teaching us that in their original state, neither Adam nor Eve was aware of his or her own mortality and, therefore, did not have to confront the ultimate death we all face.[42] If this explanation is

39. This is supported by an earlier text where God states that He has provided plants and fruit for humankind and the animals to eat (1:29–30). No mention is made at that time of any species preying upon another. Of course, if we accept the notion that all species were created at the beginning precisely as they are today (a cornerstone of creationism, though in my opinion not of Judaism) then presumably the carnivores always hunted and ate other animals. As for human beings, the Torah explicitly allows men and women to consume animal flesh (apparently for the first time) after Noah leaves the ark: "Every creature that lives shall be yours to eat; as with the green grasses, I give you all these" (9:3).

40. Since one of Adam's punishments after eating the forbidden fruit is to earn his bread by the sweat of his brow, it seems reasonable to conclude that when he first arrived in Eden, farming was not difficult.

41. This plainly suggests that as created, Adam and Eve were *not* designed to live forever, even though they had the opportunity to become immortal merely by eating a piece of fruit.

42. But this supposition, if correct, would problematically render God's threat of a

correct, it suggests that primeval man and woman were closer in nature to the other animals, which, while instinctively afraid of predators and bodily harm, are seemingly unaware of impending death or its implications.

In discussing the notion that humans are created in God's image, I suggested that this might mean that men and women, like God and unlike all other creatures, have the capacity to make willful choices. This premise is supported by God's commandment to Adam and Eve not to eat the fruit of the Tree of Knowledge of Good and Evil.[43] For a commandment not to eat clearly implies that the commanded person has the ability to choose whether or not to comply.

However, if we accept the premise that Adam and Eve were created with the ability to choose between two courses of action, presumably the right or the good one and the wrong or the evil one, what would they have gained by eating from the Tree of Knowledge of Good and Evil? Accepting this premise, they already had the ability to distinguish and choose between the two! It seems to me that the difference between pre-fruit and post-fruit humankind is that originally men and women had the ability to make some choices, from the mundane "What shall we eat for lunch?" to the more significant "Should we comply with the explicit command given by God?"; but they did not have the inherent ability to distinguish between good and evil. That intuitive ability came only with the forbidden fruit's ingestion. Put another

death sentence meaningless, since Adam and Eve would not understand what the threat meant.

43. Whether God gave Adam and Eve only one commandment – not to eat of the fruit of the Tree of Knowledge – is open to question. At the very instant of their creation, God seems to have commanded them both "to be fruitful and multiply". (A literal reading of the Torah implies that this commandment was given to both the man and the woman, contrary to the current halachic understanding that only the man is bound by the obligation to reproduce, even though he obviously cannot do so alone.) However, the phrase "be fruitful and multiply" can also be read as a blessing, which would leave the negative commandment about the fruit of the tree as the only mitzvah given to the first couple.

way, in eating the fruit Adam and Eve gained a moral sense – a conscience if you will.[44]

While the name of the Tree of Knowledge of Good and Evil supports the notion that eating from its fruit endowed humanity with a moral sense, if post-fruit humankind has the ability to understand what is right and what is wrong, why is there any need for the blueprint of right and wrong actions set forth in the Torah? If we instinctively knew what was right, we would not have to be given the ground rules by God. We would inhabit a Kantian world governed by the ethical humanism implicit in the categorical imperative. That, needless to say, is not the Torah's worldview, for the Torah prescribes hundreds of laws applicable to Jews and, according to the tradition, seven general laws applicable to all of humanity.[45] Apparently, even after exercising their free will and eating the fruit, Adam and Eve are still either (1) unable instinctively to differentiate between right and wrong (which seems unlikely) or (2) able to understand the difference, but for some reason still in need of divine law to keep them on the straight and narrow. This latter possibility presents a powerful argument in favor of the philosophical position that men and women have strong urges to do the *wrong* thing. Jewish tradition refers to these urges as the *yetzer hara* (evil urge). This stance posits that, despite intuitively knowing how they should act, human beings need a strong and effective law code to ensure optimal behavior. While this reading entails what seems to me to be an overly pessimistic

---

44. In a recent book, Rabbi Harold M. Schulweis argues that humankind's conscience enables people to make correct moral decisions even when the traditional law appears to require opposite conduct. See Schulweis, *Conscience: The Duty to Obey and the Duty to Disobey* (Woodstock, VT: Jewish Lights, 2008).

45. It is, however, the fundamental premise of Mordecai Kaplan's Reconstructionist theology. As I understand Kaplan's writings, he sees God as a force within human beings propelling their conduct toward what is good and ethical without a metaphysical imposition of a code of conduct. For further elaboration, see Kaplan's *The Meaning of God in Modern Jewish Religion*, (Wayne State University Press, 1994) which delineates Kaplan's notion of God as the power that makes for salvation.

view of human nature,[46] it does help to explain the central role that repentance and atonement play in the Jewish tradition. [47]

Many readers of this story – particularly those in the Christian tradition – see the forbidden fruit as a metaphor for sexuality, thus creating a link between sex and sin. While the commandment to be fruitful and multiply was given before Adam and Eve sinned and thus would seem to imply that Adam "knew" Eve sexually before they ate the fruit, the text does contain more than a subtle hint that sex had something to do with the forbidden "knowledge" Adam and Eve obtained after they violated God's commandment. Indeed, the very name "Tree of Knowledge" alludes to this possibility; for the Hebrew verb means both possessing intellectual knowledge and engaging in sexual conduct. Thus, for instance, the Torah relates that "Adam knew his wife Eve, and she conceived" (4:1). Even more tellingly, the Torah explicitly relates that Adam and Eve became aware of their nakedness only after they had sinned: "Then the eyes of both of them were opened and they perceived that they were naked" (3:7). One need not be a devoted Freudian to regard the serpent (which seduces Eve into sin) as a phallic symbol. The sin of disobedience, in this reading, becomes a sexual one, and certain midrashim (plural of midrash) picking up on some aspects of this theme even suggest that Eve had sexual intercourse with the serpent and then seduced Adam into eating the forbidden fruit by using her feminine wiles.[48] One thing Adam and Eve clearly learn when they eat the fruit is the power of their own sexuality, a lesson that takes on great significance

---

46. It is, of course, more in keeping with the classic Christian concept of original sin.
47. Indeed, we are told that shortly before the flood God took such a pessimistic view of humanity: "The Lord saw how great was man's wickedness on earth, and how every plan devised by his mind was nothing but evil all the time" (6:5). People are constantly going to make the wrong decisions, and we all need the opportunity to start with a clean slate again, preferably not by God's wiping the slate clean with a flood.
48. *Sotah* 9b notes that the serpent coveted Eve. He wished to kill Adam and marry her. As Rashi notes (*ad locum*), Eve in her defense claims that the serpent had sexual relations with her and indeed had married her (midrashic reading of 2:13).

as the Torah (indeed, all of *Tanakh*) proceeds. For this is but the first of numerous instances in which overt sexuality is frowned upon and the woman in her guise as sexual temptress becomes the quintessential "other".[49]

As in so many other areas of the Jewish tradition, *Tanakh* displays a contradictory attitude toward sex.[50] On the one hand, the over-arching importance of producing progeny is a fundamental Jewish value. One cannot read the Abraham and Jacob stories without being aware that the desire – indeed, need – for children to carry on one's life work is a force that drives both men and women and that sexual attraction plays a significant (and quite positive) role. Sarah, we are told, is so beautiful that she must be protected from the advances of Pharaoh and Abimelech of Gerar. The same is true of Rebecca. And the sexual heat between Jacob and Rachel (at least on Jacob's part) jumps off the page.[51] On the other hand, time and again the Torah concerns itself with fear of the sex drive (more precisely, fear of the woman's ability to harness it for her own purposes). There are numerous examples. In the Torah alone, we have Potiphar's wife, who attempts to seduce Joseph, the Midianite women at Baal-Peor, who seduce thousands of Jewish men, and what seems to be a host of restrictions placed on women's sexual expression (in the guise of a family purity code).[52] Whether this code stems from the tradition's attempt to restrain women's power or its desire to protect the men who may

49. This idea appears most forcefully in *Proverbs*, which time and again warns young men to beware of the sexual wiles of alien women.
50. For a wide-ranging discussion of the Jewish approach to sexuality, see David Biale, *Eros and the Jews: From Biblical Israel to Contemporary America* (Basic Books, 1992).
51. Indeed, sexual attraction is at the heart of three of the *megillot* (scrolls) – *Ruth*, *Song of Songs*, and *Esther* – decreed by the Rabbis to be read on specific sacred occasions.
52. For example, the blood taboo invoked during a woman's menstrual period (*Vayikra* 15:19–24) seems to me to be designed to limit the woman's sexual expression. I appreciate, of course, that the premise underlying this set of rules (and the incest prohibitions of *Vayikra* 18) can be understood as designed to rein in the *man's* sexual urges rather than to limit the woman's sexuality. But I do believe that the

be lead astray by their own sexual urges and desires, the result is the same: an attitude toward sexuality premised on fear.

But what is there to be afraid of? Why should God be concerned that humankind will obtain knowledge of its own sexuality? Is there something disturbing in the raw power the libido holds? I get the sense that the Torah is so worried about the power of sex to render a human being excessively animalistic (and hence immune to the ordered boundaries that are at the core of the Torah way of life) that it not only legislates a host of rules to curb such excess but traces the root of the issue to the original disobedience in the Garden of Eden. If I am correct, God did not intend for men and women to be so vulnerable to sexual urges, and the current state of affairs is the result of Adam and Eve's eating of the forbidden fruit.[53] Even so, the possibility of sexual excess is most assuredly not a reason to elevate celibacy as a norm to be emulated by the truly devout. The first commandment (or possibly blessing) to all men and women remains to be fruitful and multiply. Deciding that the Garden of Eden story is about human beings' new vulnerability to sexual urges provides even more support for the traditional family unit, headed by one monogamous couple, as a way of curbing sexual excess while allowing people to procreate and live happy lives.

Any way we read the story the outcome is that man and woman after they eat the forbidden fruit are not the same as they were when God created them. But we still have to ask whether we are worse off than we would have been had our mythical primeval ancestors followed the rules and remained in their original condition. To be sure, if we take the text setting forth Adam

Torah's regulation of sexual matters is grounded as well in a fear of women's power to induce men to give in to those urges.

53. This explanation of the sin rooted in sexuality does not, however, account for God's fear that eating the fruit has made Adam and Eve like "one of us" (3:22). To the contrary, that declaration seems to support those who view the sin to be one of disobedience, having nothing to do with sexuality, for surely God is not subject to sexual urges.

and Eve's punishment at face value, the result is negative: pain and inconvenience surround us. Childbirth is painful; farming (indeed, all forms of making a living) requires much toil; and the realization that each of us will die haunts us virtually from our births. As for Eve's punishment of being eternally subservient to her husband, if we understand this to be a form of spousal abuse (like the serpent's punishment of being stepped on by people), it is difficult to explain how a benevolent God could conceive of such a plan.[54] Perhaps without engaging in farfetched apologetics the best that can be said about this aspect of Eve's punishment is that it reflects the reality of a woman's life at the time the words were written without providing us with a blueprint for contemporary living. Whatever the negative results of the sin, Adam and Eve's conduct appears to have brought them to a clearer understanding of humanity's potential and, if my reading is correct, a keener moral intuition which, if properly harnessed, can lead to a more meaningful and satisfying life.

Cain and Abel

Cain is the first of several people in the Torah who appear to me to get a raw deal.[55] Unasked, he brings God a present: "In the course of time, Cain brought an offering to the Lord from the fruit of the soil" (4:3). Apparently out of the goodness of his heart (and probably responding to a feeling of wonder and a sense of thanksgiving for a successful harvest), he offered God "the fruit of the soil" that he had grown. Inexplicably (both to the reader and to Cain) God rejects Cain's offering and, instead, accepts Abel's animal sacrifice: "The Lord paid heed to Abel and his offering, but to Cain and his

---

54. While I surely believe in a benevolent God, there are a sufficient number of seemingly sadistic acts attributed to God in *Tanakh* to give one pause. Job's story is only the most obvious example. The commandment to Abraham to offer his beloved son as a sacrifice – even though God apparently never intended it to be carried out – appears to be another.
55. The quintessential example of such a person is Esau.

offering he paid no heed" (4:4–5).[56] Cain is not surprisingly upset for two reasons. First, his offering was rejected without any explanation and, second, Abel's sacrifice, which, after all, seems to be an imitation of his own, was accepted. Adding insult to injury, God proceeds to warn Cain that, if he does the right thing, all will be well, but that the urge to sin (to commit a heinous act, as yet undefined either for the reader or, more importantly, for Cain) will constantly haunt him and he must be careful lest he fall victim to this urge. What follows is that Cain kills his younger brother.

This brief story raises a number of questions: Why is Cain told to do the right thing when God has just rejected what appears to be a sincere gift? Has Cain even done anything that requires God's admonition? The midrashists (BR 22:3) have little trouble deducing from the description of Abel's sacrifice as from "the firstlings of his flock" that Cain, in contrast, insulted God by offering second-rate produce. This sort of deduction is typical of the Midrash, but it has very little basis in the text and utterly fails to convince me of Cain's blameworthiness. Rather, I would argue, what we have here is an example of God's randomness and irrationality. God chooses to accept whatever He chooses to accept; there is no rhyme or reason to His choices. And in that sense Cain is a victim of Divine Providence.[57] What is more, we are given no

56. I believe that Abel's sacrifice was more pleasing to God because, unlike Cain's gift of vegetable matter, the slaughter of animals involves the ritual shedding of blood. The Torah appears at times to be obsessed with blood, as even a cursory reading of the rules governing the sacrificial cult and the dietary laws reveals. While God's enjoyment of the pleasing odor of animal sacrifices is plainly metaphorical – since God (who is pure spirit) does not smell – even as early as the Cain and Abel story the text describes a divine preference for the meat and blood of animals. Whatever the prophets may have to say about the impropriety of Temple sacrifices in their day, throughout the Torah God clearly prefers to be worshipped through the slaughter of animals.

57. Curiously, while Cain appears to be a random victim of Divine Providence, taking a longer view of things, the Cain and Abel story fits into a pattern that spans much of biblical history: Abel is the first in a long line of younger siblings who are favored over their elders – Abraham, Isaac, Jacob, Joseph, Ephraim, Moses, David and Solomon among others. Whatever the overarching logic inherent in this pat-

reason for God to warn Cain about the danger of sin "crouching at the door" (4:7). Cain surely has as yet committed no sin. All he did was bring an offering that God inexplicably chose to reject. Is God warning him that if he takes his anger out on Abel dire consequences will result? If that is the case, I would expect a clearer warning. Yet that too is absent from the text.

What we do have is an example of an angry young man taking his frustration with God out on an innocent third party who happens to be his brother.[58] Following the murder Cain responds to God's query asking him where his brother is with one of the most familiar lines in the Bible (4:9): "Am I my brother's keeper?" This line is usually read homiletically to teach us that each person is, indeed, responsible for his neighbor; that is a salutary moral lesson. But placed in the context of the Cain and Abel story, in a freshly minted world in which there was only one family living, how was Cain to know that he had a responsibility towards other members of his society? Aristotle may well be correct that man is a political animal; but when there were only three men and one woman in existence,[59] Cain could not be expected to know that he would be held responsible for the others. Perhaps that is why his punishment, at least at first blush, does not appear to be as harsh as the murder of Abel would justify. Since nobody has

---

tern of Divine Providence may be, Cain, viewed on his own merits, still seems to get a raw deal.

58. This assumes that Abel did not brag to Cain about God's acceptance of his sacrifice and rejection of his brother's. The text implies that Cain said something to Abel before killing him: "Cain said to his brother Abel. And when they were in the field, Cain set upon his brother" (4:8). Frustratingly, the text we have is merely a fragment that does not tell us what was said. Perhaps an earlier version of the tradition, lost to us, provided a more complete story explaining exactly what the brothers' motivations were.

59. Since we know that Cain married and had children after his banishment, presumably Adam and Eve had a daughter, unmentioned in the Torah. Some of the Rabbis of the Midrash (BR 22:1, 8) try to explain Cain's murdering his brother by speculating that they were fighting over such a sister – more specifically, that each of the boys was born with a twin sister to marry and that the fight was over who would marry a third sister born along with Abel.

warned him that it is wrong to kill another human being, Cain's punishment seems to present us with the first *ex post facto* law.[60] But if, as I have suggested, eating the forbidden fruit at the very least gave humanity an instinctive sense of what is right and what is wrong, Cain should have known anyway that fratricide was out of bounds, and he should have been punished appropriately for transgressing this ethical norm.[61]

Some apologists for Cain suggest that since no one had been killed before, he cannot have been expected to know what would happen to Abel if he hit him with a rock.[62] But if my reading of the Garden of Eden story is correct, Cain (as Adam and Eve's son) is aware of his own mortality and presumably of Abel's as well. And it is not a very long leap from understanding that death is a reality to realizing that a strong blow might cause it. On the one hand, Cain could surely have deduced as much from watching his brother slaughter the sheep for his sacrifice, and, therefore, he should be liable for his actions. On the other hand, the immense pleasure that God took from Abel's act of sacrificial slaughter could serve to exonerate Cain, if we suggest that perhaps Cain did not realize the difference between sacrificing a sheep and killing one's brother. If we look solely at the text, no one took the trouble to explain the difference to him.

Cain's punishment raises a number of questions. The Torah's

60. Significantly, under Jewish law the death penalty cannot be lawfully imposed unless the lawbreaker was expressly warned not to commit the capital offense before he does so. The possibility that Cain would be punished when the law had not even been promulgated is thus doubly astounding.

61. The Torah (in the Decalogue) does tell people not to commit murder, notwithstanding my argument that they should have innately understood this. The Torah's need to include this commandment supports the argument that Cain should not have been punished when he had not yet been warned. My view, however (as set forth in the text above) is that humankind's intuitive sense of right and wrong should have sufficed to warn Cain that a murderous attack on his brother would end badly for him as well.

62. The text makes no mention of how or even if Cain hit Abel only stating that "Cain set upon his brother Abel and killed him" (4:8). Although there is no source for this in the text, the Midrash suggests that Cain used a rock (BR 22:8).

normative view of the appropriate treatment of murder – set forth in numerous places – is that the intentional, unjustified killing of another human being is properly punished by death. Yet Cain receives what seems to be a much milder sentence. Is this because of the inherent unfairness of punishing him for violating an as yet unpromulgated rule, or is his punishment harsher than one might think? While being forced to wander the face of the earth is a far cry from capital punishment, it is nonetheless more severe than might appear at first blush; for Cain is a farmer, and no successful farmer can move from place to place on a regular basis. He has to stay put in order to do his job – in Cain's case the only job he knows. But Cain is told that he can no longer be a farmer because the earth will not grow anything he tries to plant. It's like telling a musician he may no longer make or listen to music.[63] In an existential sense, that is a very harsh punishment indeed.

The Nephilim

The Torah's first *parasha* (weekly Torah reading), *Bereshit*, ends with a strange story about sexual relations between some divine beings (literally, sons of God) and beautiful women, the result of which is offspring called Nephilim – who are said to have been heroes and men of renown: "When men began to increase on earth and daughters were born to them…. It was then, and later too, that the Nephilim appeared on earth – when the divine beings cohabited with the daughters of men, who bore them offspring. They were the heroes of old, the men of renown" (6:1–4). It's hard to decide just what to make of this. I am reminded of a book I saw many years ago called *Chariots of the Gods* which suggested that the Bible's prehistoric stories are reports (distorted over time) of an alien invasion of Earth. More significantly, I think, this story serves as a prime example of the Torah's strong distaste – one might accurately say revulsion– for mixtures. The cosmos that God carefully separated from chaos at the time of creation does

---

63. I am indebted for this point to Professor Diane Sharon.

33

not tolerate mixtures – be they of wool and linen, oxen and donkeys, or women and divine beings.[64] While the text itself does not disapprove of this particular mixture in so many words, I nonetheless detect the Torah's natural antipathy to mixtures at work.

Another interesting point about this story is the text's failure to give us any further information as to precisely who these sons of God were. Were they angels? Aside from the cherubim who guard Eden against an attempted return by human beings (and there is no hint in the text that the cherubim are angels, although they are clearly some sort of divine creature), we haven't as yet encountered angels. And when we do in the Abraham stories, they are referred to as *malakhim*, messengers who act as if they were human, even though we know they were sent by God to carry out certain tasks. As for the Nephilim, since the world's entire population (aside from Noah and his family) was wiped out by the flood,[65] presumably we need not worry about who they were, since they became extinct.[66]

The penultimate paragraph of *Bereshit*, before we commence the Noah story, reports that God decided to wipe out all of humanity because of its wickedness: "The Lord saw how great was man's wickedness on earth...And the Lord regretted that He had made man on earth...The Lord said 'I will blot out from the earth the men whom I created...for I regret that I made them'" (6:5–7). These verses raise a significant theological issue. For contrary to some statements by respected authorities (including the prophet Samuel)[67] that God is the model of constancy, never changing

---

64. Wearing clothing containing a mixture of wool and linen is forbidden in *Devarim* 22:11, and the interdiction against yoking an ox and a donkey together for the purpose of plowing is found in *Devarim* 22:10.
65. This excludes the aquatic animals, which were spared.
66. Curiously, the Nephilim are again encountered in *Bamidbar* when the spies return from Canaan and report that they saw Nephilim in the land (*Bamidbar* 14:33). Since only Noah and his family survived the flood, how this is possible given that they were not descended from Noah is difficult to explain. The text offers no clarification.
67. Samuel clearly espouses this position when he tells Saul that God has irrevocably

His mind, in this verse the Torah pithily describes a God who does exactly that. The text is clear. Having originally determined that the creation of humankind was good (1:31), God nonetheless changes His mind and concludes that humanity is evil and worthy of destruction. Some commentators who posit that God is indeed constant try to explain this statement away by suggesting that the Torah uses "the language of men" to describe God. For after all, the only tools we have for characterizing God and His actions derive from our understanding of human beings and how they act.[68] That is to say, these commentators claim that God did not really regret creating humanity; that is just the way the Torah describes it, for this is how a human being would feel. Notwithstanding the logic underlying this explanation, it strikes me as an after-the-fact rationalization.

What we really have here is a bold description of a deity who is experimenting and learning about His creatures as He goes along. This characterization of God is borne out by developments in the next parasha where humanity's diet is changed (from strictly vegetarian to include the flesh of animals) and God, for the first time, begins to teach people how to live by instituting a law code, albeit a primitive one. By the end of the next parasha, we have entered a new world, one where God relates very differently to humanity than he did in the Garden of Eden where he promulgated only one negative commandment!

"torn the kingship over Israel away from you" (*1 Sam.* 15:28) for not having followed His command to eliminate the Amalekites and destroy all their possessions. Rejecting Saul's entreaties, Samuel declares: "Moreover, the Glory of Israel does not deceive or change His mind, for He is not human that He should change His mind" (15:29). Paradoxically, in this same chapter, God tells Samuel that "I regret that I made Saul king, for he has turned away from Me and has not carried out My commands" (15:11). However we may explain the dissonance between these two verses, it is still striking.

68. Many scholars have adopted this rationalization to resolve various disturbing anthropomorphic references to God throughout the Torah. A prime example is Maimonides, who speaks highly of this approach in the *Guide for the Perplexed*.

NOAH

The Earth's Corruption

The flood story begins with God's realization that the earth's creatures have become so corrupt and wicked that they must be destroyed: "The earth became corrupt before God…When God saw how corrupt the earth was, for all flesh had corrupted its ways on earth, God said to Noah, 'I have decided to put an end to all flesh, for the earth is filled with lawlessness because of them: I am about to destroy them with the earth" (6:11–13).[1] We are not told precisely what evil things the people did to deserve annihilation. The midrashists, of course, fill in this gap with all sorts of suspect practices, many having to do with sexual misconduct (both among human beings and, interestingly, among animals as well).[2]

One might suppose that, having eaten the forbidden fruit

---

1. God seems to be saying that he will destroy all of the earth's creatures, human beings and animals living on both the land and in the sea. However, since the method of destruction is a universal flood, the sea creatures were ultimately spared. The text does not tell us why, as a matter of divine providence, land animals deserved to be destroyed while sea creatures did not. I suppose the tradition of destruction by water was so well grounded that, logical or not, that outcome was the one that had to be described.

2. Rashi summarizing several midrashic traditions writes: "It means lewdness and

of knowledge, humanity should have been aware enough of the difference between right and wrong to avoid such practices and, therefore, deserved to be punished; but God's punishment of the animals is incomprehensible. They did not eat from the Tree of Knowledge and had no inborn faculty enabling them to make such a distinction.[3] Like Abraham, I ask: "Shall the judge of the entire earth fail to act justly?" (18:25) The Jewish tradition, reflecting its pet taboo against improper mixtures, explains that one species cohabited with another, so the resulting abominations (and the transgressing animals) had to be destroyed.[4] However, I reject this extra-biblical midrash and am forced to conclude that the animals' destruction is morally indefensible.[5]

Furthermore, even if humanity gained some sort of intuitive perception enabling men and women to distinguish between good and evil after eating the forbidden fruit, God's harsh punishment for humankind's evil ways is hard to fathom within a biblical tradition that extols the virtues and necessity of a legal system designed to regulate behavior. Aside from the commandments to reproduce and not to eat the fruit of one particular tree, as far as the Torah teaches us God had not yet taken the trouble to give human beings any instruction whatsoever with respect to permit-

---

idolatry…robbery…even cattle, beasts and fowl did not consort with their own species" (6:11–12).

3.   Traditionally this is the principal difference between humans and animals.

4.   I read this midrashic explanation as a rationalization by Rabbis who couldn't quite accept a divine decree of destruction against thousands of animals for no reason at all. An important strand of the Jewish interpretive tradition posits that nothing happens in God's world without a reason, so the Rabbis had to provide one for this wanton slaughter. The belief that every earthly event has a reason is, however, belied by many stories in the *Tanakh*. As I argued above, God's rejection of Cain's sacrifice is a prime example of this irrationality.

5.   Indeed, the only logical defense would seem to be to contextualize the Torah and argue that it does not sanctify animal life or concern itself with animal suffering the way we do. Not only does this offend our twenty-first century sensibilities, it also appears to contradict Torah laws that mandate treating animals kindly; so it is not a very satisfactory answer. Alternatively, one might argue that the Torah sees no purpose to animal life if the "crown of creation", humankind, has been wiped out. But even if this were true, it would not justify the animals' cruel destruction.

ted and forbidden behavior.[6] Such legislation is not provided until *after* the flood. Yet it is apparently appropriate for God to wipe out virtually all of humanity (men, women, and even children who certainly did not sin!) because it has violated principles as yet unpromulgated. Surely a God of justice would not act in such a cavalier manner.[7]

Since I cannot conclude that God is unjust, the upshot is that the flood story is a homiletic myth, a story written to teach a certain lesson, not a factual account of what actually happened. Having suggested this, it is worth noting that the flood story can be read as a reversal of the first creation narrative. Just as God created cosmos out of chaos by, among other things, separating the water above from the water below, He destroys the world by eliminating the separating firmament, thus permitting the upper waters to descend and cover the Earth. Noah, in this reading of the story, becomes a second Adam – the common ancestor of everyone alive today. The message contained in this second creation story and embodied by its second Adam may provide the key to understanding the post-deluge world we live in.[8]

6. To be sure, Cain is told that sin is crouching at the door, but God fails to explain what sin is and how Cain must act to avoid it.
7. This of course raises the question of whether we can assume that an oral tradition – replete with material implied in the Written Torah but not explicitly stated – existed alongside the written one and that at least a part of it had already been transmitted to Adam and Eve (or some of their descendants). If so, we could justify God's actions by arguing that a code of law had been given and breached, according to this oral tradition. However, even if such an oral tradition existed, we would still have a difficult time explaining why the Written Torah did not supply us with this critical information.
8. Significantly, both Adam and Noah are commanded to "Be fertile and increase, and fill the earth" (1:28, 9:1), and both have three named sons, one of whom (Cain and Ham, respectively) acts reprehensibly. Curiously though, Adam is commanded to "master…[the earth] and rule…all the living things" (1:28), while Noah's role seems more passive: "the fear and dread of you shall be upon all the beasts of the earth" (9:2). Does this difference provide some insight into the new world Noah lives in?

Noah's Character

Noah himself is an interesting character. Much has been made of the text's reference to him as righteous and blameless "in his time" (6:9). Rashi states that he was a righteous person only when compared with his truly evil contemporaries; in the company of such stalwarts as Abraham and Moses, Noah would hardly shine. Undermining this negative characterization of Noah, the Torah states that "he walked with God" (6:9) – not a description usually applied to people. In fact, the only other person said to have "walked with God" (5:24) was Enoch, Noah's great-grandfather, a man so saintly that we are told "God took him" (ibid.), suggesting that he was transported to Heaven like Elijah without having died.[9]

In any event, Noah is righteous enough to warrant an exemption from the universal destruction God has determined is needed to purge the world of evil. And it is not surprising that this exemption included Noah's immediate family – his unnamed wife, his three sons, and their unnamed wives. First of all, their exemption from the flood can be viewed as necessary to preserve Noah's sanity; second, if Noah and his wife are past childbearing age they will be needed to provide the means for future propagation of the species. While understandable, this reprieve provided to Noah's family raises an interesting question. Given that all the other human beings in the world were so evil that they all had to be annihilated – even infants who had not yet had time to learn the evil ways of their parents – it is surprising that the text tells us nothing at all about the moral stature of Noah's wife, his sons and their wives. Are we to assume that they too were righteous and blameless in their time?

Given Ham's reprehensible behavior described in the text af-

---

9. Rashi reads the Enoch text this way, adding that God took Enoch so that he would not have to live longer and risk sinning. That's a strange remark to make about a man who "walked with God". Rashi seems to assume yet again that everyone, no matter how righteous, is open to sin given the right circumstances. This stress on the power of the yetzer hara seems to me to presage the pessimistic Christian notion that every human being is born in original sin.

ter the deluge (9:22), this seems unlikely. This raises yet another question about the justice of God's decision. It is one thing to save a righteous individual from destruction directed at the truly evil; and it makes some sense to bring his family along both to preserve his sanity and (if he is too old to bear children) the possibility of continuing the human species through his bloodline. But it is quite another to ignore whatever moral traits the family members may or may not have. Either God seems to have made a mistake (at the very least, an error of omitting to consider the moral status of the sons and their wives) or we must ask why God wanted a relatively evil individual among those slated to populate the new world.

The Ark, the Animals, and the Covenant: Lessons of the Flood

God commands Noah to build a wooden boat (an ark)[10] and specifies exactly how to construct it.[11] Some biblical scholars are troubled by the discrepancy between God's original command to Noah to take "[two] birds of every kind, [two] cattle of every kind, [a pair of] every kind of creeping thing on earth" (6:20) and the command as it is phrased when Noah is told to enter the ark: "Of every clean animal you shall take seven pairs, males and their mates, and of every animal that is not clean, two, a male and its mate; of the birds of the sky also, seven pairs, male and female" (7:2–3). I have no problem with this so-called discrepancy. It makes perfect sense for the Torah first to set forth the general commandment and then to provide specifics, distinguishing between the numbers to be taken of clean and unclean animals. But I do wonder how Noah could have known which animals were clean and which were not, if God did not explicitly tell him. Fur-

---

10. The word for "ark" – *tevah* – is rare in biblical Hebrew. It is also used to describe the wicker basket that carried the baby Moses down the Nile to be discovered by Pharaoh's daughter. The parallel between Moses and Noah is plain, for Noah saved humanity and Moses saved the children of Israel.
11. This is the first of the Torah's architectural blueprints – the most elaborate being the plan for the sanctuary in the desert.

thermore, I wonder if Noah understood why God wanted him to take extra clean animals. Did God explain that they were to be used for sacrifices offered after the flood (as the tradition teaches)? If so, why doesn't the Torah explicitly tell us these things?[12]

The flood was universal – that is, according to the text the entire planet was covered with water and only those creatures residing in the ark (or those animals who could live in the sea) survived. Presumably, that means that all non-aquatic life in the Americas, Oceania, Australia, and Antarctica as well as those animals living in Asia, Europe, and Africa were wiped out. Once we accept the notion that God destroyed virtually the entire world, this mass annihilation goes without saying. But I wonder how Noah, living somewhere in Mesopotamia, managed to gather animals from across the globe. As ridiculous as this might sound when compared with the enormity of the moral question of global destruction, how did the penguins from Antarctica and the kangaroos from Australia get to the ark?[13] Notwithstanding the miraculous manner in which all the animals could have been drawn or transported to the ark (and were, in the recent Hollywood caricature of the flood story, *Evan Almighty*), the Torah makes no mention of any miracles when God commands Noah to save himself and the animals. Indeed, Noah is commanded to take wood

12. The Torah's use of the terms clean and unclean in the weekly Torah reading of the Noah story might baffle not only Noah but the reader as well; for these terms are not defined until *Vayikra* 11 (the Torah's third book relating events several hundred years later in biblical history). The terms, as used here, thus seem to be anachronistic, so much so that modern biblical critics see them as evidence that the section containing them was interpolated by a Priestly author into an earlier version of the flood story.

13. I suppose the animals from North America might have migrated over the land bridge we are told was located west of Alaska where the Aleutian Islands now are. However, this would not explain how animals from the islands in the Pacific or from Australia managed to get there. If the hypothetical supercontinent referred to as Pangaea by scientists still existed at Noah's time, this would provide an explanation for how all the other animals reached Noah's ark. However, scientists themselves date the break-up of this supercontinent to long before the arrival of human beings on the stage of history.

and tar and build the ark with his bare hands. So the ingathering of the animals should also have taken place without miracles.

If a rational explanation for the ingathering cannot be provided, the conclusion appears to be inescapable that the flood story, like the creation and Garden of Eden narratives, is not intended to teach history, but, rather, is homiletic in nature. The flood provides us a two-part lesson. First, we learn that God is willing to punish evildoers harshly,[14] and second – and I believe more importantly – we learn that God does not forget about the people he cares for and sometimes treats them very generously.

The text's critical observation that when the flood waters reached their zenith, God remembered Noah and the creatures in the ark (7:24–8:1) is central to the Rosh Hashanah liturgy, playing an important part in the *Zichronot* (Remembrance) section of *Mussaf* (additional prayer service for the High Holiday). My rebbe, Rabbi Samuel J. Chill, in a memorable sermon that I heard when I was a teenager,[15] taught that the essence of Jewish belief can be found in the *machzor* (High Holiday prayerbook), particularly in the *Malchuyot* (Kingship), *Zichronot*, and *Shofarot* (Shofar Blasts) sections of the Rosh Hashanah *Mussaf Shemoneh Esrei* (the central prayer recited in the additional High Holiday prayer service). Zichronot, he explained, teaches that the one God of the world is interested in human events and plays a role in history. This fundamental Jewish teaching, which forms the backbone of the entire

---

14. Taken together with God's comparatively lenient punishment of Cain for fratricide, I suppose the lesson should be tempered: God can be merciful or harsh. At this point in the Torah, which option God follows seems to be totally a matter of whim. We, as of yet, have no notion that human beings can use prayer or *teshuvah* (repentance) to affect God's decision. Indeed, as I read the *Tanakh*, the idea that penitence can totally eliminate punishment for wrongdoing doesn't appear until the book of *Jonah*.

15. Of all the rabbinical sermons I have heard in my life, only two remain with me: this one about the Rosh Hashanah Mussaf and a sermon I heard Rabbi Reuven Grodner deliver years later explaining that to be observant does not necessarily mean to be religious; that being religious means to be God-aware; and that observance is not an end in and of itself, but rather is designed to help us become religious.

Tanakh,[16] first reveals itself in the flood story. God brings the flood because of his disappointment with humankind's immorality; He saves Noah's family and the animal kingdom to provide continuity, to enable a "new" creation to arise from the old, and when the flood has accomplished its deadly task, He remembers Noah and the creatures in the ark and brings them to a safe haven in Ararat. What is more, he makes a covenant with humankind (represented by Noah, the new Adam) not to destroy the world with another flood and sets the rainbow in the sky as a sign of that covenant. It is this act of remembering along with the forging of the covenant with humanity that I believe are the central lessons of the flood story. God is not only interested in what is going on in the world He created; He also cares about the people in it and goes so far as to make binding promises to them.

The covenant with Noah is particularly significant. It is the first of a number of pacts God makes with human beings in the Torah, and unlike the other parochial covenants – with Abraham, Isaac, Jacob, and then the entire Israelite community – it is made with a representative of all humanity. The concept of a covenant between God and humankind is not an easy one to comprehend. Firstly, how could a deity who is transcendent – infinitely "other", intrinsically not of this world – enter into a covenant with human beings living in it? Secondly, if God, the creator of this world, is infinitely more powerful than His creatures, why would He limit himself by assuming obligations to them? Thirdly, since most contracts presume that each contracting party can require the other to live up to its obligations, what is the meaning of a contract en-

---

16. For those who posit that God is so transcendent, so "other" that by definition He could not – or, perhaps more accurately, would not – split the Red Sea to save the Jews or stop the sun from setting to allow Joshua to complete his rout of the enemy, the idea of God's playing an active role in history is difficult to swallow. And I share some of that concern. But one cannot read the Hebrew Scriptures without a keen awareness of God's role in history. For that is what the book is about: God's historical relationship with humankind, in general, and Israel, in particular. At the very least, it seems safe to say that the *Tanakh* embodies the Jewish people's understanding that God takes an active role in history, particularly its own.

tered into with an omnipotent God, which by its very definition is unenforceable by the human parties?

The answer to these questions may be found in God's unique nature and in the relationship He is trying to establish with humanity. God's promising not to destroy the world again by water reflects His abiding concern for humanity, a concern so great that He is willing to limit His otherwise untrammeled freedom of action. In this sense, at least, the transcendent God of the first creation story (*Elokim* in the text) is simultaneously the immanent deity of the second creation narrative (*YHWH* in the text), who shaped Adam from the clay of the Earth and walked with him in the Garden of Eden.[17] Support for this meshing of two aspects or notions of God exists among the traditional Jewish commentators who also point out that one may refer to God as *Adonai* (a form used in place of *YHWH*) *Elokim* to illustrate His diametrically opposed propensities to mete out strict justice (a more transcendent act) and to act mercifully (a more immanent one).[18]

Significantly, unlike the covenant God makes at Mount Sinai with the Israelite nation, the pact with Noah is unilateral. The text does not set forth any obligations on humankind's part that must be performed in order to bind God to His side of the arrangement. All we have is God's promise not to destroy the world again by water. God does not demand anything in return; He seems merely to be rebuilding His relationship with humankind by assuring Noah that there won't ever be another universal flood.[19] This not-

---

17. If nothing else, these two versions of the creation story demonstrate that the Torah is not of one mind when it comes to describing the nature of God.

18. For a description of different biblical characterizations (what Rabbi Neil Gillman refers to as word pictures) of God that deviate from our normative notion, see James Kugel's *The God of Old* (The Free Press, 2003).

19. There is one important similarity between this covenant and the more parochial ones that follow it. There is a sign designated to symbolize the covenant – the rainbow. Like the later commandment of circumcision given to Abraham (17:11) and the tablets of the covenant (*luchot haberit*) given to Moses and the Jewish people, the rainbow constitutes tangible evidence of an agreement with the invisible deity.

withstanding, a critical question about the covenant with Noah remains: what's in it for God?

It seems that God is so emotionally tied to His creation that He has to assure Noah and his family that their progeny will be safe from this kind of destruction again. Of course God's promise, as set forth in the text, does not explicitly extend to other types of destruction. But as I read it, the import seems to be clear that God is promising humankind that He will never again destroy the world.[20] Indeed, while God – when formalizing the covenant – promises only that "the waters shall never again become a flood to destroy all flesh" (9:15), He had earlier "said to Himself" (8:21) after Noah offered his sacrifices: "Never again will I doom the earth because of man…nor will I ever again destroy every living being, as I have done" (ibid.). He thus seems formally to have promised only not to flood the earth, but unofficially he seems to have forsworn other methods as well.

More importantly, the story seems to teach us that God, while we think of Him as totally self-sufficient, is in dire need of humanity. Men and women were created to fill some need in God's essence for interrelationship – what Abraham Joshua Heschel denotes as God's "pathos".[21] And even when the evil that men and women do is so great as to become intolerable for God, rather than wiping out humanity entirely, He deems it necessary to preserve the species and start over.[22]

20. Unfortunately, it is unclear whether God is also promising to prevent humanity from destroying itself. Given the weapons of mass destruction humankind has managed to invent, we can only pray that God did indeed intend to override humankind's free will should such a horrific possibility present itself.

21. God, to use Heschel's felicitous phrase, is "in search of man". See Abraham Joshua Heschel, *God in Search of Man: A Philosophy of Judaism* (Farrar, Straus and Giroux, 1955). Notably, this concern for a relationship with humankind was not sufficient to provoke God into overriding free will and preventing the evils of the Holocaust or of other acts of genocide with which human history is stained.

22. Curiously, God adopts a similar tactic after the Jewish people sin by worshipping the golden calf. He wishes to destroy the Jewish people and rebuild it through Moses (*Shemot* 32:10). Unlike Noah, Moses rejects this offer, declaring that he would rather be stricken from God's book (id., 32:32).

God's post-deluge covenant with humankind is accompanied by the first introduction of divinely ordained law, a new factor in humankind's relationship with the deity. While God did prohibit Adam and Eve from eating the forbidden fruit, this commandment was specific to one type of fruit in one place. Here for the first time, God issues instructions governing human life wherever and whenever it may take place. The text limits this set of laws to two. First, having permitted men and women to eat the flesh of animals, God stresses that humans may not eat the animal's blood as well (9:4). Secondly, God prohibits homicide and using the starkest possible language designates it a capital crime: "whoever sheds the blood of man, by man shall his blood be shed" (9:6). The Rabbis derive from the Torah text a set of seven laws applicable to all of humanity.[23] These so-called Noahide commandments are a significant feature of the new world after the flood. Humankind can no longer be trusted to live a proper life; God must step in and teach human beings how to live. This is but the beginning of a process resulting in the Torah's complex code of detailed legislation applicable only to God's selected family, the people Israel.

The Flood's Aftermath – Drink and Curse

The first thing that the text describes Noah as doing after making the covenant with God is planting a vineyard. While he presumably planted other crops as well, it is curious that the Torah tells us only about the grapes. Did God realize that after witnessing the horrors of the deluge, Noah needed to find a way to forget? Or is the biblical narrative typically providing only the information its readers must have – in this case information crucial to the ongoing plotline? For Noah makes wine from the grapes, gets

---

23. These include the prohibition of idolatry, blasphemy, illicit sexual relations, murder, theft, and the eating of a limb cut from a living animal (which seems to be derived from the text's prohibition against eating the blood with the meat). Crucially, included in these laws is the requirement that a court system be established to bring offenders to justice (perhaps, alluded to by the biblical promise that a homicide will have his blood shed by his fellowman).

drunk, and is seen in this state by his son, Ham. Noah disowns Ham's son, Canaan, who is the progenitor of the Canaanites. Shem plays the role of the good brother covering up Noah; Abraham is descended from Shem and inherits the land of Canaan. So the opposing behavior of Ham and Shem plays out through the tradition's view of history.

Since the premise of the entire story is that Noah was a righteous man, I gather that he had no idea what would happen to him when he drank this new beverage that he apparently invented (or discovered). The Torah's attitude toward alcoholic beverages is at this point clearly a negative one. We are given no reason to believe that there is any virtue in winemaking. The idea that wine can be sacramental[24] or play a significant role in the legitimate pursuit of happiness is introduced later.[25] Here Noah gets drunk and uncovers himself while asleep (9:21). Ham sees his father's nakedness and, while he informs his brothers about it, does nothing to remedy the situation (9:22). It is Shem and Japheth who walk into Noah's tent backwards (to avoid seeing their father's nakedness) and cover him (9:23). The upshot is that when Noah wakes up and finds out what happened,[26] he proceeds to curse *not* Ham but Ham's son Canaan, whose progeny will henceforth be doomed to serve the offspring of Shem and Japheth.

This is a strange incident. It is not at all clear exactly what it is that Ham did to deserve such opprobrium. "Uncovering nakedness" is a euphemism for illicit sexual relations in other parts

---

24. It will later be used for libations in the Temple and has been used for two thousand years in Jewish rituals such as weddings and the sanctification of sacred days.

25. "Wine gladdens the heart of man" (*Psalms* 104:15).

26. We are not told how Noah learned of the incident, but it seems clear to me that Shem and Japheth were quick to inform their father of what their younger brother had done – another example of the Torah's ongoing interest in sibling rivalry. Interestingly, in this case it is not the younger sibling (Ham) who is favored, but this may be an exception which proves the rule, for Ham loses favor only because he acts reprehensibly. Indeed, the verse actually refers to Ham as "the youngest son" right before Noah curses Canaan, so perhaps had Ham not erred, he would have been destined for greatness.

of the Torah (*Vayikra* 18, 20). Is there a suggestion here that Ham engaged in homosexual relations with his father while Noah was in a drunken stupor?[27] That would violate two cardinal Torah taboos – homosexual conduct and incest – and could account for the severe curse that followed. If, on the other hand, we take the text at face value, Ham's sin was to look at his father's immodesty, thereby acting in an immodest way himself and failing to give his parent due respect. Neither reading, however, would explain why it is Canaan, not Ham, who becomes the object of Noah's curse. For all the text tells us, Canaan was not even there. Without resort to Midrash, I cannot explain it.[28]

The Tower of Babel

Following the story of Noah's cursing Canaan, the Torah presents a brief genealogy of Noah's descendants. This rendition seems designed to provide the reader with the origins of such important biblical nations as Egypt, Canaan, Babylon, and Assyria. The rendition culminates with the verse: "These are the groupings of Noah's descendants, according to their origins, by their nations" (10:32). The Torah then relates the story of the Tower of Babel. We learn that the new post-flood version of humanity was not much better than the antediluvian one. The text tells us that (what seems to be) the entire human population migrated from the east to Shinar (Babylon, located in present-day Iraq),[29] and

---

27. If this is the correct reading of the text, it presages the incestuous relations Lot's daughters have with their drunken father after the destruction of Sodom.
28. Rashi (based upon BR 36) teaches us that Ham is referred to as "the father of Canaan" in verse twenty-two, when he tells his brothers about their father's nakedness, because Canaan is the one who saw Noah and told his father about it. Thus, according to Rashi, Canaan is the sinner, not Ham. While Ham's designation as Canaan's father is unusual, drawing such a conclusion from it is, to say the least, farfetched.
29. This is a bit bewildering. The ark alighted in Ararat which, if it is anywhere near the present-day mountain of that name, would be in Eastern Turkey. This would mean that humanity should have migrated due south to reach Shinar, so they should have come from the North. Perhaps, the Torah relates that they came "from the east" because its point of reference is Canaan. Thus, someone living in Canaan (west of

decided to build a tower to reach the heavens. The stated reason for this construction project is that the people wanted "to make a name for ourselves; else we shall be scattered all over the world" (11:4). This suggests a prideful effort to assume God-like power over things. Indeed, the Midrash (BR 38:6) immediately suggests that they wanted to build a tower to reach the heavens so that they could conquer heaven and prevent another flood.

The text does not clarify the exact nature of their transgression, but God states: "If…this is how they have begun to act, then nothing that they may propose to do will be out of their reach" (11:6). However we read this verse, what we have is a Promethean effort by humankind to overcome its inherent limitations – in a word, hubris. And God refuses to condone such behavior. He confounds the speech of the builders, so that they cannot communicate with one another. Consequently, the tower does not get built and the people are scattered throughout the world.

This tale is, of course, an etiological one designed to explain to the Torah's readers how even though everyone alive descended from Noah and his sons, a plethora of languages are spoken. The story also seems to be a relatively gentle reminder that, as noble as people may be, human beings cannot become like God. Tangentially, the story also seems to be teaching that, at least at this stage in civilization's history, cities were to be discouraged. Indeed, the text never mentions that the people stopped building the tower, just that "they stopped building the city" (11:8). The ideal existence appears to be a pastoral one.[30]

Ararat) could refer to Mount Ararat as in the East. (Similarly, in later times, the Talmudic sages living in Babylon referred to those living in Israel as "in the West", that is to say, west of Babylon. In contrast, Rabbi Judah Halevi, who lived in Spain, famously wrote that his heart was in the East [the Land of Israel] while he was at the most westerly point in Europe.)

30. Modern biblical scholars have suggested that the story was written from an Israelite perspective. The Israelites, as opposed to the Babylonian urbanites, still lived in pastoral bliss and found the hustle and bustle of a big city offensive; see James Kugel's *How to Read the Bible* (Free Press, 2007) 84–85.

LECH LECHA

Abram's Election

The text now shifts from the universal to the particular. Having discussed the origins and prehistory of humanity, the Torah's focus moves to what will become its raison d'etre: the people Israel and its relationship with God. The Torah already introduced us to Abram at the end of the previous parasha (11:31). There we were told that Terach left the city of Ur with part of his family – his son Abram, Abram's wife, Sarai, and Abram's nephew, Lot – to travel to the land of Canaan. But when they arrived in Haran (situated in present-day Turkey, just north of Syria), they went no further, settling there. This is where the story stands when, out of the blue, at the beginning of *Lech Lecha* (12:1) God speaks to Abram and the history of the people of Israel begins.

God commands Abram to leave his native land and his father's house to go to a land that God will show him: "The Lord said to Abram: 'Go forth from your native land and from your father's house to the land that I will show you'" (12:1). The first part of this command is perplexing. God tells Abram to leave his native land even though the Torah has informed us that he had already left Ur, his native land, with his father some time before.

My feeling is that God's command should be read symbolically; Abram is being told to leave everything pagan symbolized by Ur behind him.[1] Even though Abram is actually leaving from Haran, God's point is that he must put his pagan past behind him.

The other surprising feature of God's call to Abram is that the Torah does not tell us why Abram was chosen. In contrast to Noah, whom the Torah describes as finding favor with the Lord and introduces as "righteous...blameless in his age" (6:8–9), we are given no reason for Abram's election. I am reminded of the arbitrary nature of God's decision to accept Abel's offering and reject Cain's. Indeed, throughout *Tanakh* there appears to be a dichotomy between those instances where God's favor is deserved by its recipients and others (like this one) where God's decision to single out a particular person has no apparent reason behind it.[2] That's just the way things are!

Even though rabbinic Judaism posits that God rewards the righteous and punishes the wicked, there is textual support in the Torah for God's granting His favor arbitrarily. When, after the incident of the golden calf, Moses asks God to reveal his true nature, God replies: "I will be gracious to whom I will be gracious, and I will show mercy to whom I will show mercy" (*Shemot* 33:19). In other words, according to this text a person is not necessarily entitled to divine favor because he is righteous; nor is everyone who receives divine favor necessarily deserving of it. Predictably, that state of affairs does not seem to have sat well with the Rabbis. Concerning Abram's election, the midrashists go to town in

---

1. Similarly, New York is often referred to as Sodom in literary works. Supporting this notion, James Kugel points out that the place Abram came from, "Ur of the Chaldeans" (11:31), or at least the term "Chaldean" itself was synonymous with astronomer or astrologer in Greek and Aramaic. Thus, leaving Chaldea could be read symbolically as leaving the Chaldean pseudoscience and turning toward God (id., 93).

2. The Calvinist view of the election of some people to the exclusion of others seems to derive from the second branch of this dichotomy. The idea that reward comes to those who deserve it (and its concomitant notion that repentance can lead to salvation) appears to derive from the other.

constructing stories of his youth designed to show that he was indeed special and most deserving of God's call and blessing;[3] but none of these appears in the Torah itself. Only later, *ex post facto*, does the Torah explicitly praise Abraham (the new name given to Abram by God) as a person who will educate humanity on the path to a righteous and just life. Perhaps the clearest justification for Abram's election at this point is his response to God. He immediately packs his bags, takes his family, and goes.

In any event, God selects Abram and tells him that he will be blessed: God will make him a great nation and will condition His blessings to the rest of humanity upon their attitude toward Abram, blessing those who bless him and cursing those who curse him (12:2–3). This first covenant between God and Abram is pretty much one-sided. Abram and his descendants receive a cornucopia of divine blessings and all Abram has to do is continue the journey his father had already started years before and go to Canaan. Needless to say, he does this, taking his wife and his nephew Lot with him.

The text is careful to note that Abram was a wealthy man and that he took his wealth and the "persons…he had acquired [literally, made] in Haran" (12:5). Taking this text at face value, it appears that Abram brought his slaves along with him. The reader might wonder why the text needs to tell us that Abram brought his slaves. Coupling this seemingly extraneous information with their zeal to give Abram an extra-textual history justifying his election by God, the midrashists tell us that the patriarch had literally "made" these people, converting them to the monotheistic

---

3. For example, the Midrash tells us that Terach was an idol manufacturer and that Abram, while minding the store, destroyed the idols; there is another story that Nimrod, king of Ur, saw Abram as a threat to the state pagan religion and sought to have him executed only to be thwarted by divine intervention (BR 38:28). These stories not only provide a midrashic basis for God's election of Abram but also plainly support the rabbinic view (which has no support in the Torah text) that Abraham intuited God's oneness prior to his being called to leave his father's house and go to Canaan.

religion he espoused. Whether this midrash is taken as historical truth or not, clearly Abram's caravan was a wealthy one.

When the group arrives in Shechem (today the city of Nablus), God appears again to Abram and promises that He will give the land to Abram's offspring (12:7). This covenant is totally unilateral. God does not require anything of Abram or of his offspring in exchange for the promise of the land (which, significantly, had not been mentioned when God told Abram to go there). Scholars designate this type of contract a royal grant (or a covenant of grace). God, the king, promises to give and the recipient merely has to accept.

Abram, Sarai, and Pharaoh

At this point in the narrative, Abram, Sarai, Lot and the camp followers travel south into the Negev desert (12:9). Here the Torah, for the first time, describes Egypt as the source of food during Middle Eastern famines; the text reports that there was a severe famine in the land (of Canaan) and that Abram traveled south to Egypt in order to survive it (12:10). What happens next raises some serious questions about Abram's moral character, as yet undemonstrated in the text. And it occurs at an especially critical juncture, when Abram undoes the only positive action he has taken so far – going to Canaan – by fleeing to Egypt when the first hint of adversity strikes.[4]

As they are about to enter Egypt, Abram tells Sarai that her striking physical beauty poses a threat to his life. The Egyptians, he says, are likely to kill him in order to get him out of the way, so that they can take her – presumably to Pharaoh's harem. Abram devises a plan. He asks Sarai to say that she is his sister. She does this and is taken into the harem. On the one hand, Abram's fear is palpable and understandable; however, as the scenario plays

4. Nachmanides (Ramban) in his commentary on the Torah (*Bereshit* 12:10) rebukes Abraham for the sin of leaving the land at the time of the famine and for the sin, which will be discussed shortly, of putting his wife at risk in Egypt. For Ramban, both sins were a result of his lack of complete faith in God.

out, all his scheming appears to be nothing more than a business stratagem. In exchange for pandering his "sister" to Pharaoh, Abram is given livestock and slaves – a veritable fortune.[5] To protect Sarai, God has to step in and afflict the Egyptian court with a plague. Significantly, Pharaoh manages to deduce the reason for the plague and he immediately upbraids Abram for deceiving him: "What is this you have done to me! Why did you not tell me that she was your wife!" (12:18) Pharaoh, wanting nothing more to do with either Abram or Sarai, returns Sarai to her husband and sends the two of them back to Canaan together with all of Abram's possessions, including those he obtained by virtue of the ruse.

The ethical hero of this story is clearly Pharaoh, the supposedly decadent king of Egypt, not Abram, the man of God. Pharaoh seems to be following a moral code. In his world, unmarried foreign women may be taken to the harem as long as their brothers (or other male guardians) are showered with gifts. Concomitantly, women who are truly off limits must immediately be returned unsullied. Abram, the man of God, seems to have far fewer scruples. Abram showed callous disregard for Sarai's well-being in his zeal to save his own skin and enrich himself. Indeed, even if Abram believed that God's promise to him would protect Sarai, so that he could both enrich himself and not really put her in harm's way, he placed his wife in an awful situation. Did he think that Pharaoh would not molest her in any way after he had paid good money to obtain her for his harem? What did Abram think was going to happen as the result of his deception? Surely, nothing truly good could come of it. Indeed, if he was so sure of God's protection, why engage in the deception at all? This is a far cry from the Abram we will encounter in the next parasha who argues with God on behalf of the righteous people of Sodom (assuming there were any). To be sure, God's promise of blessing seems to come to fruition even in

5.   Curiously, Abram actually says to Sarai: "Please say that you are my sister, that it may go well with me because of you, *and* that I may remain alive thanks to you" (12:13). The verse seems to imply that Abram expects two payoffs from his ruse: that it may go well with him (riches) and that he may remain alive.

Egypt. Abram gets to keep the assets he obtained by fraudulently selling his wife into the harem while she maintains the purity of her marital relationship throughout the ordeal. But one thing is certain: the Torah does not pull any punches when it comes to portraying the patriarchs. We get a full picture, warts and all!

Abram and Lot

Abram and Sarai head north from Egypt as rich herders, with cattle, gold, and silver – presumably some of these assets being the price Pharaoh paid for Sarai. The text makes no apology for Abram's obtaining all this wealth under false pretenses.[6] Out of the blue, the Torah tells us that Abram's nephew, Lot, left Egypt with them. This information is a bit surprising at first, since the text did not even mention that Lot had joined Abram and Sarai in Egypt; but on second thought it reveals the Torah's tendency to provide details only when necessary. The story in Egypt was about Abram and Sarai so Lot was not mentioned; much of the next few chapters concerns Abram's relationship with Lot, so the Torah reintroduces him. Even more crucial to the upcoming plot, the Torah tells us that Lot was also a wealthy man, possessing flocks and herds (13:5). But nowhere does the text explain where or how Lot came by his wealth.

Perhaps, the Torah had to posit Lot's wealth as a plot device to explain how he wound up living in Sodom apart from his uncle's family. Indeed, the Torah mentions Lot's wealth and then declares "that the land could not support them [Abraham and Lot] staying together" (13:6). Apparently, an ongoing dispute between Abraham and Lot's herdsmen over grazing rights finally led Abram, the senior of the two, to suggest that Lot and he separate. Abraham

---

6. This reminds me of the Israelite slaves despoiling Egypt of its gold and silver – admittedly at God's behest – when they left (*Shemot* 11:2). According to the Rabbis, they were merely taking their due, in lieu of the wages withheld from them during their years of bondage. One might just as well say that the Egyptians withheld wages to gain recompense for the wealth that Abram had fraudulently obtained from them when he sold Sarai into the Pharaoh's harem.

offers his nephew the opportunity to choose the land he wishes as his own.[7] Lot shows himself to be a selfish nephew (and an ungrateful one to boot, for his uncle had plainly taken responsibility for him since leaving Haran) when he selects the choicest region, the well-watered Jordan plain, and moves to Sodom.

The text foreshadows the troubles Lot will have in Sodom by noting that the Jordan plain was only fertile before God destroyed Sodom and Gomorrah and by noting, without explaining itself, that the Sodomites were evil, "very wicked sinners against the Lord" (13:13). Since God had as of yet promulgated only the seven Noahide laws, presumably the people of Sodom were violating those most fundamental principles. Most importantly, this rift with Lot is the first instance recorded in the Torah illustrating Abram's generosity. This is the first time that Abram – in offering Lot first choice – demonstrates what a special person he is, endowed with character traits that justify the divine blessings bestowed upon him. Indeed, while the text has referred to righteous men in the past (notably Enoch and Noah), Abram is the first to explicitly act righteously.[8] The Torah, in recounting the rest of Abram's life, tells a number of stories designed to emphasize this aspect of his character.[9]

After Lot and Abram separate, God reiterates his promise to give Abram and his descendants "the land" (13:16), even expanding

---

7. Clearly, Abram is confident that God will keep his promise to give the land to Abram's progeny, for even though "the Canaanites and Perizzites were then dwelling in the land" (13:7) Abram, without a thought that he was dealing with other peoples' property, splits the grazing rights with Lot.
8. Significantly, Noah, as far as the text informs us, made no effort to warn any of his neighbors about what was going to happen to them. Some of the Rabbis of the Midrash (BR 30:7) dispute this, explaining that there were 120 years between God's first approach to Noah and the beginning of the flood; according to the midrashists, this time was set aside for Noah to warn the people.
9. The incident previously described with Pharaoh in Egypt (and its echo in the later incident with Abimelech of Gerar, *Bereshit* 20) does point in the other direction. And, when we get to the defining moment of Abraham's life – the *Akedah* (where Abraham binds Isaac to be sacrificed at God's apparent command) – his behavior becomes even more difficult to understand, much less venerate.

the promise to include the territory visible in all directions from Abram's tent located between Bethel and Ai. Indeed, God expands the blessing. While at the beginning of *Lech Lecha* God promised to make of Abram "a great nation" (12:2), here, after Lot departs for Sodom, God specifies that Abram's descendants will be so numerous that they will be too many to count, "as the dust of the earth" (13:16). However, I am not sure whether the promise of the land includes the eastern area given to Lot. While God tells Abram to look in all directions (including the East) – "'Raise your eyes and look out from where you are, to the north and south, to the east and west, for I give all the land that you see to you and your offspring forever'" (13:14) – the uncle and his nephew have just completed a division of the land, with the eastern Jordan plain going to Lot. This description of the metes and bounds of the Promised Land bears comparison to later descriptions given to Moses.

Abram the Military Leader

The Torah's prehistory – from creation through the flood and the dispersion of the nations after the building of the Tower of Babel – is replete with narratives about the origins of much of what we know as human life. But it is not until this stage in Abram's story (*Bereshit* 14) that the Torah first mentions that blight on human existence, war. Perhaps, there were wars before, but the Torah does not see fit to mention them. Even here, the war is somewhat incidental to the plotline. Nine kings engage in a war, five against four; in the course of the battle, Abram's nephew, Lot, (who had settled in Sodom, one of the warring kingdoms) gets captured. When Abram is informed of this, he musters a small army of three hundred and eighteen men and heads north to rescue his nephew. Traveling all the way to Damascus, this small band of marauders is successful; they free Lot, his compatriots, the women, and all of their possessions and return to the area of Sodom.

The king of Sodom offers Abram a large share of the spoils, but Abram declines, declaring that he does not want anyone to be able to say, "It is I who made Abram rich" (14:23).[10] In the course of his triumphal journey home, Abram is met and greeted by Melchizedek, king of Shalem and priest of God Most High (*El Elyon*). Melchizedek is a fabled character – he plays a significant role in the complicated theology set forth in the New Testament *Epistle to the Hebrews* and in the ceremonies surrounding the ordination of Roman Catholic priests. The reference to Shalem must be to the place we know as Jerusalem (*Yeru-shalem*). It is interesting to note that the monotheism practiced by Abram is not limited to the patriarch and his family. There is plainly a cult of the one God being practiced in Shalem, and Melchizedek is its priest.[11] Melchizedek brings out bread and wine – the first mention in the text that Noah's discovery of alcohol can have a positive, sacramental use – blesses Abram and blesses God for having delivered Abram's enemies into his hands. Significantly, Abram recognizes Melchizedek's legitimacy as God's priest by giving him a tithe of the war's spoils (this before giving the spoils to the king of Sodom).

This military escapade seems to be a strange digression, particularly since it separates God's promise to Abram "between Bethel and Ai" (discussed above, 13:14–17) and the mystical theophany Abram experiences at the Covenant Between the Pieces. It appears that this digression has three functions. First, it introduces Jerusalem and anchors that city's sacred status in the early history of the Jewish people (here as the seat of Melchizedek, the first priest mentioned in the Torah). Second, for what appears to be the first time, the Torah introduces us to one of its fundamental lessons: God's guiding hand has more to do with the outcome of historical events (particularly, military ones) than

10. This is somewhat ironic, since Abram's wealth came, in large measure, from the property he was given in exchange for Sarai in Egypt. Perhaps, in declining the king of Sodom's offer he was being diplomatic, the real reason for refusing the spoils being that he did not want to accept wealth from the evil kingdom of Sodom.

11. Later on, in *Shemot*, we find another instance of a non-Israelite priest (Jethro of Midian, Moses' father-in-law) who also recognizes the God of Israel.

the conduct of the human beings engaged in them does.[12] And third, Abram's humility and generosity shine out. Not only does he tithe a share of the spoils to the priest, he also refuses to benefit personally from the remainder. His only reason for fighting in the first place was to rescue Lot and his family. Once that goal was accomplished, Abram wanted nothing more. Abram was, after all, no ordinary general![13]

The Covenant Between the Pieces

The biblical narrative continues in *Bereshit* 15 with a mystifying description of either one or two epiphanies (or, perhaps more appropriately, theophanies). The first section comprises verses one to six, while what may be the second stretches from verse seven to verse twenty-one. The traditional division of the Torah reading on Shabbat starts the sixth *aliyah* (section of the Torah reading) with the beginning of the second section, so tradition seems to support the notion that there were two events. As a matter of convenience, I will refer to the two sections as separate man-God confrontations. After discussing them, I will return to the question of whether there were one or two.

At the outset of the episode, Abram for the first time apprehends God in a vision ("Some time later, the word of the Lord came to Abram in a vision"[15:1]) – a marked difference from the earlier revelations in which the text merely states that God spoke to Abram. What is more, in this vision Abram speaks to God – also a departure from the previous revelatory experiences (and a precursor of his dialogue with God concerning the fate of Sodom). Abram complains that despite God's promise of in-

---

12. Indeed, Melchizedek's blessing of the victorious Abram explicitly credits the military success to El Elyon: "And blessed be God Most High, who has delivered your foes into your hand" (14:20).

13. Contrast this with the Exodus story, where the freed Israelite slaves take gold, silver, and other property from their Egyptian neighbors. To be sure, the text states that God told them (*Shemot* 11:2) to "ask" for the property, but the contrast with Abram's conduct after the war is most striking nonetheless.

numerable progeny, he has no offspring and will have to leave his property (and his future expectations) to Eliezer, his major domo. God's response is categorical: Eliezer will not be Abram's heir. To the contrary, Abram's own progeny will inherit both his goods and his blessing. In reconfirming this promise, God reiterates the innumerable quantity of Abram's descendants and likens them to the stars.[14]

Following this response and Abram's apparent acquiescence God (perhaps beginning a second epiphany) tells Abram just who He is: the Lord who brought Abram *out of Ur* of the Chaldeans (15:7). This is a strange way for God to describe Himself, since Abram was in Haran, not Ur, when God first spoke to Him. The Torah seems to be intimating that Abram's father, Terach, left Ur with his family at God's behest, whether or not he was aware of it at the time. This is somewhat odd in light of the midrashic notion mentioned above that Terach was an idolater. But it is squarely in keeping with the rabbinic belief that God wills everything that happens in the world. As noted above, I believe that the city Ur symbolizes the pagan worldview that Abram was commanded to leave. If so, it is fitting that God describe Himself as having brought Abram out of Ur.

Abram asks for proof that his progeny will indeed inherit the land: "O Lord God, how shall I know that I am to possess it?" (15:8) God's response is the Covenant Between the Pieces, an arcane ceremony involving the slaughter of five animals, the separation of four of their carcasses into two pieces and the appearance of a magical fire that passes between the pieces. Apparently, this ritual reflects an ancient Near Eastern covenant ceremony. God is legally formalizing his promise.[15] Again, as with God's covenant

---

14. The previous simile (used in 13:16) was the dust of the earth.
15. This interpretation of the covenant between the pieces is supported by Jeremiah's use of the identical ceremony (*Jeremiah* 34:17–22) in his description of a covenant between God and the people Israel. The ceremony also bears a close resemblance to the contest Elijah holds with the prophets of Baal (*1 Kings* 18:20–40).

with Noah, the divine promise is unilateral; Abram assumes no reciprocal obligations.

God's promise is accompanied by a prophecy: Abram's descendants will be enslaved in a strange land for four hundred years, after which God will free them and they shall return to the land. Integral to the Covenant Between the Pieces is yet another description of the Promised Land's boundaries. This time God actually provides geographical landmarks to delineate the land: "from the river of Egypt [the Nile] to the great river, the river Euphrates" (15:18). The land described here is a good deal larger than the territory Abram was able to see after Lot left for Sodom. These boundaries clearly include within the promised territory present-day Gaza and the Sinai Peninsula, as well as present-day Jordan and parts of present-day Iraq.[16] I doubt whether the Jewish polity at its height under Solomon ever incorporated all this territory.

A key to determining whether the text describes one or two epiphanies is Abram's state of wakefulness. At the beginning of the first section, the Torah explicitly states that Abram receives a *machazeh*, a dream or vision. At the beginning of the second section, God has a conversation with Abram, and Abram clearly appears to have woken up as he slaughters animals and drives off a bird of prey. Only after doing these things does Abram fall into "a deep sleep" (15:12). From this we may conclude that two distinct epiphanies took place: the vision described in section one and the Covenant Between the Pieces (which included Abram's slaughtering the animals and falling into a "deep sleep") in section two.

Hagar

So far the Torah has shared Abram's concern that God's promise

16. The reader may recall that I was unsure whether the area east of the Jordan (which Abram could see, but Lot had taken) was included in the boundaries of the Promised Land. Here there is no such ambiguity. The deed includes all the land from the Mediterranean to the Euphrates. Whether or not this biblical description should have any impact on twenty-first century Middle Eastern politics is, of course, a different kettle of fish.

to give the land to his progeny will be meaningless if Abram and his wife, Sarai, die childless. In this section, the text for the first time addresses Sarai's inner turmoil, mainly by detailing her actions.[17] Apparently distressed that she has not given her husband any children, Sarai suggests a surrogate motherhood arrangement to Abram: "Consort with my maid [Hagar]; perhaps I shall be built up through her" (16:2). Abram will take Sarai's Egyptian servant Hagar to bed and any offspring will be credited to Sarai. Without recording Abram's reply, the text tells us that Abram listened to her and took Hagar (either as a second wife or as a concubine). Hagar immediately conceived.

Up to this point in the biblical narrative, the Torah has not alluded to one of *Bereshit's* principal narrative themes – jealousy between rival women (wives or concubines) over the ability to conceive.[18] Here, this theme appears with a vengeance. Hagar, the erstwhile servant girl, starts lording it over her barren mistress. The text reports that Sarai became "lowered" in Hagar's eyes (16:4), but it is plain that the Egyptian girl condescended to her mistress and Sarai did not like it. Sarai complains to Abram, and for the second time Abram's behavior in the face of a personal crisis is less than saintly.[19] Seeing how angry Sarai is at the upshot of her own surrogate motherhood scheme, Abram tells her to do whatever she wants with Hagar. The next thing we know, the pregnant Hagar has fled from Sarai into the desert – obviously as the result of harsh treatment (if not outright banishment) by her mistress.

While it may be tempting to excuse Abram's conduct here as demonstrating loyalty to his principal wife and a salutary concern for *shalom bayit* (domestic peace), it seems to me that his

17. Even during the Egyptian episode when she was taken (perhaps more accurately sold) into Pharaoh's harem, the text gave us no hint of what, if anything, Sarai had to say about her predicament or how she felt about it. Until this point Sarai has been a two-dimensional character, significant only because she is Abram's wife.
18. The principal example of this theme, of course, is the rivalry between Leah and Rachel for Jacob's affections. The same theme appears elsewhere in *Tanakh*, most significantly in the account of Samuel's birth (*1 Sam.* 1).
19. The first was the incident with Pharaoh.

permitting Sarai to drive Hagar out of the household was unjust and essentially cowardly. Having decided to take Hagar into his bed – at Sarai's urging, no less – Abram is ethically obligated to protect her from her mistress' enmity. Problematically, the Torah does not censure Abram's behavior, at least not explicitly. For even though God sends an angel to rescue Hagar and her unborn son, nowhere are Sarai's and Abram's actions called into question (16:7–15). As we shall soon see, Abraham takes a different tack after Hagar's child is born, questioning Sarah's[20] determination to drive out both the slave-woman and her son; but in that instance, as the text (21:11–12) takes the trouble to tells us, Abraham is anxious on account of the child, *not* on account of the treatment to be meted out to Hagar. Perhaps the Torah's message is that surrogate parenting is not such a good idea.[21] It is certainly telling us that God did not choose Abraham because he is an unflagging paragon of virtue. [22]

As it turns out, God has plans for Hagar's unborn son and intervenes. An angel of the Lord finds her by a spring and asks her where she has come from and where she is going. Hagar replies: "I am running away from my mistress Sarai" (16:8). God's messenger tells her to return and "submit to her [Sarai's] harsh treatment" (16:9).[23] Hagar receives the blessing of innumerable progeny, and for the first time in the Torah, God (through the angel) instructs a mother on the name she is to give her son – Ishmael ("God hears" [16:11]).

20. By that time, Sarai has become Sarah and Abram, Abraham.
21. Yet it is only through four instances of surrogate parenting that Jacob's sons reach the magical number of twelve – the tribes of Israel.
22. On the other hand, given that the angel who saves Hagar advises her to return and "submit to her [Sarai's] harsh treatment" (16:9), we must ask whether the Torah is telling us that even God assents to Sarai and Abram's ethically repugnant behavior, thus by definition rendering it ethical. We must conclude that either God ascribes to a surprisingly unethical, ethical code (as he did at the time of the flood, and Abram's actions are judged righteous), or He has his own reasons for allowing Abram and Sarai's unethical behavior (and Abram's actions are censurable).
23. Where is the morality in this? See the previous note.

This choice of names is in and of itself interesting, for there is nothing in the text intimating that Hagar had prayed for deliverance.[24] Is it possible that what God heard was Abram's plaint that he had no children to inherit the divine blessing? That would be a difficult conclusion to reach in light of God's later insistence that the progeny to receive the blessing will come from Sarai's offspring, not Hagar's (17:19). Perhaps the text is suggesting that Hagar indeed prayed for help. One thing, however, is quite clear. Even after the advent of Abraham and the commencement of the special relationship between God and what will become the people of Israel, God, on occasion, appears to others. In other words, we have here a hint – albeit a small one – of the universal God of the creation story who relates not only to Israel but to all of humanity.[25]

At the conclusion of this episode, Hagar returns to Abram and bears him a son. The text reports that "Abram gave the son that Hagar bore him the name Ishmael" (16:15). That statement is surprising, for the angel told Hagar that *she* – not Abram – should call her son by that name. To be sure, there is no reason to suppose that Hagar didn't tell Abram about her meeting with God's messenger in the desert. But for the literal-minded, the fact that it is Abram who names the baby "God hears" does underscore the question raised above: Just what and whom did God hear? Did God hear Hagar, or did He hear Abram's plaintive cry for a son? Or, even more tellingly – returning to another issue raised above– did God hear Abraham (partially) redeeming himself by praying on behalf of his suffering slave-woman and her unborn son?

Circumcision

Following Ishmael's birth (when Abram was eighty-six), there

---

24. Indeed, the text tells us that God heard Hagar's suffering, not her prayer.
25. Perhaps the text is suggesting that even without praying to God, Hagar's suffering itself "was heard", meriting divine intervention. If so, the Torah would be teaching a critical lesson: God perceives the unjust suffering of his creatures (whether they pray to Him or not) and responds to it.

appears to be a thirteen-year gap before God appears again to Abram (when he is ninety-nine years old). God reveals himself with a new name – *El Shaddai* (which I understand to mean God the Powerful) – and commands Abram to be a righteous person by walking in His ways: "Walk in my ways and be righteous" (17:1).[26] In return, God reiterates yet again the promise to make Abram the father of a multitude of nations and make his progeny exceedingly numerous. In recognition of this enviable fate, Abram is given a new name – Abraham (literally, father of a multitude). In this reiteration of the covenant, the borders of the Promised Land seem to be limited to the land of Canaan, as no mention is made of the Nile to the south or the Euphrates to the east. Most significantly, this time the covenant is no longer unilateral. Not only must Abraham walk in God's ways and be righteous; additionally, he and all of his male offspring (those alive today and those to be born in the future) are commanded to inscribe "the sign of the covenant" (17:11) on their very flesh by circumcising the flesh of the foreskin on the eighth day after birth.[27] Indeed, any male who does not undergo this rite of circumcision is to be "cut off from his kin" (17:14).

This version of the covenant is also unique because Sarai is mentioned. Sarai receives a new name – Sarah (some translate this as princess), and, what is more, Abram is told "I will bless her; indeed, I will give you a son by her" (17:16). The promise that Abraham shall have an heir by Sarah is repeated with an explicit statement that she will bear Abraham a son. Abraham is incredulous and laughs, thinking that he and his wife (who the text tells us is ninety) are much too old to have children. Assuming that the

26. The Torah does not tell Abram (or us) what these ways are. Presumably, God had informed Abram precisely what those ways were at an earlier time. Note that this potentially implies an oral tradition existing alongside the written biblical one and posits that important material is left out of the Bible's textual record.

27. The importance of this outward sign of the Abrahamic covenant is underscored by the command that, in addition to all male offspring, all slaves in the household must also be circumcised (17:12–13). To belong to Abraham's tribe one must, quite literally, be circumcised.

promise of a son by Sarah is fatuous, Abraham asks God to favor Ishmael. God's response is to repeat the promise that Sarah will indeed have a son, and Abraham is commanded to name the child Isaac (which derives from the Hebrew verb "to laugh").[28] God further tells Abraham that Isaac will be born in one year's time. Not forgetting Abraham's concern for Ishmael, God promises that he too will father "a great nation" (17:20) – traditionally understood to be the Arab nation. After this epiphany has ended, Abraham proceeds to circumcise himself and Ishmael (who is thirteen) as well as all of the household's male servants.

The circumcision commandment has been central to Jewish identity since Judaism's very inception. Today it is the center of some controversy. There are medical opinions suggesting that it is beneficial to one's health (for example, some consider it to be prophylactic in avoiding penile cancer and there is even recent evidence that suggests it assists in preventing AIDS) and there are other opinions labeling it barbaric and claiming it is harmful to one's health.[29] Either way, its importance in the Jewish world is beyond dispute. Some midrashic commentaries even suggest that a few blessed men were born in a perfect state, already circumcised.[30] The idea that a circumcised organ is perfect finds expression in a common biblical metaphor suggesting that an uncircumcised organ is less than perfect. For instance, Moses refers to his uncircumcised lips (*Shemot* 6:30); there are a number of biblical references to those sinners who possess an uncircumcised heart

---

28. Unlike Ishmael, whose mother was commanded to name him, Abraham himself is commanded to name his son Isaac.

29. The traditional practice of applying oral suction (*metzitzah*) to the wound is also a matter of some controversy. Traditionally, the practice may have been salutary, but given our knowledge of how infection is spread, the potential danger to the baby and the *mohel* (ritual circumciser) has led rabbinic decisors for much of the last two hundred years to search for a method to replace actual oral suction, such as through the mohel's use of a sponge or a pipette. Some ultra-Orthodox halachic decisors still reject such technical solutions. For a review of the historical controversy within the Jewish community, see J. Katz "The Controversy Over the Mezizah," *Divine Law in Human Hands* (Magnes Press, 1998).

30. *Midrash Psalms* 9:7 names thirteen individuals who were born circumcised.

(*Vayikra* 26:41; *Devarim* 10:16; *Ezekiel* 44:9); and one reference refers to those who have uncircumcised ears and cannot hear the word of God (*Jeremiah* 6:10). Such a metaphorical reference to the final product of the act of circumcision seems to me to reflect a misunderstanding of the rite. It is the act itself – not the resulting physical condition – that represents the Jew's acceptance (through his father's action) of the nation's covenantal relationship with God. That the rite is performed on the flesh of the organ of procreation does serve to underscore its importance, especially since it is an act a father performs on his newborn progeny; but I do not think that the sexual reference is at its core.[31]

---

31. Several midrashim in the Talmud do make this connection arguing that circumcision helps to curb sinful lust. For those Rabbis it made sense to position the mark of the covenant at the root of potential sin. See *Sukkah* 52a, *Nedarim* 32a, and *Menachot* 43b. Obviously, there is no reference whatsoever to this notion in our parasha.

VAYERA

God Visits the Sick

God appears to Abraham while he is sitting at the entrance of his tent in Elonai Mamre in the heat of the day. No reason is given for God's visit, so the midrashists search for one in the Torah's immediately preceding episode: Abraham's circumcision. Though there is no reason in the text to link these two events so closely, they explain (*Bava Metzia* 86b) that God was fulfilling the commandment of *bikur cholim* (visiting the sick). In fact, this story becomes the rabbinic model for performing this *mitzvah* (commandment). While the Talmud is, of course, expressing a lovely sentiment, I find it difficult to believe that God's visitation is related to visiting the sick. Indeed, as the story unfolds, it becomes clear that it has two purposes, neither of which has anything to do with bikur cholim: (1) to announce that Sarah will have a child the following year; and (2) to announce the impending destruction of Sodom and Gomorrah.

The Annunciation of Isaac's Birth

Traditional commentators have dwelt upon the fact that Abraham interrupts his conversation with God to tend to three travelers who appear at his tent: "He asked God to wait for him while he ran and invited the travelers" (Rashi, 18:3). While Abraham's apparent rudeness to God might be explained by his desire to help the travelers (and, according to the Midrash, convert them to monotheism), it is still surprising.[1]

After Abraham notices the travelers, he immediately assumes the role of host and prepares a massive lunch of milk, cheese, and veal. Rabbinic commentators (who are fond of positing that the patriarchs observed the as-yet-unrevealed Torah whenever they were in the Land of Israel)[2] suffered great angst over Abraham's apparent violation of normative *kashrut* rules (Jewish dietary laws) by serving milk and meat products together. Some explain his actions by noting that he must have served the milk products first and then the veal, in keeping with normative Halacha. Even if this were true, there is no suggestion that any appreciable time elapsed between the milk and meat dishes, so there might still be a problem.[3] I find the conclusion virtually inescapable that Abraham had no problem serving his guests meat and milk products simultaneously. Indeed, not all the classical commentators were so certain that the patriarchs observed all the mitzvot, even in the Land of Israel.

During the meal, the visitors ask where Sarah is and are told that she is in the tent. One says that he will return in a year and Sarah will have a son. This prophecy could hardly have come as a surprise to Abraham, since God had already told him precisely

1. I suggest below that Abraham was not rude at all because it is easy to find hints in the text that these men were some sort of manifestation of God, or, to make a more audacious claim, one of them was actually God Himself in human form. If so, Abraham did not interrupt his conversation with God at all, but merely continued it.
2. See, for instance, *Yevamot* 21a, *Yoma* 67b, BR 64:5, and *Nachmanides* 26:5. A more extensive discussion will be found below in the context of Abraham's treaty with Abimelech and Isaac's consumption of Esau's venison.
3. Although, as I understand it, no less an authority than the *Shulchan Arukh* permits the eating of meat directly after milk if the "meal" is over – as represented, for example, by washing out one's mouth – there is no hint of such a separation between the eating of milk and meat products in the text here.

this before commanding him to circumcise himself and his household. But this time the annunciation of Isaac's impending birth is overheard by Sarah; she laughs when she hears it – precisely as Abraham had when God told him. Sarah remarks to herself that she is long past her childbearing years and wonders whether at her and Abraham's advanced ages the couple could even have sexual pleasure (as I understand it, whether the procreative act itself could even be performed). The fact that the Torah abandons the conversation between Abraham and the visitors to tell us that Sarah overheard the annunciation and reacted with disbelief is somewhat surprising. We would have expected Abraham's response to the news. Even more astonishing is the fact that, instead of the visitors telling Abraham about Sarah's reactions or responding to them, the text states that God breaks into the conversation, speaking to Abraham and responding to Sarah's questions: "Then the Lord said to Abraham, 'Why did Sarah laugh …? Is anything too wondrous for the Lord? I will return to you at the time next year, and Sarah shall have a son'" (18:13–14). Why is God suddenly speaking to Abraham again when the travelers seem to have assumed this role in the story? Furthermore, God's promise to return "at the time next year" is particularly surprising, since earlier the text makes it quite clear that one of the visitors would return in a year: "Then one [of the visitors] said: 'I will return to you next year, and your wife Sarah shall have a son!'" (18:10). Who is supposed to return next year, the visitor or God?

The simplest, yet most non-traditional, resolution of this textual puzzle seems to be that God Himself was one of the three visitors – God possessed or took human form – a conclusion that the Rabbis are quick to dispute since it suggests that God has a body (or, at the very least, can assume one). Such a reading, however, resolves two problems in the text: (1) how Abraham could have abandoned the conversation with God when the travelers appeared, and (2) why both God and the traveler stated that they would return next year. Simply put, at least one of the travelers is God Himself, so Abraham does not interrupt his conversation with God, and God promises to return (in human form) next year.

To be sure, one could water down this answer by suggesting that the travelers were angels, either embodying God Himself or carrying His message. However, this approach would still not explain how Abraham could have abandoned his conversation with God at the beginning of the story. One does not abandon God to talk to men (even if they are actually angels). Furthermore, while the verse stating that God spoke to Abraham about Sarah's reaction might mean that He spoke through the traveler/angel (in the same manner that the prophets introduce their prophecies by declaring, "Thus sayeth the Lord"), this is not the plain meaning of the text; for it explicitly states, "Then the Lord said". Had God been speaking through the angel, the Torah should have explicitly said so.

Additionally, there is some textual evidence supporting the notion that one of the "men" was indeed God himself. According to the text, three "men" visit Abraham (18:2); the "men" depart for Sodom while God remains behind to talk to Abraham (18:16, 22); and only two "men" arrive at Sodom to see to its destruction and Lot's salvation (19:8, 10). The Rabbis, sensitive to these discrepancies, explain that the third visitor's mission was solely to announce the impending birth of Isaac and, having done that, he left; but the text makes no mention of this. Taking the text at face value, the missing traveler seems to be God. Indeed, when the "men" first arrive in Sodom, the Torah refers to them as "angels" (19:1). Perhaps the Torah referred to them previously as "men" because it could hardly refer to them as "two angels and God". Now that God has departed, the two remaining angels can be referred to as such. Whether God was actually one of the travelers or not, this story certainly describes an immanent God who has personal relationships with some humans – particularly the forbears of Israel.

Be that as it may, the esoteric question of God's physical immanence or incorporeality is less significant here than the text's reiteration of the laughter theme in connection with Isaac (whose name, as noted above, connotes "laughter"). One might well ask why the Torah, so soon after reporting Abraham's laughter at Isaac's annunciation, takes pains to repeat an almost identical story with Sarah as the protagonist. To be sure, two separate etiological traditions may have existed explaining Isaac's name (one featuring Abraham and one featuring Sarah); however, the text does appear to be somewhat repetitive on this point. In any event, in the annunciation of Isaac's birth we have what appears to be an archetypical annunciation scene – with one important differentiating feature. The normal annunciation – like the announcement to Hagar about the birth of Ishmael or the announcement of the impending birth of Samson – is delivered to the mother-to-be. Both annunciations of Isaac's birth are made to the father, and the mother hears about it only by listening from inside her tent. Are we being told that the relationship between God and Abraham, to some degree, excludes Sarah? We shall return to this question soon enough in connection with God's commandment to bring Isaac as a sacrifice and Abraham's reaction to it.

Abraham's Battle for Sodom

Following the second annunciation of the impending birth of Isaac, we come to perhaps the most sublime incident in the Abraham story. God has decided to destroy Sodom and states that he cannot keep that decision from Abraham because the patriarch has been singled out to teach his children and his posterity what is just and right in order to obtain what God has promised to give them: "Now the Lord had said, 'Shall I hide from Abraham what I am about to do.... ? For I have singled him out, that he may instruct his children and his posterity to keep the way of the Lord by doing what is just and right, in order that the Lord may bring about for Abraham what He has promised him'" (18:17–19). That God conditions fulfilling his promises to Abraham's descendants upon their conduct is very surprising. In the past, He has made no such stipulation. Time after time, with the one exception of the commandment of circumcision, God has made unilateral promises (so-called covenants of grace) to Abraham, without requiring that Abraham (or his descendants) do anything in return. The Torah's new tone suggests that this omission may merely have been an oversight that is now being corrected. This helps explain why no *quid pro quo* was mentioned before.[4]

In any event, because God views Abraham as His partner in spreading the monotheistic message to the world,[5] He feels compelled to let the patriarch in on His plans to destroy Sodom and Gomorrah[6] because of the gravity of their inhabitants' sins.[7] Abraham argues with God about this plan, asserting that the "Judge of all the earth" (18:25) must act justly and that it would be unjust to destroy the innocent along with the guilty. Rather than suggesting the obvious, that the innocent be relocated before the destruction, Abraham demonstrates a deep concern for humanity and suggests that the presence of fifty righteous people in Sodom should suffice

4. Abraham's questionable behavior with regard to defrauding Pharaoh and mistreating Hagar (and both incidents will repeat themselves soon with Abraham defrauding Abimelech and banishing Hagar), leads one to wonder whether it was fortunate that God did not establish a *quid pro quo* of righteous behavior on Abraham's part. How Abraham's behavior, or similar conduct on the part of his descendants, might affect the covenant between God and Israel deserves serious consideration. Perhaps we are being told that the unilateral covenant of grace was merely a foreshadowing of the more important covenant of mutual obligation that took place at Sinai, where the community of Israel agreed to follow the Torah's precepts. This, of course, is precisely the opposite of what Saint Paul concludes, in his Epistle to the Galatians, where the apostle argues that it was the unilateral covenant of grace (which requires only faith on the part of the recipient) and not the covenant at Sinai (which requires works, that is, the performance by Israel of mitzvot) that was significant.

5. He does not say this in so many words; He merely talks about Abraham's "keeping the way of the Lord" and teaching it to his progeny.

6. I have often wondered why the name of the city is always transliterated into English as Gomorrah when the Hebrew appears to be Amorah. Someone recently suggested to me that this anomaly derives from the Greek Septuagint translation. Another possibility, suggested by my brother-in-law, Michael Bohnen, is that the Hebrew letter *ayin* may have been pronounced gutturally – which would account not only for Gomorrah but also for the biblical city of *Aza* being referred to as Gaza.

7. The text at this juncture does not tell us anything about the nature of those sins. Interpreters, since antiquity, have inferred the Sodomites' sinful ways from their conduct when the angels arrive at Lot's house.

to save the entire city, innocent and guilty alike. God acquiesces and then Abraham and God engage in a fierce bargaining session, the upshot of which is that God will spare the city if He finds ten innocent people there.[8]

I wonder whether Abraham's concern was engendered by the fact that Lot and his family were living in Sodom. Given the lofty sentiments Abraham expresses in his plea for God's mercy on the city, I am inclined to dismiss that unkind thought. This episode provides a clear glimpse of Abraham's deep concern for humanity that justifies his election by God. This is not the first time that God has been recognized as "Judge of all the earth"; after all, it is as judge of humanity's conduct that God decided to unleash the flood. But this is the first time that the Torah describes a human being as referring to God in that manner and, in effect, trying to embarrass him into behaving more justly.[9] In his concern for humanity and his desire to protect even the wicked, Abraham becomes a paradigmatic figure for his descendants.

Lot in Sodom

The two angels – for that is what they obviously are[10] – arrive in Sodom and find Lot sitting at the city gate. This is often understood to suggest that Lot was an important person in the city – indeed, according to some, a judge.[11] Emulating his uncle's earlier hospitable behavior, he invites the angels into his home and feeds

---

8. Presumably, God knows that He will not find even ten innocent people in Sodom, so the bargaining seems to be mostly for Abraham's sake and is very one-sided. God makes no counteroffers and merely allows Abraham to bargain Him down to sparing the entire city if only ten innocent people live there.

9. I think this dialogue bears close comparison to the numerous occasions on which Moses pleads with God to save Israel using a variety of different arguments – often based on embarrassing the deity – in an effort to be persuasive; for instance, see *Shemot* 32:11–14, Moses' prayer in the wake of the golden calf incident.

10. Actions aside, the text actually refers to the "men" (18:16) who left Abraham's dwelling as "two angels" (19:1) arriving in Sodom.

11. In biblical times, the city's elders or judges sat at the city gates. Lot's sitting there thus implies that he was a city elder or judge. See Rashi 19:1.

them, though not so lavishly as did Abraham.[12] The residents of Sodom surround the house and demand that Lot send his guests out so that they "may know them" (19:5), apparently a euphemism for having sexual relations with them. In making this demand, the people of Sodom exhibit not only aberrant sexual desires but also a disregard for the niceties of the host-guest relationship and the norms of hospitality. Lot, in diametrical opposition, appears to have an exaggerated view of what the bonds of host and guest demand. In order to protect his guests, who are absolute strangers, he offers to satisfy the populace's sexual cravings by offering them his two virgin daughters: "I have two daughters who have not known a man. Let me bring them out to you…but do not do anything to these men, since they have come under the shelter of my roof" (19:8). The offer is rejected, either because the men of Sodom want only male carnal victims or because the mob is so beyond control that nothing short of their original demand will satisfy them.[13] The upshot is that the mob storms the house, the angels pull Lot inside and shut the door, and the men of Sodom are miraculously barred from entry by a blinding flash of light.

The angels ask Lot who else lives with him and tell him to get everyone out of the city because it is about to be destroyed. Lot has two married daughters, but their husbands think their father-in-law is joking; so they do not heed his warning. As far as we can tell, Lot's immediate family is made up of eight people: his wife, himself, two unmarried daughters, two married daughters and two sons-in-law. Even if all of them are righteous, this number still falls two short of the ten righteous people needed to save the city. While the text does not tell us that the angels scoured the city looking for a few righteous people, given that "all the people to the last man" (19:4) had made up the mob seeking to rape the

---

12. Commentators have compared Lot's apparent stinginess unfavorably with Abraham's generosity, but it seems to me that Lot's poorer offering may merely reflect a difference in the two men's wealth.
13. Perhaps Lot knew that the offer of his daughters would be rejected because the Sodomites were homosexual. Of course, if this is the case why did he make the offer?

visitors, their assumption must have been that all the inhabitants of the city were rotten to the core.[14]

The Aftermath of Sodom's Destruction

Lot himself does not turn out to be so righteous after all. Even when, the following morning, the angels tell him that the destruction of Sodom is imminent, Lot hesitates to leave the sinful city: "Still he delayed. So the men seized his hand, and the hands of his wife and his two daughters" (19:16). The angels expressly warn the refugees not to look back on the destruction. Lot's wife disobeys this warning, looks back and is immediately transformed into a pillar of salt. It isn't difficult to understand why Mrs. Lot would want to look back. After all, she is leaving two daughters and two sons-in-law behind, not to mention friends she may have made in the wicked city.[15] She seems to me to receive an extremely harsh punishment for acting upon simple human curiosity or empathy. It is easy to say that the pillar-of-salt story is meant to explain the existence of a particularly fine-looking pillar of salt near the Dead Sea, but that does not in the least explain why God, in the process of destroying two cities and the entire Plain, also proceeds to kill off Lot's wife because of her normal human curiosity. Perhaps the lesson is simple: when it comes to obeying a divine decree – even one promulgated by an angel, not God Himself – excuses based on normal human emotions are not acceptable.[16]

With his wife no longer in tow, Lot arrives in Zoar with his

---

14. There is no reference whatsoever to Gomorrah. However, positing that Lot's family was righteous, we must assume that that city had fewer than two innocent people.

15. Since no mention is made of Mrs. Lot before this episode, Lot may even have met and married her in Sodom. So she might have been looking upon the destruction of her native city and her parental family.

16. This type of thinking is particularly pertinent in the context of the Akedah story as discussed at length below. Likewise, the shocking deaths of Nadav and Avihu who "offered before the Lord alien fire" (*Vayikra* 10:1) and of the people of Beit Shemesh who "looked into the Ark of the Lord" (*I Sam* 6:19) seem to result from the transgression of a divine command. However holy their motivations may have been, they violated a divine command and paid for this with their lives.

two virgin daughters, but soon leaves it – "for he was afraid to live in Zoar" (19:30) – and sets up housekeeping in a cave. The text tells us that in light of the destruction of Sodom, the daughters believe that the entire world has been destroyed and that the three of them are all that is left of humanity: "Our father is old, and there is not a man on earth to consort with us in the way of all the world" (19:31). Their reasoning seems disingenuous. Even if like Abraham, the next day they looked from afar and saw "the smoke of the land rising like the smoke of a kiln" (19:28), they knew that Zoar had not been destroyed because they had fled there. All I can suggest is that perhaps the shock of such devastation led them to conclude that the end of humanity was near. In their shocked eyes, even Zoar's destruction was imminent.[17] Credible or not, the young women's fear that they will have no opportunity to bear children because there are no men around other than their father seems to lead them to hatch a plot to have incestuous relations with Lot. They get the old man drunk and "have their way with him" on two consecutive nights.

For the second time in the Torah, drunkenness leads to or enables reprehensible behavior (the first was Noah's post-flood drinking spree that led to Ham's dishonorable actions and the cursing of Canaan).[18] In this case, the result of Lot's drunkenness is the birth of two of Israel's ancestral enemies: Moab and Ammon. The incestual origin of Moab and Ammon leads me to consider the possibility that the motivation for this story was originally etiological; perhaps it was designed to cast aspersions upon the beginnings of two nations closely related to the Israelites, but nonetheless their enemies. This supposition would also explain the illogical behavior of Lot's daughters; they acted hei-

---

17. Perhaps this is why Lot and his daughters left Zoar. If this is so, Lot is partially to blame for his daughters' fear and their subsequent actions. He should have believed the angels when they said that he could live safely in Zoar.

18. Curiously, in both cases the intoxicated individual is not a "mean drunk"; rather than taking the initiative and committing a crime, the drunken individual is a victim who is taken advantage of by others.

nously both because they were raised in Sodom and because they were the matriarchs of Moab and Ammon.

I find the contrast between the treatment of Lot's wife, on the one hand, and his daughters, on the other, troublesome. Lot's wife, for curiously looking back to see what was happening to her hometown and its inhabitants (including two of her children), suffers immediate death. The daughters, for their intentional and blatant violation of one of the seven Noahide laws forbidding illicit sexual relations, suffer no punishment at all, as least as far as the text tells us. This appears to be yet another example of God's arbitrary nature, administering justice on a whim, when and how He sees fit.

Abraham, Sarah, and Abimelech – Déjà Vu All Over Again

Following the destruction of Sodom, the biblical narrative continues with Abraham again moving his family, this time into the Negev desert. He arrives at Gerar, southeast of Gaza in the land of the Philistines.[19] This area is ruled by an individual referred to as King Abimelech (this compound name, meaning "my father-king", must be a hereditary title adopted by the ruler of the place, for years later Isaac interacts with a ruler of the same name). In what is almost a carbon copy of the story we discussed above involving Abraham, Sarah, and Pharaoh (12:10–20), Abraham, afraid of being killed so that Sarah could be taken, tells Abimelech that she is his sister. While Sarah was silent last time, this time the text strongly suggests that she too lied about her status, for Abimelech declares as much in his defense: "She also said, 'He is my brother'" (20:5).

---

19. Gerar, according to Nachmanides (22:32), was the royal capital. The Bible makes no mention of the Philistines during this encounter, but at the end of the next chapter Abimelech returns from making a compact with Abraham in Beersheva to "the land of the Philistines" and Abraham is described as residing "in the land of the Philistines a long time" (21:32, 34). This seems to be an anachronism since scholars believe that the Philistines had not yet arrived in Canaan in Abraham's time.

Rather than visit Abimelech with a plague (which had been Pharaoh's fate), God appears to the King of Gerar in a dream and announces that he must die for taking a married woman. Abimelech responds to God's decree by loudly proclaiming his innocence (he had not even touched her) and declaring that he had been duped by Abraham and Sarah into thinking that she was Abraham's sister; God should not punish him because his "heart was blameless and [his] hands were clean" (20:5). Remarkably, God replies that, knowing this, He kept Abimelech from touching Sarah,[20] and He demands that Abimelech return Sarah to her husband on pain of death. If Abraham prays for Abimelech, he will be saved.

When Abimelech does so, he confronts Abraham, who tells him that technically he had not lied because Sarah was actually his half sister.[21] In a slight twist on the previous story where Pharaoh gave Abraham presents when he took Sarah and then banished Abraham and his household when the truth came out, here Abimelech gives Abraham and Sarah sheep, oxen, and slaves to make up for the "offense" of innocently taking Abraham's wife only after the truth comes out and, in addition, gives them the freedom to settle wherever they wish in his domain.

This story is surprising for a number of reasons. To begin with, assuming the biblical narrative follows chronological order, Sarah is at least ninety years old, as the Torah tells us that she was ninety when Isaac's birth was announced to Abraham (17:17). She is well into menopause, so old that she laughed at the thought of having sex with her husband (18:11–12), so it is more than a bit surprising that Abraham is still frightened that her beauty will

20. If that is the case, one can well wonder why God threatens an innocent Abimelech with punishment.
21. Interestingly, Abraham tells Abimelech that he has routinely asked Sarah to tell anyone they meet on their travels that she is his sister. Are we to understand that Abraham has been traveling the area pandering out his wife and that the incidents with Pharaoh and Abimelech are not the only instances of this behavior? I do not think so, but this text does give one pause.

lead to his murder.[22] Furthermore, it does seem strange that the identical story is told about the patriarch and his wife twice, with only the name of the offending monarch changed. And, perhaps most problematically, the Torah states that as a result of his innocently taking Sarah, Abimelech and his entire household are punished with a bout of infertility that does not disappear until Sarah is returned; Abraham is "compensated" for his fraud; and Abraham prays on Abimelech's behalf. While I suppose it should not be surprising that Abraham, who is obviously God's favorite, gets special treatment from the deity, there surely does not appear to be any semblance of justice in God's dealings with Abimelech. As for Abraham's conduct, it is just as reprehensible here as it was earlier in Egypt – possibly more so because he apparently did not learn anything from the incident with Pharaoh and felt perfectly within his rights to perpetrate the same scam a second time.[23]

This story together with its Egyptian predecessor is what biblical scholars call a type scene. Indeed, it recurs yet again when Isaac and Rebecca pull the same trick on another Abimelech of Gerar (26:6–11). I do not understand the significance of the type scene technique here. If there is any historicity to the story, it is highly unlikely that this kind of thing would occur twice to Abraham and Sarah[24] – and certainly not when Sarah had reached so advanced an age. I can only think of a few reasons why the scene might be repeated in Abimelech's time. Perhaps the Torah is trying to explain how Abraham attained such great wealth (not-

---

22. One solution to this difficulty is that the incident took place at a much earlier time. Jewish tradition teaches that the Torah was not written in an exclusively chronological fashion, so this might be the answer. Alternatively, Nachmanides (20:2) suggests that maybe after the angel's annunciation of Isaac's birth, the blush of youth miraculously returned to Sarah's cheeks along with her menstrual cycle.

23. Nachmanides (20:12) also takes Abraham to task for this repeated immoral conduct. The only point one might make in Abraham's defense is that God speaks very harshly to Abimelech in his dream. If Abimelech was as innocent as he appears, he would not have needed such a stern warning to make him return Sarah.

24. Much less a third time when the characters are Isaac, Rebecca, and another Abimelech.

withstanding the damage these stories do to his moral standing), or maybe the stories are designed to underscore Sarah's remarkable beauty, even in her old age (which I find more than a bit counterintuitive).[25] Of course, the simplest – though least traditional – explanation may be that the story was enshrined in two separate traditions. The redactor of the Bible simply could not allow himself to omit either version.

Isaac's Birth – Hagar and Ishmael's Banishment

God fulfills his promise to Abraham and Sarah, and the elderly wife gives birth to a son whom Abraham names Isaac.[26] The name derives from the Hebrew for "laughter" and obviously recalls both Abraham's and Sarah's having laughed at the thought that they would have a child this late in their lives. Isaac is duly circumcised, and Abraham holds a feast. Note that the feast is made at the weaning, not at a later stage in the child's development, which might parallel a modern bar mitzvah celebration.[27]

We are now told that Sarah sees Ishmael (who by this time

25. Even the first time in Egypt, Sarah could not have been a young woman. Since Abraham was at least seventy-five years old when he arrived in the land of Canaan (12:4) and Sarah was ten years younger than he (17:17), she would have been no less than sixty-five when they arrived in Egypt. Even though she lived to be one hundred and twenty-seven years old (23:1), she would hardly have looked young enough to be snatched up for Pharaoh's harem at the age of sixty-five unless she was extraordinarily beautiful (which, of course, may be the very point the text is trying to make).

26. In the course of five sentences, the text mentions Abraham being Isaac's father no fewer than three times. One commentator has suggested that this appears to be overkill possibly to dispel any possibility that it was Abimelech, not Abraham, who fathered Sarah's child. It is true that the Abimelech episode immediately precedes Isaac's birth in the text, but I find it difficult to believe that anyone would think a miraculous birth to an elderly woman well past her menopause – which makes sense only in the context of God's promises to Abraham – would occur if Abraham were not the father.

27. The midrashists (*Sanhedrin* 89b) use the mention of a feast to provide a reason for Abraham's "test" in the Akedah narrative, which follows shortly after this episode. They suggest that Satan – the heavenly accuser– pointed out to God that despite the large feast, Abraham did not bother to offer any sacrifices of thanksgiving. God responds that he is sure of Abraham's devotion and that Abraham would even sac-

is a teenager) "playing" (21:9). The word "playing" used by the Torah is derived from the Hebrew verb for "laughter", thus creating a linguistic link between Ishmael's actions and Isaac's name. This "playing" results in Ishmael and his mother being banished, estranged from Isaac and his progeny forever, so it deserves our attention. If Ishmael was merely laughing or playing, it would be hard to understand why Sarah got so upset. Perhaps, a clue may be found in Sarah's words: "'Cast out that slave-woman and her son, for the son of that slave shall not share in the inheritance with my son Isaac'" (21:10). Perhaps, even seeing Ishmael happy and carefree might have been enough to cause Sarah to get him out of the way if the inheritance was at stake. One commentator suggests that the linguistic link between Ishmael's "playing" and Isaac's name suggests that Ishmael was "playacting" as if he were Isaac, that is, acting as if he were the heir presumptive. That would surely push Sarah over the edge. Rashi (21:9; citing the Midrash) does not make such an interpretive leap. He suggests that Ishmael engaged in various forms of misconduct based upon verses elsewhere in *Tanakh* where the laughter verb is used to describe the commission of various evils: idolatry, illicit sexual behavior, and murder.[28] Such a dire description of Ishmael makes sense only if we consider him to have been the progenitor of the Arab nation, one of Israel's perennial enemies. As such, the Sages would have been eager to portray him as a bad (if not evil) young man.

Whatever it was that Ishmael was doing, Sarah runs to her husband and demands that he banish both Hagar and Ishmael for fear that the elder child might get the inheritance she wants for Isaac. This text is subject to two different readings. If Sarah is concerned that Ishmael might inherit all of the worldly goods that Abraham had amassed (and we know from previous sections

---

rifice his beloved son if God asks him to. What follows, of course, is the Akedah story.

28. The same verb is used to describe the Jews worshipping the golden calf (*Shemot* 32:6); Isaac "fondling" or "sporting" with his wife Rebecca in the third "sister-not-wife" episode (26:8); and armed combat (*II Sam.* 2:13).

that he was indeed very wealthy), then Sarah would be revealing herself to be an avaricious materialist. If, on the other hand, what she was worried about was the possibility that Ishmael might inherit the spiritual legacy that God had promised Abraham through Isaac, while her motives would be exemplary, her lack of faith in God's promise to Abraham that Isaac would inherit the divine covenant (17:19) would be surprising.[29] Either way, her behavior seems far from praiseworthy.

Unlike his earlier readiness to send Hagar away at Sarah's urging, this time Abraham does not like the idea at all – perhaps because it is one thing to banish a pregnant concubine and quite another to send away a teenage son whom one presumably loves dearly. The Bible uses classic understatement in describing Abraham's reluctance: "The matter distressed Abraham greatly, for it concerned a son of his" (21:11). But God tells him not to worry. Abraham should listen to Sarah, and God will take care of Ishmael and make him the father of a great nation. So Abraham gave Hagar "some bread and a skin of water" – scant provisions for a sojourn in the desert wilderness, but presumably Abraham relied on God's promise to take care of them – "placed them over her shoulder, together with the child, and sent her away" (21:14). The commentators are split on whether Hagar carried only the bread and water "over her shoulder" or also her son. Rashi, adding to the pathos, explains that Ishmael had suffered a heat or sunstroke and could not walk. However, Saadiah Gaon rejects that reading. What happens next is a bit strange. The text relates that after the water ran out Hagar left the boy under one of the bushes. Since Ishmael was fourteen when Isaac was born and the story has now taken us beyond Isaac's weaning, Ishmael is probably fifteen or sixteen years old.[30] Heat stroke aside, we would have expected him

---

29. Of course, it is possible that Abraham never told Sarah about the particular promises God had made to him. I find that possibility highly unlikely. Surely Sarah must have known that her husband had a special relationship with the deity that would explain her miraculous conception of Isaac so many years after menopause.
30. Ishmael was circumcised at the age of thirteen, one year before Isaac was born

to lead his mother on the trek; indeed, he later grows up to dwell in the wilderness and becomes an archer, a skilled hunter. Why is he pictured here as a weak, helpless child? Is this for dramatic purposes? If so, why does the Torah want to create this effect? I am not sure why, but what is clear is that the Torah also depicts Isaac at the *Akedah* as a child when the tradition teaches that he was a man in his thirties. So the Torah is consistent in painting such dramatic pictures where Abraham is concerned.

Returning to our story, Hagar sits down and, unwilling to look at her child in what are presumably his death throes, starts to cry. But it is not her tears that God notices.[31] While the Torah tells us nothing about Ishmael's reaction to the situation, it declares that God heard "the cry of the boy" (21:17), not that of the mother. This is, to say the least, a little odd. Is this an implicit criticism of Hagar? Is the text suggesting that she should have comforted her son in his agony rather than crying, in an understandable but inappropriate reluctance to watch him suffer? That critique, in my opinion, would not justify God's failure to hear her cries. Rather, it seems to me that Hagar's anguish in and of itself exhibits a lack of faith in God. For when, during her pregnancy, she was visited by an angel and told to return to Sarah, Hagar received a divine oracle telling her that Ishmael would grow up to be "a wild ass of a man" and that he would have many offspring (16:12). She has either forgotten this promise or lost faith in it, which would explain why God ignored her tears. As for Ishmael's "cry", perhaps he cried out and perhaps the cry was merely internal. But God hears it and sends his angel to Hagar a second time. A well miraculously appears, and God's promise to make of Ishmael a great nation is repeated.

I have often thought about why this incident was chosen as

(17:17, 24–25). His teenage status at this point in time makes the suggestion that Hagar was carrying him all the more farfetched.

31. Ironically, the previous time God heard Hagar's cries which were not mentioned explicitly in the text; this time, God seems to ignore Hagar's explicitly mentioned crying.

part of the Torah reading for the first day of Rosh Hashanah. The traditional reason given is that the reading begins with the birth of Isaac, since God traditionally "remembered Sarah" and allowed her to conceive on that date, the first day of Tishrei. But I find that answer less than satisfying, since the bulk of the reading deals, not with Isaac, but with Hagar and Ishmael. The answer, I think, is found in the tradition that Rosh Hashanah celebrates the creation of the world. Humanity, of course, is not limited to the people of Israel; this story, which recounts God's concern for Ishmael – forefather of the Jews' Arab enemies[32] – serves to underscore the universality of God's relationship with humankind and, thus, is more than appropriate for reading on the world's birthday.

Abraham, Abimelech, and Gaza

The next mini-episode (seemingly an unimportant interpolation before the climax of the Abrahamic saga in God's command-ment that the patriarch bind up his son Isaac as an offering) has, I think, some significance in the context of current events in the Middle East. Abimelech, the king of the land of the Philistines,[33] approaches Abraham and requests that he take a loyalty oath: "swear to me here by God that you will not deal falsely with me or with my kith and kin, but will deal with me and with the land in which you have sojourned as loyally as I have dealt with you" (21:23–24). Abraham takes the oath, apparently ceding his and his descendants' right to take the land in question by force from Abimelech or his descendants. When Abimelech's servants sub-sequently seize a well that Abraham had dug, Abraham demands a formal pact between Abimelech and himself in which he seems

---

32. Rashi (21:17; citing *Rosh Hashanah* 16b) explains that God heard Ishmael's cry "where he is"; that is to say, Ishmael was judged and saved based upon his own actions up until that time, and the manner in which his Arab descendants would mistreat the Jews in the future was not taken into account. This is a surprising statement coming from Rashi, who had interpreted Ishmael's offensive conduct, critiqued by Sarah, as the most dastardly of crimes.

33. This time the text is explicit in identifying Abimelech's kingdom as the land of the Philistines.

to renounce what, up until this point, had presumably been part of the Promised Land, ceding Gaza to Abimelech and his descendants in exchange for eternal rights to the well Abraham has dug.

It seems to me that if biblical references have any modern political meaning (which I am certain is not the case), this is a strong precedent supporting the Israeli government's decision to remove its settlers from Gaza (which, of course, is in the land of the Philistines). After all, Abraham has already promised not to take this land by force. And his willingness to cede it to Abimelech seems to imply that it is not part of the Promised Land. Ironically, those rabbis and other supposedly religious supporters of the Gaza and West Bank settlers who believe that it is forbidden to abandon any part of the geographic Land of Israel *including Gaza* appear to be contradicted by this treaty entered into by Abraham, an individual who, these self-same "authorities" would assert never violated any Torah precepts while in the Holy Land.[34]

This argument might, however, be mitigated by two factors: (1) the Talmud (*Sotah* 9b–10a) suggests that the Philistines broke their promise to Abraham at the time of Samson and later of King David. If so, it could be argued, that this abrogated Abraham's promises to them; furthermore, another passage in the Talmud (*Chullin* 60b) suggests that the covenant was now null and void because the Philistines had been displaced by another people, the Avvim, so the Israelites had no obligation to maintain the patriarchal covenant with them; and (2) Rashbam (22:1), willing to criticize Abraham's actions, actually claims that God was exceedingly angry at Abraham for making this covenant with Abimelech and

---

34. The theory apparently is that, while the Torah had not yet been given, God imparted its precepts to Abraham, Isaac, and Jacob who followed them while in the Promised Land. This interpretive tour de force (*Yevamot* 21a; *Yoma* 67b; BR 64:5), from a rabbinic perspective, is the plain meaning of the text in *Bereshit* 26:4–5 where Abraham is commended for keeping God's "commandments...laws, and... teachings". That the patriarchs did not observe the commandments outside of the Promised Land is a rabbinic concession necessitated to explain such obvious violations as Jacob's simultaneous marriage to two sisters in Haran (Nachmanides, 26:5).

his descendants because this land of the Philistines was considered to be within the boundaries of the Land of Israel. Rashbam even notes that in Joshua's time the people are told that "very much of the land still remains to be taken possession of…namely, those of the five lords of the Philistines – the Gazites, the Ashdodites, the Ashkelonites, the Gittites, and the Ekronites" (*Joshua* 13:1–3). Thus, one could argue that Abraham had in fact sinned by making this covenant and that according to the book of *Joshua* the nation of Israel was apparently not bound by it.[35]

The Akedah

This episode is central to the Abraham saga – indeed, to the entire Jewish gestalt. Traditionally, the passage is read every morning as part of the daily prayers, and it holds pride of place in the Rosh Hashanah and Yom Kippur liturgy. It may very well be the closest Abraham – and by extension, the Jewish people – ever come to confronting God in an attempt to understand what (or who) God is and what He expects of humankind, in general, and of Jews, in particular. Yet, after a lifetime of pondering this text, I continue to find it puzzling at best and, I fear, ultimately incomprehensible on moral, textual, and theological grounds.

The story is straightforward and uncomplicated. It is written in very simple – indeed, often understated and, I believe, sublime – Hebrew. God decides to test Abraham and commands him to take his son Isaac and offer him up as a sacrifice at a place to which God will lead him. Abraham, without so much as a verbal confirmation of God's instructions, much less a complaint, sets forth with Isaac and a retinue of young men to do as he is told; they

35. Rashbam even suggests that the horrific trial of the Akedah was God's reaction to this covenant. God, as if peeved at Abraham's presumptuousness in giving away the land (on behalf of himself and his progeny), tells Abraham to bind Isaac as a sacrifice, declaring, somewhat cruelly: after you have done so "then we will see what good you accomplished by making this covenant". For an in-depth discussion of this covenant and its parameters, see David Novack's *The Jewish Social Contract* (Princeton UP, 2005), 40–44.

arrive at Mount Moriah (traditionally believed to be the Temple Mount in Jerusalem); Abraham binds up his son and places him on the altar; he lifts the knife[36] for the slaughter, but just in the nick of time an angel stops him; a ram is conveniently found to complete the sacrifice; and Abraham and his progeny are blessed because he did not withhold his son from God.

The rabbinic tradition, as I understand it, views this story as demonstrating Abraham's complete faith in God and his willingness to do God's bidding without question. Indeed, the blessing Abraham receives at the end of the episode stresses precisely that – he is blessed because he did not withhold his son from the sacrifice God had commanded: "Because you have done this and have not withheld your son, your favored one, I will bestow my blessing upon you…" (22:16–17). And, according to the High Holiday liturgy, Abraham's merit in performing this deed was so great that we, his descendants, are able, thousands of years later, to reap benefits from it by reminding God of what happened at Mount Moriah.

I suppose the story makes sense from the perspective of a religious tradition grounded in the revelation of divine law. Like Abraham, devotees of traditional Judaism accept all the revealed precepts regardless of whether they seem moral or even logical.[37]

---

36. In a stirring bit of translation, Robert Alter translates the Hebrew word as "cleaver", thus implicitly comparing Abraham to a butcher.

37. I am reminded in this connection of the words of Samuel when he chastises Saul for failing to kill the Amalekite king and all of the captured cattle as the prophet-judge had told him was God's command. When he informs Saul that the kingship will be taken from him for disobedience, Samuel stresses that nothing is more important than blind compliance with the command of the deity (*1 Sam.* 15:22). And this is said in connection with Saul's refusal to murder a defenseless captive and to kill cows and sheep, presumably innocent animals. To be sure, the Torah nowhere prohibits the killing of animals for either food or sacrifice; but I cannot reconcile a commandment to butcher animals for no utilitarian reason with a Torah which requires that an animal's sensitivity to pain be considered when it is killed for food – which, as I understand it, is the basis for the rules governing *shechitah* (ritual slaughter). This last point apparently bothered the Rabbis because they explained the animal slaughter by positing that the Amalekites had magical powers and could turn themselves into animals (Rashi, *1 Sam.* 15:3). Accordingly, for the

From that point of view, the Rabbis could well be expected to approve of Abraham's unquestioning obedience to the divine command. Indeed, one might say that God was testing Abraham to see whether he and his children (that is, the Jewish people) were capable of accepting the Torah and following it without question – a test which (if that was indeed the test) Abraham passed with flying colors.

However, based upon my understanding of Judaism and the Torah's outlook, there is a fundamental flaw with such a reading. If Abraham's conduct exemplifies how God wants us to live a Torah life – obeying without thought or reason – one could well question what kind of people God thinks we are or, more significantly, what kind of a God He is. The human being whom Psalm 8 describes as but a little lower than the angels and the jewel of God's creation is not a robotic automaton or even a child who can be expected to obey without thought, especially when the commandment to be followed makes no sense or, as here, is morally abhorrent. In other words, if we read the Akedah as extolling blind obedience to God's commandments, we undercut the essential moral of the Garden of Eden narrative – that by eating the fruit of the Tree of Knowledge humanity learned the inherent difference between good and evil, thereby permitting each person to exercise free will and choose the good.[38] Indeed, even though the Torah later provides the Jewish people with a plethora of commandments to be obeyed (perhaps, to protect them from being swayed into temptation by the yetzer hara), ultimately free choice to follow or disregard the mitzvot is integral to the Jewish worldview. Thus, the message of the Akedah cannot be the propriety of unthinking obedience.

Abraham's blind obedience and silence in the face of this horrific command is surprising on another level as well. It does not seem to reflect the Abraham we know from other Torah stories.

midrashists, by refusing to listen to God and slaughter all the animals, Saul let the enemy get away.

38. See Schulweis, *Conscience*, cited above in connection with the Garden of Eden story.

When God told Abraham about the impending destruction of Sodom, he pleaded for the lives of its people. When Sarah wanted to banish Ishmael and Hagar (the second time), Abraham was troubled, forcing God to instruct him to listen to Sarah's advice. Here, in sharp contrast, Abraham's reaction is utter silence. He does not plead with God to change his mind, and he certainly does not consult with Sarah (probably because he knows full well what her response will be).[39] Maybe Abraham does not question the command because he knows that such a tactic would be futile. After all, despite the patriarch's rhetorical skills, God destroyed Sodom. However, it seems to me that labeling the task futile is not an adequate explanation, for it is Abraham's beloved son and the future of his people that are at stake here. One would expect him at the very least to argue the point.

Of course, there is a significant difference between the Akedah on the one hand and Abraham's going to bat for Sodom and Ishmael on the other. Here, if we accept the text at face value, God has told Abraham exactly what to do, and precisely when the task is most difficult, obedience might be considered most praiseworthy. But that is precisely the most troubling point of all – can such unquestioning obedience to a divine command that is patently immoral ever be the primary value of a Torah life? This archetypal story of obedience and "faith" has profound implications for our understanding of the nature of God, the nature of the Jewish people's mission and how we are expected to fulfill it, so we must attempt to understand it.

Biblical scholars have sometimes attempted to negate the centrality of Abraham's blind obedience by reading the entire story as an etiological myth meant to explain why the ancient Israelites did not sacrifice their children to their deity, as many of the neighboring peoples did to theirs.[40] While such an interpretation

---

39. Sarah's involvement will be explored further in the next section.
40. Most interestingly, there is at least one instance in *Tanakh* (II *Kings* 3:26–27) where such a child sacrifice to a pagan god appears to have been successful. Mesha, King of Moab, is losing a battle against the forces of Israel. In desperation, he sacrifices

is supported by the Torah's repeated abhorrence of child sacrifice, it ignores the framing message of the Akedah text. Both the text and traditional Judaism (most particularly in the liturgy) loudly declare that the moral of the story is that it was Abraham's willingness to go ahead with the sacrifice that was meritorious. An interpretation that ignores this oft-repeated message misses the point.

Attempting to mitigate the fact that God asked for and Abraham was willing to carry out human (child!) sacrifice, the Rabbis long ago suggested that God would never have really asked Abraham to sacrifice his son; indeed, they say, the language used by God indicates as much: "Take your son…and raise him up as a burnt offering" (22:2). As Rashi notes, Abraham was not told "to slay his son" and offer him as a burnt offering, but rather "to raise him up" (Rashi, 22:2), just like you would a burnt offering. Whether or not we buy into this midrashic tap dance, clearly one can argue that God was only testing Abraham; He never intended for Abraham to go through with the sacrifice, so He cannot be deemed immoral on that score, only cruel.[41] As for Abraham's willingness to commit the deed, Danish philosopher Soren Kierkegaard argues in *Fear and Trembling* that pure religious faith permits (indeed requires) man to suspend his understanding of what would otherwise be considered ethical by human society. This position, as I argue below, is outrageous. If God is meaningful at all, He must be the embodiment of the ethical and the moral. Abraham cannot have perceived Him to demand the un-

his firstborn son as a burnt offering, obviously to a pagan god. The result, *mirabile dictu*, is that the army of Israel flees the battlefield.

41. However, I would argue that even claiming that God did not really mean for Abraham to complete the sacrifice makes a mockery of the test. For if there was no command to sacrifice Isaac, what kind of a test could it have been? Surely at a moment of this magnitude, Abraham was listening carefully to God's words; if Rashi and the Rabbis he follows were able to read them as meaningless, surely Abraham could do so as well. If he did, then the "test" was only a meaningless charade.

ethical.[42] This would undermine Abraham's and our own very notion of God.

Another way to explain Abraham's willingness to proceed with the sacrifice is to suggest that God never intended Isaac to die and that Abraham, on some level, must have known this. Viewed this way, Abraham's perfect faith demonstrates itself in his willingness to undergo the test without even understanding its purpose, certain that, in the end, the God he has come to know will not permit him to carry out the deed. This reading is also unsatisfactory because it makes a mockery of the test. If Abraham went through the motions of a make-believe sacrifice knowing all the time that he was only playacting, "passing" the test would hardly seem to merit the eternal adulation Abraham receives.

No matter how we deal with the issues of blind obedience and moral action in the story, there is another paradox at its very heart. As we have already noted (18:17–19; 21:12), God has expressly promised Abraham that his progeny, *through Isaac*, will be a multitude that will bring blessing to all of humanity. Indeed, according to the midrashists, it was to preserve Isaac from Ishmael's bad influence that God instructed Abraham to banish Hagar and her son. Yet here that self-same God is telling Abraham to kill Isaac. If the man Kierkegaard calls "the knight of faith" is a rational human being, how can he carry out a divinely sanctioned sacrifice which will effectively nullify God's past promises?

A couple of answers have been offered to this paradox. Kierkegaard defines the whole situation as absurd and praises Abraham for making a "leap of faith" confident that, even if he sacrifices his son, somehow his future blessing through Isaac will

---

42. Indeed, when Mordecai Kaplan strives to find a "God" that has no metaphysical existence, he defines the deity as that force within humanity that presses toward ultimate salvation – which I read as meaning the essence of ethical and moral living. This, of course, contradicts a number of instances where the Torah understands God differently. For on occasion God is portrayed as acting immorally, such as at the time of the flood and in sending Hagar back to face Sarah's abuse – not to mention the entire book of *Job*.

still be assured. I am not enough of a philosopher to buy into that double-talk. To be sure, it is hard to disagree with Kierkegaard's assertion that faith is beyond reason; that, after all, is what faith is all about. But, ultimately, in this case, God – who miraculously restored Sarah to her youth, so that Isaac could be born "naturally"– is asking Abraham to believe that Isaac's death will not impede the fulfillment of the promise. If God, as Abraham has seen, attempts to work in natural ways, than the promise will die with Isaac. So God is essentially asking Abraham to suspend belief in the God he knows and to perform a heinous crime on behalf of a God who he clearly should not recognize. This is far more than just a "leap of faith". Certain midrashic traditions have taken a different path, suggesting that while Abraham did expect to slaughter Isaac, he may have been confident that after the murder God would resurrect Isaac so that the earlier promise could be fulfilled.[43] Both these answers demand a level of *emunah shelemah* (perfect faith) that seems to me to demonstrate naiveté of the highest order or, to put it more harshly, a level of irrational zealotry that borders on insanity.

Ultimately, aside from the questions of blind obedience, moral action and the paradox of the death of God's promise, the very notion of God testing Abraham is absurd. Why should God give Abraham a pop quiz? Does an omnipotent and omniscient God, who presumably knows the innermost secrets of every man and woman's heart (as the High Holiday liturgy constantly reminds us), have to test Abraham's belief?[44] Are we dealing here with the Supreme Ruler of the Universe or with an immature par-

---

43. See Shalom Spiegel's *The Last Trial: On the Legends and Lore of the Commands to Abraham to Offer Isaac as a Sacrifice, The Akedah* (Jewish Lights, 1993) which traces this surprising midrashic tradition.

44. Note that above, in my discussion of the flood, I suggested that God "was experimenting and learning about His creatures" as he went along. If such an approach were taken, I could argue here that God was still trying to learn more about Abraham, that he really did not know. Even if on a philosophical level this answer were plausible, at this point in Abraham's life it seems unlikely that God still needed to test him.

ent who wants to be sure his child loves him before giving him his birthday present? Of course, this question was not lost on the Rabbis; Nachmanides in particular, whose Torah commentary often finds a rational approach to difficult issues, addresses this question. He argues that God did not need to test Abraham to determine whether he had the requisite faith to carry out the cruel command – God already knew. Rather, Ramban tells us that Abraham had to actualize his potential to make it real. While Nachmanides resolves the question of God's omniscience, he ultimately fails to satisfy my criterion for a successful resolution of the Akedah problem; for he accepts the notion that it can be admirable to kill your own son if God tells you to do it. As I understand it, if God is not moral, God is not God – or at the very least, not a God worthy of our worship.

In recent years there has been a great deal written about ethical relativism – the idea that what is right for one society in one set of circumstances might not necessarily be right for another whose circumstances are different. For example, many claim that the sexual mores of the Victorian era are out of date – they just don't fit the age in which we live. These mores may have been right back then (although that is far from clear in the minds of many), but as Bob Dylan wrote, "The Times They Are A-Changin'". Applying an ethically relative perspective to the Torah might solve the question of the Akedah. We could suggest that in Abraham's time, child sacrifice (and thus Isaac's sacrifice) would have been considered moral.[45] Indeed, at the time the other nations routinely sacrificed their children. Only we moderns have an ethical problem with carrying out such a command. But that kind of argument just won't do. For such an answer would strip the Torah of its universal message, applicable to all people at all times. And, needless to say, it is not an answer the Rabbis or the Torah

---

45. Indeed, the Christians who read Isaac's binding as a prefiguration of Jesus' crucifixion fervently believe that the one-time murder of a single individual brought salvation to the world.

could give. According to Jewish tradition, the Torah is a divinely revealed blueprint of what is right and what is wrong, and it does not change from generation to generation.[46] Thou shalt not murder is as valid today as it was on Mount Sinai thousands of years ago. Good is good and evil is evil! Perhaps that is what is meant by the midrashic concept that the Torah – which defines what is right and wrong – existed before the creation of the world. I would suggest that the Torah's immutable sense of right and wrong when it comes to fundamental morality stems from the Jewish belief that Torah comes from God whose very essence is truth, righteousness and goodness.

Dennis Prager, some of whose insights into the interaction between modern society and the religious community are quite perceptive,[47] likes to cite Dostoevsky's *The Brothers Karamazov* to attack ethical relativism. In the Grand Inquisitor parable in that novel, Dostoevsky writes that without God there are no limits. From this viewpoint, unless an unimpeachable authority reveals what is right and what is wrong, any behavior can be righteous depending on the circumstances; and Immanuel Kant notwithstanding, there is no logical basis for determining what is good and what is evil. While I do not go quite so far in requiring the pronouncement of the Divine to underscore morality, I find the other extreme of moral relativism equally unacceptable. Even though I do believe that a democratic society can legislate its own acceptable mores, I am well aware that Hitler's regime in Germany gained power in a democratic election, as did Mussolini's in Italy. Even if we were to presume (as some scholars do) that the major-

---

46. I do not mean to suggest that the legislation set down in the Torah must always be followed without deviation, notwithstanding changing circumstances. The halachic process, as I understand it, is designed to evolve along with humanity's maturity. As we attain a better understanding of what it is that God wants from us, halachic decisors are empowered to reconstitute the law, so that it conforms to the true spirit of the Torah. What I am suggesting here is that on issues of fundamental interpersonal morality – murder being a prime example – Torah truth is eternal and immutable.

47. On the other hand, I am not a fan of Prager's political opinions.

ity of Germany's citizens were not troubled by the Holocaust, no legitimate moral system can possibly condone it.

To state my position succinctly, I believe that there is such a thing as absolute right and wrong. And I believe that Judaism teaches us that the ability to distinguish right from wrong stems from God – whether gained by studying His Torah or by eating from the Tree of Knowledge and thus gaining an intuitive understanding of good and evil. For me, that is where the crux of the Akedah story's incomprehensibility lies. For, in short, the story presents in bold relief the unsolvable problem of theodicy: in this case, how can God demand that Abraham act immorally? God is good and Abraham knows it.[48] The God-Abraham debate about the fate of Sodom is proof enough. In pleading for the lives of the people living in the condemned city, Abraham remonstrates with God by challenging Him to be the just God Abraham has come to know and revere (18:25): "Shall not the judge of all the earth act justly?" If God is the source of what is good and just, how can He command Abraham to sacrifice his son and applaud the result if Abraham blindly follows His instruction? The notion that killing Isaac can be a moral act is simply incomprehensible – which means that the command to murder Abraham's son (and that is precisely what we are talking about here) calls into question everything Abraham must think he knows about God. Put another way, if whatever God says should be done is good by definition then it must be good to sacrifice one's child. Yet such an act is the very antithesis of what Abraham inherently knows is God's way.

---

48. Of course, the other possibility is ever-present – that God is not necessarily good but merely *is*. Certainly the God portrayed in the book of *Job* leaves a great deal to be desired when it comes to goodness. He punishes Job (indeed, permits his children to be killed) for no apparent reason other than to win a bet; and when it comes to explaining to Job the "justice" of it all, relies solely on the fact that He is so powerful and all-embracing that no human being can possibly understand Him, which to this reader at least appears to be the ultimate cop-out. Suffice it so say, that this view of an all-powerful but not necessarily good or just God is not the Torah view as expressed in the Pentateuch, the Prophets and virtually all of Scripture, excluding *Job*.

Since the entire Jewish idea derives from Israel's acceptance of the Torah as the embodiment of goodness and morality, a divine commandment to commit murder is the ultimate contradiction.[49]

While I have carefully examined several other possible solutions to this contradiction, every effort I have made runs aground on the language of the text. First, I wondered whether the story could be read as Abraham's testing God, not *vice versa*. Abraham, after all, is living in a world in which child sacrifice is fairly common. Having received God's instructions, he might well have asked himself whether the God who took him from Mesopotamia to a strange land – in order to make of him a great nation and a blessing to all humanity – wants (or even permits) him to commit an act so antithetical to everything he knows God stands for. Read this way, it is God who passes the test by repealing His commandment at the last minute and providing a ram for the sacrifice.[50] That would be a version of the tale I could live with. But, of course, that is not what the text says. The language could not be clearer; God is testing Abraham, and Abraham passes the test by being willing to sacrifice his son.[51]

Rather than suggesting (as above) that Abraham knew that God did not want him to kill Isaac and just went through the charade as ordered, I also wondered whether God was testing Abraham, hoping that he would not be willing to commit this evil deed. God wished to know whether Abraham had sufficient

---

49. Kierkegaard, as mentioned above, solves this problem by asserting that pure religious faith permits (indeed requires) the suspension of what is otherwise considered ethical by human society. Since I equate God with what is right, good, and moral, this explanation takes me nowhere.

50. Indeed, there is a tradition that the ram had been ready since the creation of the world to perform that very function.

51. This problem is not avoided by positing, as do a number of scholars, that the second appearance of the angel to Abraham after the sacrifice has been averted is a later addition to the original story. For even in the angel's first appearance, he states that God now knows Abraham is a God-fearing man because he did not withhold his son from the deity – making it crystal clear that the test was whether Abraham would indeed be willing to go through with the killing of his son and that Abraham passed the test.

moral maturity and free will to stand up to Him and refuse to do that which he knew was immoral even in the face of the divine fiat. Again, such an interpretation though beguiling is belied by the text which tells us that Abraham was indeed willing to murder Isaac and that he *passed* the test by demonstrating that willingness.

Perhaps the most satisfying explanation of this disturbing story is that it never happened but was merely a dream in which Abraham questioned his understanding of God's nature and concluded that God abhors human slaughter and will not permit it. That would turn the story into an "interior dialogue" exploring the nature of God and what is expected of humanity. Such a reading would convert the narrative into a morality play of sorts – maybe even a courtroom drama, a trial between competing conceptions of divinity, with the view that God sanctifies human life and desires moral conduct ultimately prevailing. That approach would be most satisfactory to the modern sensibility. Indeed, no less an authority than Maimonides views the episode as having been dreamt.[52] But I cannot accept this explanation either. There is no suggestion in the text that Abraham is dreaming. When the Torah wants to let its readers know that a Divine revelation is taking place in a dream or trance, it does so; thus, Abraham's epiphany at the Covenant Between the Pieces and Jacob's dream of the angels ascending and descending the heavenly ladder. The Akedah story is recounted as a straightforward narrative and, as much as I might like it to be, cannot be read as a dream.

Finally, I suggest that the Akedah narrative might be sensibly explained by focusing on the nature of Abraham's experience in receiving the command. Perhaps the test to which he was subjected was to see whether he could discern the difference between a true command from God and a temptation from other sources.

---

52. Maimonides has his own compelling reasons for maintaining this position – an entire framework in which all prophets, excluding Moses, receive divine inspiration through dreams or trances; nonetheless, his understanding turns out to be useful in this exegesis of the Akedah story.

I must confess that this approach stems from a great, yet unrecognized, biblical authority, Woody Allen. In his humorous retelling of the story, Allen has God chastising Abraham when it was all over for actually going out to do this crazy thing. And when Abraham argues that his actions proved his love for God, God responds, "it proves that some men will follow any order no matter how asinine as long as it comes from a resonant, well-modulated voice".[53] Despite Allen's plain effort to get a laugh, I find some profundity in this version because it stresses the obligation of human beings to use the reason God gave us to be certain that putative commandments which offend our inherent moral sense in fact come from God before we hasten to perform them[54] – a lesson too infrequently learned by those with excessive religious fervor, as world events have proved time and again.

There are two apparent problems with this solution to the Akedah's insoluble nature, one of which bothers me more than the other. The first is insurmountable since once again this interpretation of the Akedah story cannot be squared either with the text or with the liturgy's use of it, both of which stress that God tested Abraham by commanding him to sacrifice Isaac and that Abraham passed the test by demonstrating his willingness to do so. The second runs afoul of classic rabbinic Judaism. For if God grants human beings the right to reject his wishes, this reading followed to its logical conclusions would permit each human being to decide which mitzvot to accept and which to reject. The option of rejecting those commandments we find personally unappealing is the hallmark of classical Reform Judaism but not, in my opinion, a traditional Jewish viewpoint. In fact, the rabbinic

53. Woody Allen, "The Scrolls" in *Without Feathers* (Random House, 1983).
54. Rabbi Gordon Tucker makes much the same point in his recent discussion of the nature of Halacha. Rabbi Tucker argues that when the community experiences a collective religious intuition that God wants something other than what the Tradition has taught, this "prophetic" voice should be listened to. See Tucker, "Can a People of the Book also be a People of God?" *Conservative Judaism*, Fall-Winter (2007–08): 4–25.

tradition posits that both the Written and Oral Laws were transmitted to Moses on Sinai, thus clearly obviating our right to pick and choose. So I am not entirely comfortable with this reading of the Akedah. However, since I believe that the law was not given at Sinai precisely as it is worded today, viewing the Akedah as Abraham's test of the authenticity of (what appears to be) God's command, falls within my understanding of the Torah's content and meaning for modern Jews. Indeed, since I believe that we are constantly striving – within the framework of over two thousand years of tradition – to understand what God expects of us, it makes sense for Abraham, the patriarch, to have been doing the same.[55]

Curiously enough, Jerome I. Gellman of Ben-Gurion University has offered a reading of the Rabbi of Izbica (the Hasidic Rebbe Mordechai Joseph Leiner; 1802–1854)[56] that is, in some ways, similar to the one I have reached under Woody Allen's inspiration. Adopting what can only be termed a radical theological position, the Izbicer suggests that Abraham was indeed torn with doubt about the ethical nature of God's command. However, rather than concluding that Abraham became a Kierkegaardian knight of faith and rose above these doubts by suspending the ethical, the Izbicer proposes that the *process* of going to Mount Moriah and binding Isaac was Abraham's method of uncovering the divine will (that is, of questioning it respectfully). Abraham's trial thus becomes his willingness to undertake the journey in an attempt to determine what God really wants from him. When he reaches the end of the journey, the voice of the angel wells up from within him to explain the real thrust of God's command and tell him not to slay Isaac. Abraham's ability to stay the course (though

---

55. For me, Halacha is a constantly evolving system inviting human beings to continually strive to understand what it is God expects of us. As a result of this outlook, Franz Rosenzweig's view of the nature of mitzvot – that we are commanded to do that which, in an existentialist sense, we feel commanded to do – resonates strongly with me.

56. J. Gellman, "A Hasidic Interpretation of the Binding of Isaac" in *Between Religion and Ethics* (Bar Ilan University Press, 1993), XXIII–XXXIX.

racked by doubt) and find out what God truly wants is, according to Gellman's reading of the Izbicer, the true act of "a knight of faith". Yet again, however, this attractive interpretation of the Akedah runs aground on the text's praise for Abraham's willingness to make the sacrifice.

One other aspect of the Akedah story deserves mention. Throughout Jewish history the Akedah has served as a paradigm for martyrdom. Focusing on Isaac rather than Abraham,[57] numerous Jewish poets have called on this story to provide a model for *kiddush Hashem* (martyrdom in God's name) in the face of religious persecution. While the story unquestionably teaches that God does not want child sacrifice, the rabbinic tradition is clear that, despite the doctrine of *pikuach nefesh*, which abrogates almost all commandments when life is at stake, martyrdom is required when the alternative is public desecration of God and His covenant with Israel. And it is God's commandment to Abraham to sacrifice his son that is often cited in support of this principle. I am of two minds regarding this aspect of the story. On the one hand, we can read the Akedah narrative cynically as reflecting what appears to be an eternal syndrome – fathers and mothers sending their children to confront death in order to satisfy the parents' zeal for their own obsession.[58] On the other hand, however, we must bear in mind the millennia of persecution confronted by the Jewish people and the genuine heroism and courage displayed by those who chose martyrdom rather than rejection of their heritage and covenant with God. The Akedah story resonates from both perspectives – yet another aspect of its paradoxical nature.

In the final analysis, the story remains powerful, affecting,

---

57. The traditional view (Rashi, 23:2) that Isaac was a grown man in his thirties and not the boy described in the text makes the focus on his willingness to suffer martyrdom more meaningful. If, as the tradition presumes, Sarah died at the time of the Akedah, then we can definitively state that, according to the text, Isaac was thirty-seven years old at the Akedah, since he was born when Sarah was ninety and she died at the age of one hundred and twenty-seven.
58. Many would say that the Vietnam War was an example of this syndrome.

and on a moral level essentially incomprehensible. We read it in the synagogue twice a year, and each time it is beautiful, moving, and terrifying. As my teacher Rabbi Neil Gillman poignantly puts it, this is *our* story and we have to come to grips with it. Thus far I have been unable to do so. Perhaps in the world to come,[59] Elijah the Prophet can explain it to me.

59. Assuming, of course, that I get there despite my failure to believe that each of the six hundred and thirteen mitzvot was commanded by God.

CHAYEI SARAH

Sarah's Death and Burial

This portion begins with the death of the first matriarch at the age of one hundred and twenty-seven. The Rabbis of the Midrash, seeking to explain the cause of Sarah's death and its textual juxtaposition to the Akedah story, explain that she died suddenly when she heard about Abraham's plans to sacrifice Isaac.[1] Given what we have learned about her, that story seems plausible. She does not appear to have been told about God's Akedah command. In fact, the text is remarkably silent about Sarah's reaction to the incident, which may well explain why the midrashists were anxious to fill in that blank by supposing that the news was the cause of her death. Sarah was extremely protective of her son – virtually a paradigmatic caricature of the Jewish mother in current humor. One can well imagine her shock at learning what his fate was to be at the hands of her husband (Isaac's father, no less). It is interesting to speculate what would have happened if Abraham had consulted Sarah on the matter. No doubt she would have objected most forcefully, and I am not sure how Abraham would have dealt

---

1.   *Pirkei de-Rabbi Eliezer* 32; cited in Rashi 23:2.

with that. Indeed, God had previously told him to follow Sarah's advice and banish Hagar and Ishmael, in order to protect Isaac from Ishmael's negative influence. So maybe Abraham was afraid that God would have wanted him to listen to Sarah again. Given what I have posited were his own doubts about the command, perhaps Abraham wanted to avoid such confusion.

At this juncture it seems appropriate to devote a few words of summation with respect to Sarah. The Torah paints an interesting picture of this woman. She appears to have been strikingly beautiful even in old age – so much so that Abraham fears for his life when he travels with her.[2] She is also fairly docile – at least prior to the advent of Hagar and, later, the births of Ishmael and Isaac. We see no hint of rebellion when her husband tells her that they have to pick up and leave Haran for (literally speaking) God knows where; nor does she have anything much to say when Abraham asks her to lie routinely about her marital status in order to save his neck, even when the price is her entry into the harems of (at least) two potentates. She does not appear to be a person of strong faith, as her skeptical laughter at the thought of God's giving her a child in her old age demonstrates.[3] On the other hand, it is when we turn our attention to her position in Abraham's household (most particularly to her role as Isaac's mother) that her strength of character appears. Even though Hagar's entry into Abraham's bed was Sarah's idea in the first place, she becomes inordinately jealous of the servant girl and first forces her to flee and then, after Ishmael's birth, insists on her banishment together with the child (with no reason to believe that either of them will survive a stay in the desert). Significantly, it is Abraham, not Sarah, who is told by God that there is no need to worry about Ishmael. For all Sarah knew, Hagar and her son were being condemned to death.

2. *Midrash Lekach Tov*, picking up on this trait, explains that Sarah was as beautiful at the age of one hundred as she had been at twenty.
3. To be fair, we should note that even Abraham (the paradigm of faith) laughed when he received the same news.

Perhaps this apparent failure of charity towards Hagar can be excused by Sarah's zealous devotion to Isaac.

At the end of the day, the tradition treats Sarah with enormous respect and admiration. On the one hand, this may be a knee-jerk reaction. The matriarch of our people who was married to Abraham our patriarch, who miraculously gave birth in her nineties, must have been a saintly woman. No matter what the text seems to say, there are no two ways about it. On the other hand, it is no surprise that our culture – which has always venerated motherhood – should have venerated Sarah for her devoted role as Isaac's mother. However, as I believe the Hagar incident reveals, Sarah's role as a mother also teaches a cautionary lesson: excessive motherly zeal has its negative aspect. As in other areas of life, there can always be too much of a good thing.

Having announced Sarah's death, the text returns to Abraham and his purchase of a burial plot. Since Hebron appears to be the closest thing Abraham had to a permanent residence (and, significantly, Sarah had died there), it is not surprising that he decides on that location. One might ask why he has to purchase property at all in light of God's promise that he will receive the entire land.[4] But, of course, that promise has not as of this point in the narrative been fulfilled, and Abraham is merely a resident alien in what the Torah describes as land owned by Hittites.[5] So he proceeds to participate in a rather strange real estate negotiation. When Abraham announces that he wants to purchase a burial plot, the Hittites respond that, since he is chosen by Elokim he can have whatever he wants for nothing. It is a Torah truism that the inhabitants of Canaan were idolaters, which makes it somewhat surprising that they would refer to Abraham as one chosen by Elokim. Perhaps, as believing polytheists, they regard Elokim

---

4. As noted above, he didn't make any purchases when he "gave" half of the land to Lot.
5. As I understand it, the historical Hittites had not as yet arrived in Canaan, so the reference is either anachronistic or actually refers to another Canaanite people of the same name. In either event, the point is not significant to the story.

as Abraham's god and view the prospective purchaser as someone who does enjoy some sort of divine favor.[6] In any event, Abraham flatly rejects this generous offer and insists on buying the cave of Machpelah from a Hittite named Ephron, and at the full price to boot. Ephron repeats the offer his kinsmen had made, stating his willingness to give Abraham the cave as an outright gift, to which Abraham repeats his insistence on paying for it. So Ephron disingenuously names the price by telling the "buyer" what the land is worth and stating that, of course, he wants nonetheless to give it away. Abraham promptly weighs out the money and the transaction is completed. On first reading, this appears to be an exercise in double-talk. But I think that these verbal shenanigans probably reflect what at the time was a ritualized negotiation formula. Courtesy would not permit the seller to ask for money or actually name the asking price. So a formula appears to have been devised to facilitate commerce in real property.

The Midrash teaches (BR 58:4) that Machpelah, where Abraham himself is later buried (as are Isaac and Rebecca and Jacob and Leah), is the place where Adam and Eve had been interred. The text makes no such claim; but the legend tends to exalt the place's importance.[7] Today Hebron and Machpelah have become controversial – a sore point exacerbating tensions between the Israelis who venerate the place in light of its biblical associations and the Palestinians who comprise the bulk of the city's population and who, like the Jews, venerate Abraham (Ishmael's father) as their progenitor. It is also the site of a horrific massacre of praying Moslems by a Jewish fanatic in 1996 (and, to be evenhanded, an earlier Arab massacre of the Jews living in Hebron in 1929).

6. Alternately, perhaps they used the term Elokim to refer to their pagan deity as well; or perhaps the reference was to all of the gods in which the local populace believed. After all, in Hebrew, "Elokim" while a singular noun when it refers to God, is in form plural.
7. I think the same process is evident in the traditional identification of Mount Moriah (the site of the Akedah) with the Temple Mount in Jerusalem. This correspondence is explicitly drawn in *II Chronicles* 3:1 where Solomon begins building the Temple on Mount Moriah.

However the political dispute is ultimately resolved, reliance on the text's description of a purchase by Abraham from the resident Hittites does not, I think, move the ball very far. If the text is accepted as authoritative in today's political realm – a very unlikely proposition – God's grant of the entire land to Abraham's descendants would appear to be a lot more authoritative; and if metaphysical deeds of real property don't do the trick, it is hard to see how a three-thousand-year-old text will do it.[8]

A Wife for Isaac

At the end of the Akedah story the text tells us that Abraham "returned to his servants [who had accompanied him to Mount Moriah], and they departed together for Beersheva" (22:19). Isaac goes unmentioned. That omission may be a vestige of an earlier text in which Isaac was in fact sacrificed;[9] the midrashists explain it by recounting that Isaac went off by himself to study in a yeshiva that was being operated by none other than Noah's son, Shem (who must have been a very old man by then!) and his grandson, Eber.[10]

---

8. As long as Palestinian propaganda clearly attempts to rewrite history, claiming no Jewish temple ever existed on the Temple Mount and that the Holocaust never happened, the Bible's historical testimony is clearly irrelevant to resolving the present conflict. However, even if this pernicious form of historical revisionism were abandoned, the present-day political argument over the Promised Land may have its antecedents in the biblical and Koranic versions of the Akedah story. Since Islamic tradition places Ishmael on the altar at the Akedah, instead of Isaac, the Arabs could argue that the promise made there applies to Ishmael, as Abraham's true heir. I have never seen such an argument made on behalf of the Palestinian position; but if Scripture is to be the basis for contemporary agreements and peace treaties (which I believe is a dubious proposition), it is certainly one that would have to be addressed.

9. See Spiegel cited above in the context of the Akedah.

10. BR 56:11. It is possible that the Midrash only refers to this institution as Shem and Eber's because they had founded it, not because they were still running it. Alternatively, Shem did live to be six hundred years old according to the biblical record (having been born when Noah was five hundred [5:32], so he still could have been heading the yeshiva. Either way this is an excellent example of the midrashists' penchant for reading their contemporary values and institutions into the biblical texts. That Shem, Noah's righteous son, was a *rosh yeshiva* (head of a talmudical

In any event, after Abraham buries Sarah he turns his attention to procuring a proper wife for Isaac, which demonstrates that Isaac was indeed around. Abraham summons his steward Eliezer (who, it will be remembered, stood to inherit all of Abraham's property before Isaac was born) and requires him to swear an oath that he will not choose a wife for Isaac from among the Canaanites.[11] Rather, he is to go back to Abraham's birthplace to find an appropriate woman.

In light of the traditional Jewish taboo against intermarriage – with Canaanites in the book of *Bereshit* and with any "foreign women", as legislated by Ezra after the first return to the Land of Israel[12] – this is not surprising.[13] But it does seem strange

academy) would come as a surprise to none of the midrashists; that a yeshiva existed centuries before the giving of the Torah also raised no eyebrows. What were they studying in this yeshiva? A tractate from the Babylonian Talmud?

11. The oath is formalized by having Eliezer – who is actually not referred to by name even once in this entire story – place his hand under Abraham's thigh (which I understand is a euphemism for his genitals). James Joyce, picking up on this image in *Ulysses*, has Leopold Bloom swear by "placing his right hand on his testicles" in "Oxen of the Sun" and "Circe" (episodes fourteen and fifteen respectively).

12. *Ezra* 10.

13. Of course, there was to be no intermarriage whatsoever between the Israelites and the seven Canaanite nations (mentioned in the Covenant Between the Pieces) because they were to be driven out or destroyed. The classic passage forbidding intermarriage with the Canaanites is found in *Shemot* 34:15–16: "You must not make a covenant with the inhabitants of the land, for they will lust after their gods…and when you take wives from among their daughters for your sons, their daughters will lust after their gods and will cause your sons to lust after their gods". A parallel to this passage appears in *Devarim* 7:3–6. According to the text in *Devarim* 23:4–9, the interdiction is slightly more complicated. Even Moabites, Ammonites, Edomites, and Egyptians who presumably convert are not permitted to marry Jews until the tenth and third generations respectively. *Devarim* 23:5 explains that this is because the Moabites and Ammonites "did not meet you with food and water on your journey after you left Egypt, and because they hired Balaam…to curse you." While no reason is given for the length of the respective waiting periods, note that in the Decalogue, God visits the "guilt of the parents upon the children, upon the third and the fourth generations of those who reject Me" (*Devarim* 5:9), so perhaps until three generations have passed offspring is still considered to belong to its familial antecedents. This, of course, does not bear at all on the ten-generation waiting period for Moabites. Interestingly, the Rabbis had to engage in some fancy footwork to deal with the fact that King David was the direct descendant (by far

when one considers the fact that God had instructed Abraham to leave his birthplace and go to Canaan. Now, at the critical moment when Abraham must build the family that will continue the blessed legacy which led him to leave Haran in the first place, it is only from that rejected location that he will accept a wife for his son. Eliezer, a careful servant, asks what he should do if he finds an appropriate woman but she is unwilling to come back with him to Canaan. Should he return and bring Isaac to her? That was an unthinkable option for Abraham. It would, in his view, be better for Eliezer to return empty-handed than for Isaac to leave the Promised Land. The fact is that Isaac never leaves Canaan – unless one believes that he indeed spent some time at Shem's yeshiva and that the house of study was situated elsewhere. This, of course, cannot be a prerequisite for patriarchal status, since Jacob spends a goodly number of years in Haran (and, of course, Abraham had visited Egypt when in need of food in time of famine). But it does show us Abraham's conviction that the blessing he had been promised is attached to the land – so that he wouldn't risk losing it by sending Isaac away from Canaan.

What follows is a beautiful story. We are treated to the first of a series of archetypal betrothal scenes situated at a well. Eliezer, who has gone on his journey with a string of camels and lots of gifts for the hoped-for fiancée, arrives in Haran (referred to in the text at this point as Aram-naharaim) and stops by a well. He prays for a sign from God that one of the young women coming to draw water will be Isaac's future wife: "'O Lord, God of my master Abraham, grant me good fortune this day…. Let the maiden to whom I say "Please, lower your jar that I may drink,"…be the one whom You have decreed for Your servant Isaac" (24:12–13). No sooner has he finished this prayer than, lo and behold, Rebecca (Abraham's grandniece, that is, the daughter of his nephew Betuel) arrives at the well, responds to Eliezer's request for water in the affirmative,

---

fewer than ten generations) of Ruth, a Moabite woman. Reading the Torah prohibition as applying only to male Moabites readily dispensed with that glitch.

and even offers to draw some for his camels precisely as Eliezer had hoped. He asks whether he can impose on her family's hospitality for the night, but not before he has given her some jewelry (presumably to impress her with his or, more likely, his master's wealth). She says yes and tells Eliezer who she is.

Betuel and his son Laban agree to the match. Eliezer gives them some gifts and lavishes more jewelry on Rebecca. They ask whether she can stay in Haran for a few more days before her departure; Eliezer demurs, and Rebecca agrees to go at once. I think this willingness to disregard her family's wishes demonstrates Rebecca's independence, which will be a critical (and most significant) character trait later in her life. When they arrive back in Canaan, Isaac is "out in the field toward evening" (24:63). Some translate the verb for what he was doing there as meditating, thus permitting the midrashists (BR 60:14) to say he invented *Minchah*, the afternoon prayer service. Whatever he is doing, it must have had some effect because the text tells us that Rebecca falls off her camel when she sees him.[14] She asks Eliezer who it is and, when she learns it is Isaac, she veils herself, presumably out of modesty. In any event, Isaac doesn't quarrel with Eliezer's choice, takes her into his mother's tent and, as the text takes care to inform us, loves her.

Aside from God's reference to Isaac in the Akedah command as the son Abraham loves, this is, I believe, the first use of the verb in the Torah. We were not told that Adam loved Eve, or that Abraham loved Sarah. I read this text – both Rebecca's falling off the camel at her first sight of Isaac and the statement that he loved her – as suggesting a strong sexual attraction between the two of them.[15] What is more interesting is the statement that

14. Some translate the verb employed in the verse as "alighted" which lessens the dramatic impact of the scene, but the literal translation is "fell". Of course, she may have been impressed by Isaac's spiritual aura or his good looks, and not by what he was doing at the time.
15. This would of course depend upon Rebecca's age at the time Isaac met her. We know that Isaac was "forty years old when he took to wife Rebecca" (25:20); how-

"Isaac brought her into the tent of his mother Sarah" (24:67). At this time, Isaac was living in the Negev region, and since Sarah had been living with Abraham in the Hebron area, there is no reason to conclude that her tent was in the Negev desert. The usage must therefore be figurative. Abraham had remarried (as we are about to learn) and Isaac was establishing his own household. Given the strong mother-son attachment he must have had with Sarah – remember what a doting and protective mother she was and Abraham's apparent apprehension of telling her about God's Akedah command – the text is informing us that Rebecca's arrival allowed him finally to get over Sarah's death and move on with his own life.

From all we know about Rebecca at this juncture she is a well-brought-up young woman who knows how to treat strangers and yet is sufficiently her own person to defy her family and agree to leave immediately for her new home. We also get the sense from Eliezer's experience in finding her that God has intended her to marry Isaac all along. But we have no hint as yet of the headstrong, virtually fanatical woman we shall meet in the next parasha when she induces her younger son to defraud both his twin brother and his father in order to further what she considers his (that is, the younger son's) divinely intended destiny.

Abraham's (Inter)marriage

Abraham doesn't waste much time after Sarah's death in finding

ever, Rebecca's age is unclear. The Torah (22:23) tells us that Abraham heard about Betuel's birth after the Akedah. If Betuel was actually born at that time then Rebecca, his daughter, must have been several decades younger than Isaac. However, if the verse means to imply that Rebecca was born at the time of the Akedah, she might have even been in her twenties at the time Isaac and she got married. This would all depend on how many years elapsed between the Akedah and Isaac and Rebecca's marriage. If only three years elapsed (because Isaac was thirty-seven at the Akedah and forty when he got married) Rebecca would have been three years old at the time of her wedding! However, if Isaac was only thirteen at the time of the Akedah then she could have been twenty-seven when they got married. In short, trying to determine the age of the Bible's characters through a careful reading of the text does not always provide a decisive answer.

another wife. He marries a woman named Keturah who bears him six more children. Since there is no mention of any miracles at this point, the text apparently does not consider it at all unusual for a man of such advanced years to have children – which contrasts sharply with its earlier treatment of Abraham's impending fatherhood of Isaac ("Can a child be born to a man a hundred years old …?" [17:17]). The midrashists tell us that Keturah was none other than Hagar, the rejected Egyptian slave-woman and mother of Ishmael. That seems to be a bit of a stretch given the way Abraham had treated her and his rejection (at Sarah's – and, indirectly, God's – urging) of her son in favor of Sarah's. I also think it unlikely that Hagar would at this point in time, absent miraculous divine intervention, be of child-bearing age. Since we know that Ishmael was about fourteen when Isaac was born and Sarah died when Isaac was thirty-seven and Ishmael was about fifty-one (since she was ninety when she gave birth to Isaac) then even if Hagar gave birth to Ishmael when she was fifteen, she would at least be in her sixties. Absent a miracle similar to that performed on Sarah's behalf, it is unlikely that a woman at that stage of life would be able to bear six children.

More interesting is the fact that Abraham thinks nothing of marrying a local woman – which he deemed unthinkable for Isaac.[16] This raises the interesting question of why intermarrying with the local Canaanite population was so taboo. If the Canaanites were an inherently impure or unworthy people, as Noah's curse of Canaan seems to indicate, than neither Abraham nor his descendants should intermarry with them. Presumably, it was this understanding that led the midrashists to suggest that Abraham remarried his Egyptian slave-woman Hagar, and not a local woman. However, if intermarriage was taboo because it would

---

16. If we accept the Rabbis' traditional view that Abraham, while in the land of Canaan, followed all of the Torah precepts (even though they had not yet been given), his marriage to a Canaanite woman raises yet another question.

lead to assimilation with the local idolatrous culture, as *Shemot* 34:16 ("their daughters will lust after their gods and will cause your sons to lust after their gods") seems to indicate, then once Isaac had been born and the divine covenant safely passed on to the next generation, Abraham could safely do what he pleased. (Indeed, one might argue that Abraham could always have done so, since he would have had the strength of character to remain immune to the idolatrous blandishments of his local wives.) While Abraham was also opening up a can of worms by siring more children who might compete with Isaac for the coveted inheritance, this does not seem to have bothered him, as he made it clear that Isaac was his sole, legitimate heir and "he sent them [the sons of his concubines] away from his son Isaac eastward, to the land of the East" (25:6).

Another problem with marrying a local Canaanite woman would have been the question of how Abraham's descendants – had they intermarried with the local Canaanite population – would have ever been able to banish the Canaanite side of their wives' families (not to mention their own children, if they followed Abraham's model) when it came time for God's promise to be fulfilled and the Canaanites to be dispossessed. As we know, in Ezra and Nehemiah's time (*Ezra* 10; *Nehemiah* 13:1–3), the Jewish men who "had married foreign women, among whom were some women who had borne children" (*Ezra* 10:44) did expel them. But the emotional toll this must have involved is unfathomable.

Abraham: A Few Parting Words

At the age of one hundred and seventy-five, Abraham dies and is buried at Machpelah by Isaac and Ishmael. While the appearance of Isaac and Ishmael (the progenitors of the Jews and the Arabs) as joint mourners at their father's funeral gives rise to nice homiletics, I find it a bit disturbing that Isaac shows up to bury his father but was nowhere to be found when his mother died. Of course, if we accept the midrash that he was studying Torah at the yeshiva run by Noah's son Shem, perhaps he couldn't have made it to Sarah's funeral unless it was near Hebron.[17] Short of that kind of fantasy, we have a stark and ironic contrast. Isaac does not appear at the death of the mother who doted on him, but he respectfully buries the father who, at what he thought was God's command, tried to kill him. I suppose that those who view the Akedah story through traditional eyes would say that Isaac had been a willing participant in the attempted sacrifice and had no reason to resent his father on account of it.[18] But I think of a young man bound on an altar with his father brandishing a weapon, intending to kill him with it, and I cannot imagine that he would have no resentment.

A few words about Abraham appear to be in order. The tradition exalts the first patriarch as the quintessential man of faith, the discoverer (or, more appropriately, the rediscoverer) of the one God and the first Jewish hero. There are glimpses of such a person in Abraham's story – particularly the dialogue with God about the fate of Sodom, his dealings with Melchizedek and his generosity with Lot. But we also see an opportunist (in his dealings with Pharaoh and Abimelech with respect to Sarah); a weakling, when he meekly allows Sarah to banish the pregnant Hagar; and, most significantly, a fanatical zealot, who is so sure he is in direct communication with God that he blindly follows what he believes is a command to kill his beloved son despite that act's patent immorality. In short, as with all biblical characters, Abraham is a multi-faceted personality whose life presents us with a perplexing complex of problems. Perhaps the Jewish tradition is

---

17. On the other hand, if the yeshiva was somewhere in the Holy Land (which was necessary if we are to accept the midrash that he never left Eretz Yisrael), Isaac would likely have been able to get to Hebron for his mother's burial. But the text makes no mention of his having attended a yeshiva at all, much less where it was located.

18. The Midrash (cited in Rashi 22:8) teaches that when the verse repeats the phrase "and the two walked off together" (22:6, 8) during the Akedah episode, it is alluding to the fact that Abraham had let Isaac know what was to happen, and Isaac accepting God's command walked in the same path his father had.

better off with the Abraham of the midrashists than with the more essentially human man so vividly portrayed by the Torah text.

TOLDOT

The Story of Isaac

With the death of Abraham, the Torah commences what it calls the story of Isaac, the least vividly portrayed story of the patriarchs. While the parasha begins with the statement that it will be telling us the story of Isaac, in reality it deals with the rivalry between his twin sons, Esau and Jacob.[1] Isaac remains a passive figure throughout. He does little, hardly ever travels and is acted upon by others – primarily by his sons and his wife Rebecca. From a psychological perspective, perhaps this can be explained by Isaac's having undergone the trauma of the Akedah.[2] In any event, other than a dispute with the Philistine king about wells and a third incarnation of the "sister-wife" archetypal story, Isaac's

---

1. While the New JPS translates the opening words as "this is the story of Isaac", the word *toldot*, translated as "story", can also mean progeny. Thus, the same translation renders the Hebrew word elsewhere as "this is the line of Shem" (11:10); "this is the line of Ishmael" (25:12). Such a translation would further emphasize my point, as this parasha, which is ostensibly dedicated to Isaac's story, is really about his offspring.
2. The Midrash (BR 65:10) in an inspired moment suggests that Isaac's sight was impaired when the tears of the ministering angels fell into his eyes at the Akedah. Perhaps this is an oblique reference to Isaac's post-traumatic stress disorder.

significance appears to rest primarily on his role as the imparter of the blessing for which his sons compete. Isaac lives the life of a bridge figure, silently carrying on the traditions of his father Abraham and transmitting them to his sons (or at least to one of them).

Jacob and Esau – In the Beginning

As noted above, Isaac and Rebecca seem to have fallen in love at first sight (to be more precise, Isaac fell in love at his first sight of Rebecca; the text is silent as to her feelings for her husband, although her "falling off" her camel when she saw him suggests some level of sexual attraction). But their efforts to raise a family which can inherit God's blessing (already passed from Abraham to Isaac) are at first unsuccessful. Rebecca is unable to conceive. This continues a pattern that began with Sarah, who was also barren until God announced the impending birth of Isaac. Isaac introduces a note of compassion for his wife that Abraham never expressed: he "pleaded with God on behalf of his wife, because she was barren" (25:21).[3] The text obviously assumes that a woman's failure to conceive is inevitably because she is barren. That the husband may be sterile is not even contemplated.

Even before their birth, we are told that Rebecca's twin sons engage in a struggle for supremacy: "the children struggled in her womb" (25:22). Rebecca, desperate to discover the meaning of this struggle, seems to have gone to a divine oracle: "she went to inquire of God" (25:22). Remarkably "God answered her" (25:23) directly[4] stating that each of the children in her womb represents

3. Abraham seemed to be mostly concerned about himself (and passing on the divine covenant), asking God: "What can You give me, seeing that I shall die childless?" (15:2). Indeed, before Isaac's miraculous birth, Abraham had been willing to settle for either Eliezer (15:3) or Ishmael (17:18) as his heir.
4. Aside from Eve, who hears her punishment directly from God (3:16), Rebecca appears to be the first woman that the text tells us God spoke to. Hagar received her oracle through an angel (16:9–12). Of course, if we understand one of Abraham's three visitors to have been God in human form, Sarah directly converses with God when she denies that she had laughed (18:15).

an independent nation, and that "one…shall be mightier than the other, and the older shall serve the younger" (25:23). The oracular prophecy is clear that the "older shall serve the younger", so it is not surprising that Rebecca, upon hearing it, favors Jacob (who was born second) throughout his life and does everything she can to support his bid for supremacy.

The struggle between the twins continues at the very moment of birth as Jacob desperately hangs on to Esau's heel – apparently fighting for the right of the firstborn from the very outset.[5] As the story progresses, we shall see that the twins are actually competing for two separate, though related, prizes: the birthright, which provides the firstborn son with a double portion of his father's estate upon his death, and the family blessing (first delineated by God to Abraham in 12:2–3 and later expanded upon). As I explain below, the family blessing can also be loosely divided into a material and a spiritual one; the former paralleling the blessing Jacob steals from Esau and the latter paralleling the Abrahamic covenant Jacob receives from Isaac at the end of the parasha.

The text proceeds to describe the two antagonists. Esau is characterized as an outdoorsman and a hunter; Jacob, in sharp contrast, stays in camp and is an *ish tam*, literally a "simple" or, perhaps, a "pure" man. Ironically, Jacob, as we shall see, turns out to be neither simple nor pure. Indeed, as we read the narrative, it becomes abundantly clear that it is Esau who is the simpleton, an obvious target for his brother's clever scheming. At this point, it is sufficient to note that Esau is an alpha male who finds his pleasure in the rugged life of the hunter while Jacob is a quieter type – perhaps even a momma's boy – who likes to stay at home. Most significantly, we are informed right at the beginning of the story that Isaac was partial to Esau ("because he had a taste for [the] game" [25:28] Esau provided)[6] and Rebecca favored Jacob.

5. Ironically, had Jacob triumphed and come out first, presumably he would have been doomed to "serve his younger brother", or do oracles not work that way?
6. As I discuss below, this statement seems to belie the rabbinic tradition that the three patriarchs, while in the Promised Land, observed the commandments before they

We find the first reported head-to-head confrontation between the two brothers when Esau returns from a hunting expedition and finds Jacob cooking up a stew – in the familiar King James language, "a mess of pottage" (25:34). Esau is famished and asks for some. Instead of engaging in a simple act of brotherly kindness, Jacob seizes the opportunity to persuade Esau into selling him the birthright (that is, the right of the firstborn son to inherit a double portion of the father's estate) in exchange for the stew. The simple, emotional, and famished Esau apparently could not care less about the birthright so he accepts Jacob's offer. This "spurn[ing] of the birthright" (25:34), to use the Torah's description, contrasts very sharply with Esau's reaction when later, at Rebecca's urging, Jacob swindles him out of the family blessing. As we shall see, Esau at that time "burst[s] into wild and bitter sobbing" (27:34) and goes so far as to threaten Jacob's life. So it is difficult to understand why the text describes him as having spurned the birthright. Is the Torah biased against Esau (like the Rabbis undoubtedly were years later) or is there more here than meets the eye?[7]

In any event, far from the portrait of Esau painted by the rabbinic tradition – in which he is an enemy of all that is right and good in the Jewish way of life[8] – the man described by the Torah

---

were given on Sinai. According to Jewish law, animals, to be fit for eating, must be ritually slaughtered.

7. Modern biblical critics will of course argue that apologists struggling to validate Jacob's actions added this condemnatory line later. It certainly does not mesh with the rest of the story, which stresses (even glorifies) Jacob's ability to trick Esau into selling him the birthright. They would argue that this etiological story actually exalts Jacob as a trickster following in the footsteps of Abraham, who defrauded at least two foreign rulers. In this respect Jacob is more like his grandfather Abraham than his gullible father Isaac.

8. Rashi, weaving these midrashim into his commentary, notes that when the twins struggled in utero, Jacob struggled to get out when Rebecca passed a house of study and Esau struggled to get out when she passed a pagan temple (25:22). Furthermore, Rashi declares that Esau used to deceive others (including Isaac) with his words and that he was tired when he returned from the hunt because he had been murdering people (25:27–29). Moreover, according to Rashi, Esau spurns the birthright because it entails serving God as one of his priests (25:32, 34). Thus, in

is a caring son, who has little concern for the material things of life. Esau's rejection of the birthright (under what appears to be extreme duress) should argue in his favor, since he is only giving up the double portion of his father's estate. Nothing in the text at this point indicates that Esau spurned his claim to be the future recipient of God's blessing of the family and, through the family, of the entire world.[9] Of course, the tradition teaches (and the text, read as a whole, certainly implies) that God wants the blessing to go to Jacob, not to his older brother. Nonetheless, when we examine the conduct of the two brothers, Esau doesn't appear to deserve the bad rap that the Rabbis have traditionally given him. Furthermore, God's rejection of Esau seems to be yet another example of the deity's arbitrary nature when it comes to who receives divine favor and who does not.[10]

Isaac, Rebecca, and Abimelech – Déjà Vu Yet Again

Disrupting the narrative about Esau and Jacob, the Torah now recounts for the third time the archetypal "sister-wife" story. Yet again one of our patriarchs lies about the nature of his relationship with his wife (saying that she is his sister) to protect and, ultimately, to enrich himself. On the first two occasions Abraham and Sarah were the protagonists and Pharaoh and Abimelech were the antagonists; this time Isaac and Rebecca share the spotlight

a few short verses Esau becomes an idolater, a murderer, one who despises God's service, and an individual who deceives both his father and others. Such is the power of the Midrash. Aside from a desire to impute absolute evil to Jacob's rival, the Rabbis may also have been influenced by their perception that Esau was the progenitor of Rome. So any criticism of Esau was by extension a criticism of the Roman legions that were cruelly oppressing Judea when the midrashists wrote and that had destroyed the Temple.

9. As I explain below, complicating matters there may actually be two family blessings – one focusing upon material abundance and political strength (which Jacob tricked Isaac into giving him, and which Esau clearly wanted) and the other, the Abrahamic covenant, intentionally passed on from Isaac to Jacob at the end of the parasha.

10. Of course, it does fit into the pattern noted above in the section on Cain and Abel of younger brothers being chosen in place of their elder siblings.

and Abimelech (presumably, another king of the Philistines in Gerar who has assumed the hereditary name) is the duped ruler.

Isaac and Rebecca travel to Gerar to avoid the famine striking the land,[11] but notably unlike the two occurrences involving Sarah, Rebecca is not taken into the harem and Abimelech does not suffer any illness or plague as a result. Rather, after Isaac and Rebecca had lived there for "some time" (26:8), Abimelech sees the couple engaging in what is probably some sort of sexual behavior – the verb *metzachek* describing this behavior derives from the same verbal root (meaning laughter) as Isaac's name and has been translated variously as "fondling", "cavorting" and "jesting".[12] Upon viewing this activity, Abimelech upbraids Isaac for having lied to him, and Isaac responds by telling him that he resorted to this ruse only because he was afraid for his life. Abimelech is quite put out, noting that because of this lie someone might have unwittingly slept with Rebecca and brought guilt upon everyone. This remark and the fact that Abimelech orders all his subjects to leave both Isaac and his wife alone leads me to question whether the ruler's indignation was somewhat overstated. Perhaps, Isaac was in more danger than Abimelech admits. However, given that Isaac and Rebecca had lived in Gerar for a while and Rebecca had not been taken into the harem, perhaps Abimelech's claims are genuine. In any event, what we have here is another stark example (like Pharaoh and the earlier Abimelech) of a non-Jew behaving in a substantially more ethical manner than the patriarch and the matriarch. I see this as yet another proof of the arbitrary election of this family.

As in the other archetypal scenes, Isaac obtains substantial wealth in the aftermath of this incident. However, this time, instead of the victim enriching him, God bestows the wealth di-

---

11. Following Abraham's stratagem, they may have been on their way to Egypt; but God appears to Isaac and declares: "Do not go down to Egypt; stay in the land which I point out to you…and I will be with you" (26:2–3).
12. The same verb is used to describe the conduct engaged in by Ishmael that caused Sarah to demand that he and his mother be banished from the household.

rectly. As a result of this, the Philistines become envious of Isaac's wealth and stop up the wells in the Gerar area that Abraham had dug years earlier. Abimelech asks Isaac to leave, and he departs and sets about redigging other wells dug by his father, setting off a dispute over water rights with the people of Gerar. Finally, Isaac returns to Beersheva; Abimelech follows him there and suggests that they make a treaty. Isaac does so, thus concluding a pact with another Abimelech in the same place his father had years before with the Philistine ruler's predecessor.

As this episode suggests, Isaac seems destined to repeat his father's actions and follow in his footsteps time after time. It is almost as if he is a mere carbon copy of Abraham – following Abraham to the Akedah, praying for his own barren wife, escaping famine, playing out the "sister-wife" scene, making a covenant with Abimelech and finally passing on the blessing to the next generation. In most of this, Isaac plays a passive role, either following in Abraham's footsteps or reacting to the events and people around him.[13]

Esau's Intermarriage

In a single sentence, the text informs us that Esau took two wives, both of them the daughters of Hittites, and that both Isaac and Rebecca were unhappy about it. I find this puzzling. In discussing Abraham's marriage to Keturah, I considered the reasons why Abraham was so vociferously against Isaac's marrying a local Canaanite woman.[14] And I suggested that once the divine covenant

13. Another reading of Isaac's story could point out the differences between Abraham and Isaac: Isaac seems to have had a closer relationship with his wife (up until this point); God forbade Isaac from leaving the Promised Land, while he did not stop Abraham; Isaac was clearly not as able a trickster as Abraham or, as we shall soon see, his son Jacob. These differences emphasize the fact that while Isaac may appear to have been a carbon copy of Abraham and a passive individual, he was his own man with his own unique character traits.
14. Note that God makes no mention of any such prohibition and that conversion does not seem to have been a viable answer. Otherwise, Isaac could have married a Canaanite convert.

had been passed on to Isaac, there was no problem in Abraham's marrying Keturah even if she was a Canaanite.[15] Indeed, knowing that Ishmael would not receive the divine covenant, Abraham never put any restrictions on the women he could marry. By the same token Rebecca should not have cared whether or not Esau intermarried with the local nations. That Isaac should have found Esau's wives "a source of bitterness" (26:35) is understandable because he may have entertained hopes of Esau's receiving the Abrahamic covenant (and the covenant, apparently, had to be kept within the family, or, at least, could not include the peoples inhabiting the land of Canaan), but Rebecca, who had no such desire, should not have been so troubled. I cannot figure out why she was so upset.[16]

Isaac's Blessings

Before turning to the carefully wrought story of how Jacob received his father's spiritual blessing, a few words about the stress the Torah places on the right son receiving it. I have always found this aspect of the story more than a little bit baffling. Why should it matter whether Isaac blesses Jacob or Esau or what words he chooses? If God wants the blessing to go to Jacob, presumably that is what will happen – especially if Jacob is God's chosen one. Yet every character in the story undoubtedly thinks it vitally important which twin is standing (or perhaps kneeling) before Isaac when the blessing is conferred. Does Isaac really possess some magical (and, hence, irrevocable) power to shape the future through his words, no matter what God intends? Such a possibility, to my mind, is theologically preposterous. Surely God does not need a human mouthpiece in order to confer a blessing, and if a human being blesses the wrong person, presumably, God can

---

15. While there is a possibility, according to the midrashists, that Keturah was really Hagar (an Egyptian) no one suggests that she came from Abraham's homeland, where he sent Eliezer to find a wife for Isaac.
16. Perhaps she was not really upset and merely feigned that emotion in an effort to shift Isaac's favor from Esau to Jacob.

ignore the error. Yet the text plainly speaks as if it made all the difference in the world.

One way of answering this question would be to argue that Isaac's blessing really did have binding power, but it was a special case. God had expressly told Abraham that He would bless those Abraham blessed (at least this is the traditional understanding of the somewhat ambiguous "you shall be a blessing" [Rashi, 12:2]) – and this gift of blessing had passed to Isaac. Indeed, even if this was not what God really meant, Rebecca might have known about the promise and misunderstood it, believing that for the blessing to pass to Jacob, Isaac had to say the "magic" words to him. Even though she had received an unambiguous oracle promising Jacob's supremacy, perhaps Rebecca did not want to take the chance that Isaac's blessing could trump the oracle, so she took action. Any way I look at it, the conclusion appears inescapable that Rebecca, Esau and Jacob all believed that Isaac's words of blessing had special power, no matter what God may have actually intended. In a text positing an omnipotent deity, that is more than a bit surprising.[17]

When the time comes for the blessing to be conferred, the text tells us that Isaac was old and going blind – a circumstance necessary if Jacob and Rebecca are to trick the patriarch.[18] Isaac asks Esau (his favorite) to go out with his gear, quiver, and bow; hunt game; prepare it in the manner Isaac liked; and bring it to him so that he could bestow his blessing before his death.

From a traditional perspective, Isaac's desire to eat game killed on the hunt is itself surprising because the Rabbis teach that the patriarchs kept the commandments while they lived in

17. The same question can be asked concerning Balaam's efforts to curse the Israelites in *Bamidbar*. God clearly does not want to curse the Israelites; however, rather than simply ignoring Balaam's curses, He ensures that Balaam blesses the Israelites instead of cursing them. If what Balaam said truly did not matter, than God could have let him curse the Israelites and then ignored his words.
18. The Midrash (BR 65:10) suggests that Isaac's blindness was designed to permit him to be tricked.

the Promised Land. This would of course include the interdiction against eating meat that was not ritually slaughtered, a painstaking process that can almost certainly not be performed during a hunt.[19] Orthodox commentators on this text are indeed troubled by this anomaly. The ArtScroll Chumash, citing the *Ne'os Ha-Desheh* (a nineteenth-century work by the Hasidic master, Abraham Borenstein of Socharov) translates Isaac's request that Esau take his "quiver and bow" as his "sword and bow". By telling Esau to take a sword (the quiver is presumably implicit since a bow is useless without arrows), Isaac would seem to be suggesting that Esau ritually slaughter the game with his sword after he catches it (apparently without using the bow that the ArtScroll translators cannot eliminate from the text).[20] While the ancient Aramaic *Targum* (translation) by Onkelos also rendered this verse as "your weapons, your sword and your bow", the apologetics fueling this translation are clear. However, the desire to provide Esau with a knife to perform shechitah on the animal belies the difficulty in catching an animal and then having the time and leisure to slaughter it ritually.[21] Furthermore, since Isaac apparently enjoyed this kind of meat (remember Esau's game was the stated reason for his being Isaac's favorite), he would have had to have been doing this all the time. It seems to me that the desire to show that the patriarchs performed the commandments is but another example of anachronism in the Midrash, whereby the Rabbis presume that the form of Judaism practiced by their ancestors mirrored their own. Today, taking a similar path, ultra-Orthodox children's books routinely picture our ancestors wearing black hats and coats.

19. See similar discussions above concerning Abraham's serving milk and meat together to the three visitors and his putatively giving away part of the Promised Land to Lot and to Abimelech.

20. As I understand it, if an animal is shot with arrows before slaughter, the meat is not kosher.

21. I remember seeing a suggestion somewhere (which I have been unable to locate) that the problem of getting kosher meat for Isaac was solved miraculously when God saw to it that Esau's arrow passed directly under the deer's throat and performed shechitah on it.

Needless to say, the Jews in Egypt did not dress in the manner of eighteenth-century Polish nobility.[22]

It turns out that Rebecca was eavesdropping on the Isaac-Esau conversation. This in and of itself tells us something about Isaac and Rebecca's marital relationship. It surely wasn't one of mutual trust.[23] Rebecca apparently had not informed her husband about the oracle she received prior to the twins' birth. Perhaps, if she had done so, Isaac would not have been intent on conferring the all-important blessing on Esau. Having overheard Isaac's request for fresh game and his desire to bless Esau when he brought it, Rebecca summons Jacob and concocts a scheme designed to trick both her husband and her elder son and obtain the blessing for her favorite.

Among her other talents, it seems that Rebecca was a first-rate chef. Since Jacob is not a hunter like his brother, she cannot prepare fresh game for Isaac; but she knows how to cook goat meat in a manner that tastes like Isaac's favorite meal. Even that, however, is not enough. For Jacob is concerned that despite his near blindness, Isaac will be able to recognize him by touching his smooth skin – which is not at all like Esau's hairy body. Interestingly, Jacob's concern is for himself, not for his father. With palpable fear he tells his mother that if the ruse is discovered, he (Jacob) will be cursed instead of blessed. Here again, the power of Isaac's words is emphasized. Jacob's concern is immediately quelled when Rebecca tells him that any curse will fall on her, not him.

So, while Esau is out hunting, Rebecca steals his best clothes

---

22. My teacher, Rabbi Lewis Warshauer, is fond of demonstrating this aspect of midrash by taking out a *Haggadah* and pointing out a picture of the Jewish slaves' quarters in Egypt where there are *tzitit* (garments with ritual fringes) hanging on a washing line.

23. Of course, Sarah also overheard the conversation between Abraham and the angels from the entrance of the tent (18:10). Either she was also eavesdropping or she was in the tent preparing the food for the guests as Abraham had requested. When it came to Isaac, I have noted above that Abraham did not share everything with Sarah, so Isaac in planning to give the blessing (without consulting his wife) is following in his father's footsteps.

and puts them on her favorite. She covers Jacob's hands and neck with goatskin and sends him to Isaac with the food she has cooked. Isaac asks who it is and Jacob tells him that he is Esau. Obviously concerned with a depiction of the eponymous father of Israel[24] as a conniver and defrauder, Rashi (based on the Midrash) strives mightily to read the text in a manner that avoids the outright lie by careful punctuation. While the plain meaning of Jacob's statement is "I am Esau, your firstborn son", Rashi reads the text as: "It is I. Esau is your firstborn son" (27:19). To this reader, at least, Rashi's hyper-clever apology for Jacob does not hold any water whatsoever – particularly in light of Jacob's earlier concern that the ruse will make a trickster out of him and cause him to be cursed.

Isaac nonetheless senses that something is awry. He asks Jacob how he was able to complete the hunt and prepare the food so quickly; Jacob responds that God made it possible.[25] Isaac still isn't satisfied and asks Jacob to come close to him so he can feel his skin and establish "whether you are really my son Esau or not" (27:21) – precisely what both Jacob and Rebecca had predicted would happen. It is then that Isaac makes the oft-quoted observation that "the voice is the voice of Jacob, yet the hands are the hands of Esau" (27:22). Perhaps more confused than ever, Isaac now asks directly whether it is really Esau, and Jacob answers in the affirmative. Here as well, Rashi strives by linguistic legerdemain to acquit Jacob of a falsehood. The text states that Isaac asked, "Are you [really] my son Esau?" and Jacob responded, "I am" (27:24). Rashi points out that Jacob did not say, "I am Esau" and apparently reads his answer as merely stating that he was in

24. As we learn later on, God changes Jacob's name to Israel.
25. According to Rashi, this very statement – concocted by Jacob as an explanation for his ability to come so quickly with the desired food – gave Isaac a clue that it wasn't Esau standing before him. For Esau, according to the Rabbis, wasn't the kind of person likely to invoke God at all. Of course, this explanation disregards Isaac's understanding that Esau was indeed qualified to receive the all-important blessing.

existence – which is hardly a fair reading of what the text is telling us. Simply put, we have here a fraud on Isaac perpetrated by Rebecca and Jacob in concert. And if we are to take this conduct as exemplary because the blessing was supposed to go to Jacob all along, then the Torah is teaching us that the end justifies the means – which I do not believe is an authentic Torah principle.

In any event, Isaac proceeds to give the blessing to Jacob. It has four parts: (1) a blessing of material wealth – "May God give you of the dew of the heaven and the fat of the earth, abundance of new grain and wine" (27:28); (2) a blessing of political mastery over other nations – "let peoples serve you and nations bow to you" (27:29); (3) a blessing of political mastery over his brothers – "be master over your brothers, and let your mother's sons bow to you" (27:29); and (4) an echo of the blessing given to Abraham – "cursed be they who curse you, blessed be they who bless you" (27:29). The final part lends support to the supposition that the power to bless had been inherited by Isaac from his father and that he had now passed on this "spiritual" family blessing to Jacob. The other three parts of the blessing, however, are completely materialistic and generic, having nothing particular in common with the earlier blessings given to Abraham.

As soon as Isaac completes the blessing, drama (perhaps melodrama is more appropriate) ensues. Jacob no sooner leaves Isaac's presence then Esau appears with the food he has prepared. When Esau discovers that Jacob has already received the blessing – and, even more importantly, that for some unexplained reason Isaac cannot take it back[26] – he cries bitterly and asks his father to bless him as well. Isaac explains that it is too late to change the provision that makes Esau Jacob's servant but proceeds to give Esau a blessing of material wealth – "your abode shall enjoy the fat of the earth and the dew of the heaven above" (27:39) – and a lesser blessing, culminating in a promise that Esau will ultimately break Jacob's yoke from his neck: "yet by your sword you shall

---

26. This is another example of the apparent magical power of Isaac's words.

live, and you shall serve your brother; but when you grow restive, you shall break his yoke from your neck" (27:40).[27] Isaac makes no mention of the power to bless having been given to Jacob, nor does he make any attempt now to give it as well to Esau.

I appreciate that the episode of the fraudulent procurement of Isaac's blessing teaches us the salutary lesson that it is not enough to trust in God's providence and that human beings must act in order to fulfill their own destinies.[28] But the incident is still hard to understand. Most importantly, it is difficult to fathom how the words of human beings can control blessings that ultimately (to be effective) must come from God. To be sure, God had told Abraham that he would "be a blessing" (12:2); but it seems to me that the blessing still comes from God and that a mistake on Isaac's part should not have the magical effect that the text assumes it has. Then there is the patently unfair condemnation of Esau for no apparent reason other than his willingness to take wives from outside the clan. Such conduct didn't bother Abraham after Sarah's death; and more importantly, as we shall see a little later on, it does not turn out to be any sort of an impediment for Judah who, after all, becomes the progenitor of the Davidic royal line and ultimately of the Messiah.[29] Indeed, while Esau's Hittite wives pain Isaac, he still wishes to give Esau the blessing. To be sure, there is some evidence

27. While King David did conquer Edom (the Torah teaches us that Esau was the progenitor of the nation of Edom [36:1, 43]) and the Edomites eventually overthrew their Israelite rulers, thus confirming this prophecy, the Rabbis' identification of the Romans as descendants of Esau does not fit into this paradigm.

28. The same lesson can be learned from God telling Moses at the splitting of the Sea of Reeds to instruct the Israelites to move forward instead of passively praying to God for help. Only when the Israelites do so does the miraculous sea splitting take place.

29. As I discuss below, Judah married the Canaanite woman Shua (38:22); however, the Torah does not explicitly state that Tamar, the woman who gave birth to Judah's twin sons (Perez and Zerah), was a Canaanite. So while Judah certainly intermarried, the child who continued his line and was the progenitor of King David may not have had a Canaanite mother. Indeed, one can argue either way: perhaps the Torah did not mention Tamar was a Canaanite because it was obvious, or perhaps after mentioning that Shua was a Canaanite, the Torah assumed we would infer that Tamar was not, if it did not explicitly say she was.

that Esau, the hunter, is an impetuous man of hearty appetites and a tendency to act before he thinks; but in contrast to the wiliness of Jacob, as abetted by his mother, these shortcomings do not seem to me to justify Esau's becoming the archetype of the evil oppressor of Israel. And we certainly do not see any character traits in Jacob at this point in his life that render him worthy of becoming the eponymous patriarch of Israel, the nation of priests.

Esau's Rage, Jacob's Flight, and the Final Blessing

Not surprisingly, Esau is furious at this turn of events and, possibly thinking out loud, declares: "Let but the mourning period of my father come, and I will kill my brother Jacob" (27:41).[30] Esau's consideration for his father shows that there is more to his character than blind fury. Either out of respect for his father or concern for his mother's feelings (which surely isn't deserved considering her role in this whole affair), he is able to control his fury and delay what he thinks will be his ultimate revenge. Somehow or other, Esau's words reach Rebecca's ears and she tells Jacob to flee to her brother Laban in Haran and to stay there until Esau's anger subsides, at which point, she says, she will send for him. Rather than tell Isaac the truth – that Esau is so angry that it isn't safe for Jacob to stick around – Rebecca tells him what she thinks he would rather hear: that she doesn't want Jacob to marry a local woman. Isaac swallows the bait and, echoing Abraham's earlier instruction to Eliezer, instructs Jacob to go to his mother's family in Haran and find a wife among Laban's daughters, which is, of course, precisely what Rebecca had already told him to do, albeit for a different reason. The seemingly loving relationship between Isaac and Rebecca has reached such a low ebb that even now Rebecca does not reveal the real reason for Jacob's flight although, perhaps, she is trying to spare Isaac's feelings.

30. The text states that he "said [this] to himself" (27:41). Given that his ranting was reported to Rebecca, it seems reasonable to translate this phrase as thinking out loud.

At this point, with Rebecca's fraud already exposed, Isaac proceeds (fully aware to whom he is speaking) to give Jacob yet another and more important blessing, that of the Abrahamic covenant. The previous blessing, which Jacob received dishonestly, focused upon economic and political success (although it did include an echo of part of the Abrahamic blessing – "cursed be they who curse you, blessed be they who bless you" [27:29]). Now, Isaac gives Jacob the blessing that really matters: "May God bless you, make you fertile and numerous (so that you become a nation) and may He grant you and your offspring the blessing of Abraham and the land God assigned to him" (28:3–4). This blessing – which, to repeat, is voluntary and not elicited from Isaac by fraud – aside from alluding to the blessings of fertility and nationhood previously granted to Abraham, explicitly mentions the "blessing of Abraham" and the gift of the Promised Land. There is no doubt that this blessing transmits to Jacob the Abrahamic covenant.[31]

In light of this blessing, one cannot help but wonder what the fuss was about with respect to the earlier blessing that Isaac had intended for Esau. Apparently, Jacob was always destined to continue the family's relationship with God – for Isaac was certainly free at this juncture to give the Abrahamic covenant to Esau without in any way undoing the blessing Rebecca had stealthily arranged for Jacob. Given this insight, we might suggest that the blessing intended for Esau was always an entirely material one. But if that is the case, how can we explain the fourth part of the blessing – the promise that those who curse you will be cursed and those who bless you will be blessed? Either Isaac did intend this blessing for Esau and it was merely an amplification of the mate-

---

31. To be sure, the earlier blessing did include the provision that those who bless Jacob will be blessed and those who curse him will be cursed, an echo of God's original promise to Abraham. But that is by no means comparable to the extensive spiritual blessing Isaac bestows here. Nor does it include any reference to Abraham or the Promised Land. Curiously, the provision of the Abrahamic blessing concerning blessings and curses (which may include the power to bless others) is not repeated at this time, perhaps, because Jacob has already received it.

rial blessings, not a spiritual one endowing Esau with the power to bless others, or, more audaciously, perhaps Isaac was never fooled; he knew all along who it was standing before him with the animal skins on his hands and decided to go along with the ruse. Hinting that he knew who was really before him, he tacked on this echo of the Abrahamic blessing, but saved the complete blessing for Jacob when he was not in disguise.[32]

After Jacob leaves for his adventures at his uncle's house, Esau finally realizes that "the Canaanite women displeased his father Isaac" (28:8) and makes one last effort to make his father happy. He goes to his Uncle Ishmael and takes another wife, Ishmael's daughter Mahalat. I wonder what difference he believed this would make. It was apparently too late for Isaac to reverse the blessings he had bestowed on the respective twins, and Esau certainly couldn't have thought that he was going to win over his mother, who was so obviously partial to Jacob. Perhaps Esau felt that with Jacob gone, he should smooth over relations with his parents since he would be the only one of their children still around. Alternatively, as my teacher Rabbi Neil Gillman points out, the Rabbis, who have very little good to say about Esau, consistently note his respect for his parents. Even an evildoer, like the Rabbis' version of Esau, can excel in performing one good deed. Clearly, Esau had a special relationship with Isaac as expressed by his often hunting and preparing game for his father; his anguish at losing his father's blessing; his decision to wait until his father's death to avenge himself on Jacob; and the respect he showed in burying Isaac. In any event, this is where the text leaves him when it turns its attention to Jacob, whose saga is about to begin in earnest.

---

32. This conclusion, of course, does substantial violence to the text, which stresses Isaac's blindness and shows Rebecca and Jacob going to extraordinary lengths to receive the blessing intended for Esau. These factors coupled with Isaac's violent reaction to having been duped seem to rule out his having known; however, given the number of times that Isaac asks Jacob who he is, one might wonder how entirely convinced he was even when he gave the blessing.

VAYETZE

Jacob's Flight and First Epiphany

Jacob leaves his parents in Beersheva and departs for Haran, his mother's hometown and the residence of her brother, Jacob's uncle Laban.[1] At sunset he stops for the night and arranges a group of stones as a pillow. The Torah then recounts Jacob's famous dream of a ladder suspended between heaven and earth with angels ascending and descending on it. In the midst of the dream, God appears to Jacob (for the first time mentioned in the text) and repeats to him the promises previously made to his father and grandfather: Jacob's descendants will inherit the Promised Land, will be as plentiful as the dust of the earth, and will be a blessing

---

1. The parasha begins with the statement that Jacob "left Beersheva and set out for Haran" (28:10). This verse has served as the basis for both a classic joke and a meaningful lesson. The joke goes as follows: How do we know that Jews wear yarmulkes (skullcaps)? From Jacob, for under no circumstances would he have "left" Beersheva without a covering on his head. Rashi teaches us the meaningful lesson. Struck by the text's statement that Jacob left Beersheva (which, of course, should have been obvious from the fact that he set out for Haran), Rashi derives the interesting idea that a tzaddik's (righteous man's) departure from a place is noteworthy because his absence diminishes it – a homiletic idea often used to praise a rabbi or other important community personage upon his departure.

for the other nations. Apparently aware of the stress Jacob is undergoing as he flees to Haran, God uncharacteristically provides Jacob with an additional personal blessing: God will always be with him, will protect him wherever he goes, and ultimately will return him to the land promised to his progeny.

Rashi (28:11) predictably notes that this dream took place on Mount Moriah – where the Akedah traditionally took place and where the Temple would be built. After all the text states that Jacob "came upon a certain place"; to a midrashist that place would have to correspond to some "certain place" readers of the Bible already know about. What better place than the site of the Akedah and the holy Temple? There is, of course, nothing explicit in the text to suggest this correlation other than the fact that on a journey heading northward from Beersheva to Haran, Jacob might well have gone by way of Jerusalem. Since the text does identify the spot as one where heaven and earth are conjoined, it makes sense to interpret the place as the ultimate holy of holies. However, the fact that, as we are about to learn, Jacob did not know that this was a holy spot (one where his father had been bound on the altar!) makes me wonder whether this was indeed Moriah.

As for the meaning of this interesting dream, the Rabbis seem to have had a field day with it. For example, the ArtScroll Chumash notes interpretations ranging from Jacob's envisioning the entire history of the Jewish people (contained in a *gemmatria* [an exegesis based on manipulating the numerical values of the Hebrew letters] identifying the four ancient kingdoms that would ultimately conquer the Land of Israel) to an allusion to the ultimate revelation of the Torah at Mount Sinai (midrashically picturing the Torah as the bridge between heaven and earth). For me, its meaning is a straightforward one. God, in appearing to Jacob, stresses that He will always be present in the lives of Jacob and his descendants and that He will always take an active role in their lives.

Much more interesting, I think, is Jacob's reaction to this epiphany. He awakens and remarks (28:16): "God is present in this place, and I did not know it!" This is a surprising reaction for someone who is supposed to have been steeped in the traditions of his father Isaac and his grandfather Abraham. Why was Jacob so surprised to find God here? Surely he was not taught that God resides only in particular spots.[2] God appeared to Abraham and Isaac in numerous places in the Holy Land, and the earlier stories in the book of *Bereshit*, particularly those in the Abraham chapters, clearly reveal that God was a force to be reckoned with outside of the Promised Land as well. For example, He appeared to Abram in Haran and commanded him to leave his father's house; and He punished Pharaoh in Egypt when Sarai was sold into the royal harem.

Perhaps at this juncture in his life Jacob was not yet the religious personage he was later to become. Indeed, that conclusion is practically inescapable when we look at Jacob's next reaction to his remarkable vision. After ritually consecrating the place and giving it a new name, Jacob proceeds to take the most surprising oath. He agrees to accept God as his God, but only if God protects him, gives him food and clothing and enables him to return to the Promised Land: "If God remains with me, if He protects me.... the LORD shall be my God" (28:20–22). This oath is surprising on two counts: Firstly, God has just promised that He will do these things. Does Jacob doubt God's word? Secondly, how could Jacob possibly make his belief in God conditional? To be sure, the Rabbis go to extravagant lengths to answer these questions,[3] but I think the text speaks for itself. When viewed in the context of what we already know about Jacob, what we have is a picture of

---

2.   Those who look to contemporaneous Mesopotamian and Canaanite religions to explicate the Bible's meaning might argue that the notion of a god's being found in specific sacred spaces is a feature of such religions and is echoed here.

3.   The Midrash (BR 76:2) suggests that Jacob is not doubting God but rather doubting himself, concerned that he might in the future commit a sin that will relieve God of his promises. Nachmanides (28:20) suggests that the word translated above as "if" can also mean "when". Read that way, Jacob is neither doubting God nor making his faith conditional; he is merely stating that when this happens, God will have proven himself to be his God.

a self-centered and ambitious young man as yet unworthy of the blessings and the mantle of family leadership that he obtained (at least in part) under false pretenses. He is certainly not yet a person of pure faith in God. Whether Jacob ultimately develops into such a person is an issue we shall discuss below.

Jacob's Courtships and Marriages

Jacob arrives in Haran and comes to a well with a large stone over its mouth that has to be removed in order to permit flocks to water there. Literary Bible critics note that meeting one's mate at a well is a type scene, which recurs several times in the biblical narrative.[4] We have already encountered such a scene when Eliezer (who was seeking a wife for his master's son) meets Rebecca at a well in Haran, and Moses, in the future, will meet his wife Zipporah at a well in Midian (*Shemot* 2). The type scenes are, of course, not all the same. There is no suggestion here that the well where Jacob meets Rachel is the same one at which Eliezer met Rebecca (even though both are in Haran).[5] And unlike his descendant Moses – who confronts ruffian shepherds at the well where he meets his wife Zipporah and has to rescue her and her sisters from their harassment – Jacob's experience here is a friendly one. He asks the shepherds if they know Laban (Jacob's maternal uncle), and they inform him that in fact Laban's daughter Rachel is coming to water her father's sheep. I find it interesting that Rachel is a shepherdess (as is Zipporah later on in *Shemot*). One might think that the shepherd's calling suggests the ability to take care of people as well as animals – a point often made with respect to both Moses and David, not to mention the metaphor of God as Israel's shepherd which appears throughout the *Psalms* and the

---

4. Indeed, when a biblical character arrives at a well and he does *not* meet his beloved there – such as Saul's experience when looking for his father's donkeys (*1 Sam.* 9:11)– critics find the incident noteworthy.
5. Curiously, the Midrash (BR 70:8), unhappy with an unidentified well, explains that this is the miraculous well that accompanied the Israelites on their sojourn in the desert.

Prophets.[6] But I doubt that Rachel satisfies that description. The little we know of her from the text suggests a somewhat self-centered prima donna.[7]

When he espies Rachel, Jacob immediately leaps forward and uncovers the well, allowing her to water her flocks before the other shepherds take care of theirs. He kisses his cousin and, as the text takes pains to note, starts to cry. The midrashists (BR 70:12) provide a number of interesting reasons why Jacob is reduced to tears. One suggests that he had a prophetic vision that Rachel would die on the road back to Canaan upon giving birth to Benjamin and would not be buried with him at Machpelah; another speculates that he cried from embarrassment because, unlike Eliezer (who had come to seek a wife for Isaac bearing all sorts of extravagant gifts), Jacob was empty-handed.[8] It seems to me that the tears have a much more straightforward explanation. After a long and lonely journey, Jacob has indeed found the family he sought and cries from relief. What is missing – and surprisingly so in light of what is about to ensue – is any notion that Jacob is immediately smitten with love (or desire, or both) for Rachel. The text gives us no hint of the passion for Rachel that consumes Jacob for the rest of his life. Surely the very public kiss he bestows on her is not a passionate one, but rather a familial gesture. Yet it is Jacob's love for his cousin that becomes the moving force in the rest of his life story – which, with the exception of the long Joseph novella (and

---

6. Some readers find the shepherd metaphor somehow demeaning to humanity; for if God is a shepherd, we are naught but sheep. The author of poems such as Psalm 23 surely did not intend any such inference.
7. If so, she would be an interesting match for Jacob, who I also described as self-centered above. If shepherding really develops a caring personality, perhaps Jacob's experience as a shepherd in Laban's household made him more caring, even if it did not have such an effect on Rachel.
8. The Midrash (alluded to in Rashi 29:11) goes so far as to explain why Jacob had no gifts for Laban's family – he had started out with much wealth, but Esau in a fit of rage sent his son to kill Jacob. Instead of killing Jacob, Esau's son took pity on him and only robbed him. Even after the Jacob-Esau story seems to be over, the Rabbis cannot resist taking another jab at Esau.

the brief Judah-Tamar detour), comprises the remainder of the Torah's first book.

Rachel runs to tell her father Laban of Jacob's arrival, and Laban greets him eagerly. The Rabbis [BR 70:13], having identified another stereotypical evildoer similar to Esau, impute this eagerness to greed, explaining that Laban "ran" to Jacob to see what he had brought, "embraced him" to see if he was hiding anything in his clothes and finally "kissed" him to check if he was hiding pearls in his mouth (29:13). When all his hopes are dashed, Laban welcomes Jacob and listens to his sad story (according to the midrashists that Esau's son had robbed him on the way). While, as we shall see, Laban is not the most honest of men, the Rabbis really go to town on him. Laban, partially legitimating this approach, takes his nephew into his home and enjoys a free month of Jacob's labor before asking: "Just because you are a kinsman, should you serve me for nothing? Tell me, what shall your wages be?" (29:15).

Since it is at this point that Jacob asks for Rachel's hand in marriage, we finally find out that Laban has a second (and older) daughter, Leah. While the Torah expressly states that Rachel is "shapely and beautiful" (29:16), the best that the text can say about Leah is that she has "weak (or perhaps tender) eyes" (ibid.). The Rabbis go to extensive lengths to explain that Leah was a wonderful person – indeed, according to the midrashists she was intended by God to be Jacob's *spiritual* wife while Rachel was only his physical mate in this world.[9] But I do not think the simple meaning of the text can be so easily ignored. We are given a physical comparison between the two sisters that without ques-

9. The extent to which the midrashists (BR 70:16) are willing to go is exemplified by their conclusion that Leah's weak eyes were the result of her crying because she somehow knew that she had been destined to marry the evil Esau, a fate she avoided only by virtue of her fervent prayer. If that were the case, one might well question the Rabbis' suggestion that Leah was really Jacob's spiritual wife (see ArtScroll Chumash, note to *Bereshit* 29:22–25, citing Rabbi Aaron Kotler and *Michtav MeEliyahu*). For if God had destined her for Esau, the notion that she was supposed to be a matriarch and really Jacob's spiritual better half is a patent *non sequitur*.

tion favors Rachel. In any event, what the text makes abundantly clear is that it is Rachel that Jacob loves: "Jacob loved Rachel, so he answered, 'I will serve you seven years for your younger daughter Rachel.... and they seemed to him but a few days because of his love for her'" (29:18–20).

Interestingly, there is no textual reciprocity for Jacob's love; nowhere are we told that Rachel loved Jacob. Of course, feminist readers of this text would tell us that such a statement, whether true or not, would be superfluous in a patriarchal story that shows no concern one way or the other for women's feelings. But I find it significant that the passion Jacob feels for Rachel – which drives so much of his story from this point forward – is not explicitly made reciprocal on Rachel's part. It is as if she is merely an object and not a subject of any part of the narrative.

After Jacob has worked for seven years, Laban makes a big wedding, but he brings Leah, not the promised Rachel, to Jacob's tent. According to the text, Jacob didn't discover with whom he was sleeping until the next morning. That is a hard story to swallow, and the Rabbis were sufficiently troubled by it to construct a number of midrashim designed to explain the obvious anomaly. As I understand it, the Talmud teaches (*Megillah* 13b; *Bava Batra* 123a) that Rachel and Jacob had secret signs designed to avoid just such a deception;[10] but Rachel, in a remarkable act of sisterly loyalty, revealed them to Leah.[11] Even if that were the case, unless Jacob was so drunk that he lost all sense of discernment, I find it

---

10. I don't know whether this idea is meant to suggest that the couple were having pre-marital sexual relations (I seriously doubt it), or only that they had talked about the possibility of a switch on the wedding night and took steps to avoid it.

11. This story would support the idea that despite Jacob's overwhelming passion for Rachel, she did not have any such feelings for him. While the Rabbis use this story to illustrate Rachel's caring nature – betraying the man she loved so that her sister would not be disgraced on the wedding night – the sibling rivalry which later dominates the sisters' relationship belies such a reading, unless, of course, the rivalry begins with Rachel's selfless act and her sense that Leah never reciprocated properly. Alternatively, perhaps being married to the same man turned Rachel's love for her sister to jealousy, if not hate.

almost impossible to believe that he wouldn't recognize that the woman he was with was not the one he had worked seven years to get – even if, as the Midrash tells us (BR 70:19), Leah answered to Rachel's name while she and Jacob were together.

In any event, the next morning, when the deception becomes apparent, Jacob complains bitterly and is told that "in our place" (29:26) custom dictates that the older daughter be married before the younger one.[12] Accepting the reality of the situation and Laban's offer to give him Rachel in marriage at the end of the week, Jacob agrees not to make a fuss about his marriage to Leah and continues with the week of post-wedding festivities. Laban, true to form, demands that Jacob work another seven years for Rachel.

From the beginning, this household is doomed to trouble. The text tells us that Jacob loved Rachel more than Leah – indeed, that Leah was unloved (29:30–31). The irony here is deliberate of course. The consummate trickster and beneficiary of maternal favoritism is himself tricked into marrying and remaining married to the woman he does not love in order to obtain the one he truly wants. The deception that Jacob had practiced on his father and his brother has been avenged by a deception practiced on him, which, as we shall see, gets played out time and time again for the rest of his life. What we have here is a Torah staple – God's providence often sees to it that people get their just deserts in a manner that parallels their own misdeeds.[13]

---

12. This has a particularly strong resonance to me for it has a parallel in my family history. My parents were engaged for an exceptionally long number of years because my father's older sister was as yet unmarried; they were only finally able to wed when she prevailed on her parents (my grandparents) to permit them to do so.

13. The Rabbis refer to this as being punished measure for measure. Indeed, the Midrash (BR 70:19) has Leah rebuke Jacob by arguing that in deceiving him she had merely learned a lesson from the master. Just as Jacob had answered his father, "I am Esau..." at his mother's behest, so too she had answered to Rachel's name at her father's bidding.

The Birth of Jacob's Offspring – The Rivalry of Leah and Rachel

What follows is, in my opinion, the Torah's most sympathetic story of sibling rivalry. To be sure, the Cain-Abel and Jacob-Esau stories are classic examples of brotherly strife, one ending in murder and the other (as we shall see) in apparent reconciliation. And we will soon confront the bitter conflict between Joseph and his ten half brothers. But the Leah-Rachel rivalry, involving two sisters married to the same man who loves one and appears to be indifferent to the other, has a core of pathos and bitterness that I find absent in any of the others. Indeed, it gives substance to the Torah's blanket prohibition against a man's marrying sisters while both are alive.[14] This love triangle is compounded by God's taking pity on Leah, the unloved wife, and making her a fertile mother while the beloved Rachel remains barren.

The difficulty conceiving that Sarah and Rebecca experienced has already taught us that children are a gift from God. Here the text explicitly states that Leah has her first four sons because God wanted to compensate her for her secondary status in Jacob's household, and it underscores the point by reminding us that Rachel remained barren. Indeed we are told that Leah conceived only because "God saw that [she] was unloved and he opened her womb" (29:31). Perhaps God intended – as Leah hoped – that by providing Jacob with male heirs she would gain a place in his heart. Indeed, Leah named her firstborn Reuben to reflect her belief or hope that "Now my husband will love me" (29:32).

Rachel is so anguished and envious that she complains to her husband, demanding that he give her children: "Give me children

14. As noted above in a number of contexts, the Rabbis asserted that the patriarchs observed the commandments before they were given on Sinai. Jacob's simultaneous marriages to two sisters forced the commentators to suggest that the patriarchs observed the commandments only while in the Holy Land. In his commentary on *Vayikra* 18:25, Nachmanides even suggests that Rachel died upon entering the Holy Land because Jacob could not remain married to two sisters, and she ranked second to her sister because Jacob had married her after already having married Leah.

or I shall die" (30:1); Jacob (unlike Isaac who prayed for his wife) replies in anger that it is God, not he, that has kept Rachel barren. After all, we know from Leah's four sons that Jacob hasn't got a fertility problem. Jacob certainly seems to demonstrate a lack of empathy here, but he may have been as frustrated as Rachel was; and, while the text is silent on the point, he may, like Isaac before him, have been praying for his wife to conceive. Either way, Jacob's angry response to his beloved second wife certainly isn't a model of husbandly virtue. One might expect more patience and understanding from a man who labors fourteen years to marry the love of his life. This, I think, is just another example of Jacob's flawed character at this stage of his life.

It isn't hard to sympathize with both of these troubled women. On the one hand, Rachel, whom Jacob says he loves, is unable to provide him the sons she wants to give him; and Jacob, who is probably every bit as upset about the situation as Rachel, does not want to be held responsible for it. On the other hand, Leah after giving Jacob four sons has still failed to gain his affection. Indeed, Leah, in seeming desperation, names her second son Simeon to signify that "God heard that I was unloved and gave me this one also" (29:33), and her third son Levi in the hope that "this time my husband will become attached to me" (29:34). Finally, perhaps having given up on Jacob, she names her fourth son Judah in recognition that God deserves her praise for giving her all these sons.

Rachel finally adopts the same solution as Sarah had done. She gives Jacob her maid, Bilhah, as a concubine; and the maid gives birth to two sons. Rachel's reaction to these births, on the one hand, shows jubilation at having provided Jacob with sons ("He has heeded my plea and given me a son" [30:6]), but, on the other hand, shows an ugly streak of sibling rivalry: "A fateful contest I have waged with my sister; yes, and I have prevailed" (30:8). The presence of this sibling rivalry makes Rachel's barrenness very different than Sarah's.

When Rachel becomes the putative mother of two sons, one

might have expected Leah to have pity on her sister and leave well enough alone. But the sibling rivalry appears to be so intense that a loving gesture just isn't in the cards. As the Torah tells us, when Leah saw "that she had stopped bearing" (30:9), she gives Jacob her maid, Zilpah, as a concubine. Apparently Leah wants to be certain that the majority of Jacob's progeny would be credited to her (as, indeed, it would be, as Zilpah gives birth to two boys and Leah, as it turns out, bears two more boys and a girl). I would note, however, that the rivalry seems less intense on Leah's side as the names she chooses for the two boys Zilpah bore mean "luck" and "good fortune", not "now I have triumphed over my sister". Indeed she seems bitterer at the fact that Rachel has "take[n] away my husband" (30:15), than interested in competing with her. Rachel, on the other hand, seems very competitive.

How Leah's additional three children come to be conceived is an interesting story in and of itself. Rachel apparently hasn't given up on the possibility that she might have children of her own. When Leah's firstborn, Reuben, brings his mother *duda'im* (usually understood to be mandrakes) from the field, Rachel is so anxious to get her hands on them that she bargains away her position in Jacob's bed that night. Since the context suggests that the plant is an aphrodisiac or may enhance the likelihood of conception[15] this seems to have been a reasonable bargain from Rachel's perspective. We aren't told what Jacob thought of Rachel and Leah's bargain; perhaps he just didn't care with whom he had sex (or, recalling his first wedding night, maybe he simply could not tell the difference between his wives when it came to sex). In any event, Leah conceives for the fifth time that night and piously recognizes this to be a reward (from God) for having given her maid to Jacob. Jacob's reaction is again not provided; but he's soon

---

15. If we understand this plant to be magical, the Torah here is apparently validating magic. However, one could argue that the folk medicine under consideration here is not the same thing as magic, or that even if the story imputes magical powers to the plant, the Torah is not declaring that it had magical powers but only recording that Reuben, Leah, and Rachel believed that it did.

in bed with Leah again and, lo and behold, another son is born, followed by the only daughter mentioned in the text, the ill-fated Dinah. Whatever Jacob's reaction to the six sons Leah has given him might be, Leah, ever hopeful of Jacob's love and affection, and grateful for God's blessing, names the last boy Zebulun, signifying "God has given me a choice gift; this time my husband will exalt me, for I have borne him six sons" (30:20).

It's at this point that God steps in and finally "opens…[Rachel's] womb" (30:22). The Torah explicitly states that God has finally remembered Rachel and listened to her pleas. She gives birth to a son, and, as the text takes pains to inform us, immediately starts thinking about having another one; for she names the baby Joseph, which literally means "May God add", reflecting her desire that God grant her another son. While Rachel is clearly grateful to God for "removing her disgrace" (30:23), she still seems very self-centered and in eternal competition with her sister – character traits that we have witnessed in Jacob's relationship with Esau as well. With the birth of Joseph, Jacob's family is all but complete. He has eleven sons and a daughter; and there is every reason to believe that Rachel will have yet another son before too long.

Jacob Accumulates Wealth

With his family virtually complete, Jacob starts thinking about returning to Canaan. Interestingly, although Rebecca had told him that she would send for him to come home when Esau's anger had cooled, no such message ever arrives.[16] Laban, who apparently is quite happy having Jacob around to work for him, objects to his son-in-law's plan to leave and offers to pay Jacob for further work. This suggests that up to this time the only recompense Jacob has received is the opportunity to marry Laban's daughters. Jacob, of course, is no patsy. He knows that God blesses whatever he

---

16. This might help to explain why Jacob is so frightened of Esau's potential wrath when he does return. If Esau were no longer angry, presumably Rebecca would have called Jacob home as she had promised.

does – indeed, even Laban seems to know this as he says "I have learned by divination that God has blessed me on your account" (30:28). Instead of money, Jacob asks for title to all of the dark-colored sheep and spotted and speckled goats that will be born to the flocks he watches for Laban. Laban agrees, but clearly demonstrating the unsavory side of his nature, proceeds to instruct his sons to remove all the dark-colored and speckled or spotted animals from his flocks. He has his sons take this newly constituted, spotted, speckled, and dark-colored flock a distance of three days away from the rest of the flock that he leaves with Jacob. Under normal rules of heredity (as understood at the time the Torah was written), he has minimized, if not nullified, the chance of Jacob's finding such animals in the flock he is tending.

To foil Laban's scheme (and reap a victory over his father-in-law's trickery), Jacob engages in a classic example of sympathetic magic. He shows the goats some rods he prepares which are altered to have stripes and spots on them; and he has his sheep face streaked or wholly dark-colored animals in Laban's flock. The result is that the animals in the flock he is tending give birth to streaked, striped, and speckled offspring. Furthermore, he only does this with the stronger animals, the upshot being that the kids and lambs born to Jacob's flock are stronger. When all is said and done, under his deal with Laban, Jacob accumulates a fortune in flocks (and satisfyingly weakens Laban's flock both quantitatively and qualitatively).

I find this entire episode surprising because it is premised on the notion that sympathetic magic can be effective. To be sure, the episode is framed by passages declaring that God is the real source of Jacob's success. Indeed, in the following chapter Jacob does not even mention the "magic" he performed when he tells his wives: "God, however, would not let him [Laban] do me harm. If he said thus, 'The speckled shall be your wages,' then all the flocks would drop streaked young. God has taken away your father's livestock and given it to me" (31:7–9). But if that is really the case, one would expect the Torah – a text devoted to the principle of total monotheism – to state unequivocally that God is performing a miracle and not imply that Jacob the wizard relied on magic to get his way. Instead, what we have reads like a folk tale rather than a Jewish religious text. It is, of course, not the only example in the Torah of what we would call magic. Moses' creation of a copper serpent statue to heal those bitten by serpents also fits the bill (*Bamidbar* 21).[17] But it is a far cry from what we would expect to find in this fundamental text. What would Maimonides (who categorically denies the efficacy of any magic other than God's miracles) have to say about this?[18]

Interestingly enough, shortly after Jacob's declaration to his wives that God ensured his success, he tells them about a dream he had during the mating time of the flocks. This dream contains another account of how Jacob ended up with a streaked, speckled, and mottled flock – but this time without the sympathetic magic. According to this version, Jacob had a dream in which an angel explained that it was God who contrived that all of the sheep and goats would be streaked, speckled, or mottled, so that under the deal struck by Jacob and Laban, they would belong to Jacob. This is more in keeping with what one would expect to find in the Torah.

If we accept the documentary hypothesis, we can argue that the two theologically conflicting versions of the same story were

---

17. This, of course, posits that the Torah includes Jacob's use of the rods and the curative powers of the copper serpent under the definition of magic. Clearly there is a gray area, such as Reuben's mandrakes, where employing such methods might be considered a folk cure or folk wisdom and not the actual performance of magic. While the copper serpent does seem to have magical properties, one could argue that it was only intended to encourage prayer.

18. I am reminded of an article I read a few years ago opining that, in Maimonides' view, it is not permissible to entertain Jewish people with legerdemain. Since there is no such thing as actual magic, the Torah's prohibition of magic, according to Maimonides, must be directed to illusions such as stage magicians practice. On the other hand, I am told that there are respected Jewish sources (Abarbanel is one) that accept the reality of magic. For a classic discussion of magic and Judaism, see Joshua Trachtenberg's *Jewish Magic and Superstition: A Study in Folk Religion* (Sefer ve Sefel Publishing: Jerusalem, 2004).

both included in the final version of the text.[19] Needless to say, I find the version in which God (rather than magic) is responsible for Jacob's success more in keeping with the monotheistic idea that pervades the text.

Jacob Leaves Haran and Returns to the Promised Land

In the same dream in which the angel tells Jacob how he attained such great wealth, God proceeds to inform him that it is time to return to his native land – which is, of course, an idea he had already considered before God spoke to him. Both Rachel and Leah agree that it is time to leave, casting aspersions on their father's character in the process. As the text explains, both sisters are upset that Laban has benefited from Jacob's labor in exchange for marrying them, but they have essentially been disinherited: "Have we still a share in the inheritance of our father's house? Surely, he regards us as outsiders, now that he has sold us and used up our purchase price" (31:14–15). As a result, they tell Jacob, he has every right to anything God has given him that might otherwise belong to Laban. This is an astonishing thing for young women in this patriarchal society to be saying. It reveals sympathy for the plight of women in a male-dominated culture that I find, to a large extent, absent from most of the Genesis narrative.[20]

Having obtained Rachel and Leah's consent to leave – and it should be noted that Jacob admirably felt it appropriate to seek his wives' approval – Jacob puts them and their children on camels, gathers all his livestock and sets off for Canaan without letting Laban know that he is going.[21] Laban, who had gone off to shear his

---

19. In fact, the same explanation can be provided for other seemingly redundant, disturbingly similar, or conflicting versions of events we have already discussed. Chief among these are the two versions of the creation story and the three distinct versions of the "sister-wife" story (two involving Abimelech).

20. On the other hand, the sisters may be reflecting only on the fact that having been "sold" to Jacob, they no longer have any obligation to Laban or his household.

21. Note that even though the Torah later refers to Bilhah and Zilpah as Jacob's wives (37:2), they are not consulted as Leah and Rachel were, so clearly their status is secondary.

sheep, only finds out that Jacob had fled three days later. At this point the chase is on. However, before Laban catches up with the fleeing family (which by this time had crossed the Euphrates), God appears to Laban in a dream and tells him "to beware of attempting anything with Jacob, good or bad" (31:24).[22] At this point the biblical irony is intense. Laban, meeting face to face with Jacob, chastises him for having left without even allowing him to kiss his children and grandchildren goodbye, and he tells Jacob that it is only because of God's warning that he will do him no harm.

Before leaving Haran, Rachel had entered her father's house and stolen the household idols. This act becomes crucial to the plot at this point. While Laban is not permitted to harm Jacob, he can demand the return of his stolen idols. Laban at the end of his harangue accuses Jacob of having stolen the idols; Jacob denies the theft and declares: "Anyone with whom you find your gods shall not remain alive!" (31:32).[23] Presumably, Jacob assumed that no one had taken them (certainly not one of his presumably pious wives or children) and that Laban had just made this accusation so that he could search Jacob's tents to make sure he had not taken the family silver. Laban searches the entire camp (tent by tent) and fails to find the idols because Rachel has hidden them in her camel cushions and is sitting on them. When her father enters her tent, she apologizes for not rising because, she says, she is menstruating. Laban's search (which as Jacob expected turns up empty-handed) is apparently the last straw for Jacob, and he explodes with anger at his father-in-law. After a lengthy diatribe about Laban's years of unfair treatment and Laban's brief response,

---

22. This is somewhat surprising in light of Laban's evil character, but I suppose God does appear to bad people from time to time, as the Balaam story in *Bamidbar* demonstrates.

23. In yet another example of words (or at least of the patriarchs' words) having magical powers, the midrashists (BR 74:9) jump on this curse as the cause of Rachel's untimely death in childbirth. For the Rabbis, the words of a righteous man are always fulfilled, even if he utters them in error.

the men agree to what amounts to a non-aggression pact and Jacob's family moves on.

The denouement of Jacob's sojourn in Haran has a number of interesting aspects. To begin with, we have the irony of Jacob's complaint that Laban has treated him unfairly. After all, Jacob is in Haran because he had to flee from Esau's justified wrath at the way Jacob had treated him. No matter how hard Jacob worked or how difficult the work conditions were, he came to Laban's household empty-handed and leaves with a large family and great wealth, so his complaints are somewhat hollow. As noted above, Jacob's sojourn in Haran also provides an ironic counterpoint to his earlier fraudulent behavior in depriving his brother both of the family birthright and Isaac's blessing. The fraudulent Jacob is himself defrauded by the fraudulent Laban, and because God favors Jacob despite his shortcomings, he comes out ahead in both episodes. This is yet another example of God arbitrarily favoring those he wishes to favor, whether or not the recipients are deserving of divine favor.

Of greater interest to me is Rachel's theft of Laban's idols. To be sure, the midrashists (cited in Rashi 31:19) are quick to point out that this matriarch of Israel was stealing the meaningless idols in order to save her father from idolatry. But that explanation is hard to accept in light of the harsh things Rachel has to say about her father and her willingness to flee without even saying goodbye. She certainly does not appear protective of Laban to me. Rather, it seems clear that the idols must have been important to her. And this implies something disturbing about Rachel. We tend to view the patriarch's four wives – Sarah, Rebecca, Leah, and Rachel – as saintly Jewish matriarchs. Indeed, under the influence of feminist thought, in recent years most non-Orthodox prayer books have introduced (sometimes as a prayer's option) an invocation of the God of the four matriarchs as well as that of the three patriarchs at the beginning of the *Shemoneh Esrei* (the main prayer, containing nineteen blessings, recited three times daily). How are we to square that attitude with what seems to be a clear example of idolatry on the part of one of them (and of the fraud performed by Rebecca)? Perhaps we are being asked to recognize, but disregard, the negative aspects of the matriarchs' characters much as we do their husbands'. None of our forbears is a paradigm of virtue; and due respect for the influence of motherhood and the need for the tradition to reflect a complete inclusion of women probably justifies twentieth-century changes to the prayer book so that it reflects modern gender sensibilities.

Another surprising aspect of Jacob's decision to return to Canaan (even if God has told him to do so and promised "to be with him" [31:3]) is that up until this point he has shown no concern about what he will find there when he arrives. He has been gone over twenty-one years, but the text reveals no thought on his part about whether his father or mother are still alive or about how Esau will react to his return. Since he fled in fear of Esau, one would expect Jacob to be somewhat concerned about his brother's reaction to his return, particularly since his mother has not sent for him as she had said she would when Esau's anger had abated. Perhaps Jacob's lack of concern about Esau is easily explained. He has been promised divine protection. However, the last time God made such a promise (twenty-one years ago) Jacob still expressed concern over his safety. Has he grown spiritually to the point where he absolutely relies on God? Or has he matured in other ways as well, so that he envisions a number of ways to protect himself and his family from Esau's wrath?

VAYISHLACH

Jacob Prepares to Meet Esau

Now that Haran and Laban are behind him, Jacob turns his attention to his next problem: how to confront Esau, his defrauded and, presumably, raging brother. Jacob sends messengers to Esau to inform him of his arrival and of the wealth he has acquired over the decades since he left. Crucially, he begins the message deferentially, describing himself as "your servant Jacob" and ending with the words "I send this message to my lord in the hope of gaining your favor" (32:5–6). The very fact that he had messengers available to send gives us some idea of how wealthy Jacob has become. His household clearly includes a retinue of male and female slaves and, given the size of his flocks, probably numerous freemen (and their families) who work for him. Whether the message's obsequious tone is merely a stratagem designed to put his brother off guard or a sign of genuine fear, when Jacob's messengers return with the news that Esau himself is coming to meet Jacob accompanied by four hundred men, Jacob is terrified. He adopts three methods of defense: first, he divides his entourage into two groups (so that if one is attacked, the other can escape); second, he prays to God; and third, he sends bountiful gifts to his brother.

In his prayer, Jacob asks God to protect him and his family, carefully reminding the deity that He had told Jacob to return to his native land and promised to provide for him. Demonstrating unusual humility, he pleads with God to prevent a massacre: "I am unworthy...Deliver me, I pray, from the hand of my brother...I fear he may come and strike me down, mothers and children alike" (32:11–12). Perhaps more importantly, he alludes to the Abrahamic blessing he had received, reminding God that he had promised to make Jacob's offspring as numerous as the sands of the sea.

Having finished praying, Jacob decides that his obsequious message may not have been enough, so he plans to assuage Esau's anger by showering him with presents. He sets aside a large flock of animals, divides them into numerous separate droves, and sends them on ahead in intervals. He tells the servants accompanying each drove that when they meet up with Esau they should tell him that the flocks are a present from Jacob and that Jacob is following behind them. Jacob hopes that the gifts will propitiate Esau's presumed anger, so that when Esau finally reaches the family camp "perhaps he will show me favor" (32:21). Given what Jacob already knows about Esau – that he is a man who would give anything to achieve immediate gratification (for example, sell his birthright for a "mess of pottage") – this makes some sense. By sending the droves one by one, he will slowly wear down Esau's burning anger by constantly feeding his ego and his "bank account". But if Esau's bringing a small army with him is any indication of what is likely to happen, one might well wonder whether the gift of a flock of animals is going to make much difference. It is interesting that despite Jacob's fervent prayer, his faith in God is not so strong that he ignores taking independent action to attempt to prevent disaster from striking his family and himself.[1]

---

1. The Rabbis took a more positive view of Jacob's action. Praising his self-reliance (without impugning his faith), the Rabbis noted (cited in Rashi 32:7) that he not only prayed but also sent presents and prepared for the possibility of violence by dividing his camp.

The Wrestling Match: Jacob's Epiphany at the Jabbok River

What follows is a very strange story, yet one of the utmost significance. Jacob sends his wives, concubines, children, and possessions across the Jabbok River and then, for no stated reason, returns to the other side alone. We find him there with nothing but the clothes on his back – just as he was when he fled from Esau's anger and first dreamt of God. On the banks of the Jabbok, he wrestles with a "man" all night long until the break of dawn. Jacob's opponent, recognizing that he has not won the fight, wrenches Jacob's hip out of its socket and asks Jacob to let him go. Jacob refuses to do so unless the "man" blesses him. In an exceedingly strange conversation, the "man" asks Jacob what his name is – a question reminiscent of Isaac's questioning Jacob's identity when, in an effort to receive another blessing, Jacob pretended to be Esau. Jacob tells the "man" his name and is then informed that his name shall "no longer be Jacob, but Israel" (32:29) because he has struggled with "beings divine and human" (32:29) and has prevailed. When, in turn, Jacob/Israel asks his opponent his name, he is told that he must not make such a request. The two part company, and Jacob remarks that he has seen a divine being and has survived. The passage ends with the explanation that, in light of Jacob's hip injury, the children of Israel do not eat the thigh muscle.

What is this episode trying to teach us? On the one hand, the story may simply be etiological. It explains two things: why the Jewish people is known as the "children of Israel" (the Israelites) and why Jews do not eat the sciatic nerve of a kosher animal, even if it has been ritually slaughtered.[2] On the other hand,

---

2. Because the process of removing the sciatic nerve (porging) is time consuming and hence (in the modern day of huge slaughterhouses) expensive, it has become common practice in the United States for kosher slaughterers to sell the hindquarters of animals to non-kosher meat companies. That is why kosher sirloin is almost impossible to find and the notion of kosher sirloin has virtually become an oxymoron.

the significance of Jacob's wrestling match runs much deeper, for it marks a watershed in the development of Abraham's grandson from trickster into patriarch, and it becomes paradigmatic for the very nature of the Jewish people's relationship with God.

Given the fantastic nature of this incident, wherein Jacob struggles with what at first appears to be a man and then later turns out to have been a divine being, it is natural to ask about the text's intent in telling the story. Is the Torah informing us that the wrestling match actually happened, or is the story merely a literary device describing Jacob's inner turmoil? Of course, it does not really matter which position we take, for either way the episode portrays a sea change in Jacob's personality. Jacob confronts a manifestation of the Divine, fights it to a standstill, and obtains a blessing. Again, the text is ironic. Jacob received his first blessing dishonorably, by defrauding his father and brother, while this one he quite literally fought for with honor. Of course, one might well ask why Jacob needs another blessing in light of the several he has already received from his father and God. But this one appears to be especially significant because Jacob earned it.

Perhaps the most significant obstacle to understanding this story is the ambiguity surrounding the identity of Jacob's opponent on the riverbank. First we are told that it was a "man", but later the text clearly endows this individual with divine attributes. The "man" himself states that Jacob has "striven with beings divine and human" (32:29), a statement that leads Jacob to exclaim: "I have seen a divine being face to face..." (32:31), and then the "man" refuses to reveal his name. This reticence seems to be typical of divine beings. For example, God, Himself is chary of revealing His name to Moses at the burning bush (*Shemot* 3:13–15),[3] and the angel who visits Manoah and his wife to announce the impending birth of Samson refuses to give his name ("You must not ask my

3. To be sure, God does give Moses an answer when he asks Him what His name is. But the answer He gives while teaching us a lot about God – in fact, while identifying God with the very essence of existence – fails to include God's real name, YHWH.

name for it is unknowable!" [*Judges* 13:17]). Most readers conclude that the wrestler was an angel. Indeed, the Midrash (BR 77:3) identifies him as Esau's guardian angel seeking to protect his charge (Esau) from whatever danger might result from a meeting with Jacob (who is protected by God Himself). I do not find this explanation convincing. Why would Esau's heavenly guardian refuse to identify himself when, as we know, Jacob is already terrified at the thought of his brother's possible vengeance and the small army he is bringing with him? Furthermore, why would Esau's guardian bless Jacob (even if this was a condition for Jacob's letting him go)?[4] As I read the story, the wrestler is either God's representative or, perhaps, God himself in human form.[5] Depending upon whether God initiated this wrestling match or whether Jacob did, one of the following questions must be asked: Why at this juncture in Jacob's life did God see fit to engage Jacob in a wrestling match? Or, why was Jacob struggling, in his own mind, with the Divine at this point in his career?

A little context can be helpful here. Having fled from Canaan after defrauding his father and brother, Jacob himself has fallen victim to fraud and deceit at the hands of his father-in-law. In maturing from boyhood to manhood[6] Jacob has outgrown his earlier character flaws; and with the responsibilities of a family

4. The Midrash answers both these questions by positing that angels are not able to reveal their names because they do not have fixed names (which is somewhat surprising since the Midrash is full of references to named angels like Gabriel and Michael) and that the angel had no choice but to bless Jacob because he had to return to heaven at dawn to sing God's praises (BR 78:1–2, 4).

5. Since the verse actually states that "you have striven with *Elokim* (literally, God)", it is not such a stretch to suggest that the "man" was God in human form. Indeed, the suggestion that it was an angel conflicts with a literal reading of the text. Supporting this theory, we also suggested above that one of the three angels who visited Abraham before the destruction of Sodom was God Himself.

6. I am aware that a careful reading of the text reveals a chronology of Jacob's age that belies the notion that he was a boy when he left Canaan. But given the influence his mother had on his actions and the behavior he exhibited toward his brother, I conclude that it was not until his experiences in Haran that Jacob matured into true manhood. Furthermore, Abraham left Haran at the age of seventy-five (12:4) and Isaac married at the age of forty (25:20), and they both lived to ripe old ages (175

and substantial property (obtained in large measure in the face of obstacles that would have thwarted a lesser personality), he is now poised to enter a new stage in his life. He is now ready to become a more spiritual person, one worthy of founding a people destined to be a light unto the nations. This change has already been signaled by the way Jacob prayed to God at the beginning of this parasha. In contrast to the brash young man who made his belief in God conditional on God's taking care of him in Haran, here he thanks God for the blessings He has already imparted and humbly asks for protection from Esau. At this juncture, a direct confrontation with divinity and his own destiny seems only right and proper, both from Jacob's point of view and from God's as well. For the history of the family chosen by God for a special purpose has reached a turning point; and Jacob must be ready to lead it forward.

Thus, whether we view the wrestling match at the Jabbok to be the result of God's decision to give Jacob the opportunity to reach a higher spiritual level or of Jacob's realization that he indeed has changed, for Jacob it marks the attainment of a new plateau in spiritual understanding both of himself and of the world he inhabits.[7] When the patriarch-to-be wrestles with divinity and becomes Israel (a name which denotes his destined role as the eponymous father of the Jewish people), he demonstrates his readiness to assume a patriarchal role and replace his father as the carrier of the family blessing.

While Jacob's life is far from over, this is an appropriate point to make some observations about his character as it stands, after his transition from immature child to mature adult, from son to patriarch. Comparing him with the other patriarchs, he does not appear to have achieved the same spiritual stature as his grandfa-

---

[25:7] and 180 [35:28]), respectively), so clearly the parameters we apply to youth, adulthood, and old age do not apply to these biblical figures.

7. As we shall see shortly, this conclusion – that Jacob has now reached the higher spiritual heights expected of a patriarch in Abraham and Isaac's family – is not totally consistent with his behavior in the wake of the rape of his daughter Dinah.

ther Abraham – a man who talked with God constantly and who exhibited throughout his life a spiritual courage worthy of emulation (this notwithstanding the serious questions I have raised about his behavior in banishing Hagar and performing the Akedah). Comparing Jacob with his father Isaac is a bit more difficult, given the minimal information we have about Isaac's life and his general passivity. As noted above, I tend to view Isaac as a transitional figure, moving the story forward from its genesis with Abraham to its incipient nationhood with Jacob and his sons. Suffice it to say that Jacob (up until this point) is not like his father Isaac, who had a retiring life and was not terribly successful either at deceiving others or at ferreting out deceit.

Jacob himself is a multifaceted character. In his youth, under the influence of his crafty and doting mother, Jacob exhibited enormous self-confidence and a willingness to stretch the bounds of morality in order to get what he wanted. Taking advantage of a gullible Esau and a bedridden blind father, he wheedles out of them both a birthright and a blessing to which he is not entitled and then flees from the consequences. While the rabbinic tradition, apparently unwilling to accept dubious morality in the father of the nation, spends countless pages whitewashing Jacob's early years to excuse his behavior, the Torah text itself amply testifies to the fraud and deceit which characterize them. Suffering under the fraudulent treatment he receives from Laban, Jacob begins to mature. However, as the magical building up of his flocks and the carefully crafted messages sent to Esau demonstrate, he still has not forgotten how to take advantage of others and dissemble when it suits his purposes. In any event, by the time Jacob arrives at the Jabbok with a huge family and significant wealth, he is no longer the brash young man who was willing to cheat in order to get ahead and who promised to believe in God only if God turned out to be his protector. He is sufficiently concerned about his family's well-being to take steps to protect them from the putative revenge of his brother, and he prays to God for help in that endeavor with no remnant of his earlier bravado. His altered character – perhaps no more than a result of the normal process of maturation – is marked in the text by his confrontation with divinity and the new name he receives at its conclusion.

Jacob's Reconciliation with Esau

Immediately after reporting on the wrestling match, the Torah tells us that Jacob looks up, sees his brother coming with his four hundred men, and begins to divide his family into three groups. Given that there is no mention made of Jacob crossing back over the Jabbok this is a bit surprising. Presumably the Torah did not think it necessary to mention that Jacob had returned to his family. In any event, Jacob immediately takes precautions to ensure that his family – particularly Rachel his beloved wife and her son Joseph – are protected. He divides the family into three groups and positions each one carefully: at the front, the concubines and their sons; in the middle, Leah and her children; and, at the rear, Rachel and Joseph. The obvious purport of this arrangement is that if Esau's army attacks, the most important family members will be safest. Thus, despite his newly acquired maturity and spirituality, Jacob persists in favoring Rachel and her son. I can only imagine the trauma the men, women, and children situated at the front, and even in the middle, must have undergone at being placed closer to danger. This is but a foretaste of the mischief Jacob will ultimately cause by spoiling Joseph and favoring him over his brothers.[8]

At Esau's approach, Jacob humbly rushes forward and subserviently bows seven times. But Esau does not attack. Rather, he runs to Jacob and embraces him – falls upon his neck, kisses him, and weeps with him – and then inquires about the women and children. What is more, he steadfastly refuses to accept the gifts that Jacob proffers, stating that he has enough. It is only when

8. In Jacob's defense one should note that in his family favoring one son over another was a long tradition. Isaac was favored over Ishmael and Jacob over Esau (at least by their mother), so when Jacob tragically acts in a similar manner, at least he is following family tradition.

Jacob insists that Esau accepts the presents. Esau then invites his brother to travel with him to Seir, where he lives. Jacob begs off, claiming that the children are frail and that the flocks could not bear a forced march; Jacob, instead, urges Esau to go on ahead and promises to join him. In fact, Jacob has no intention of doing so. Instead, he settles down in Shechem, where he purchases a parcel of land.

Throughout this episode, Esau's behavior is exemplary. Rather than seeking revenge, he is utterly conciliatory. Upon learning of Jacob's arrival, he may originally have planned to open hostilities. This would explain the four hundred-man army he brought with him. But by the time his brother arrives, whatever anger Esau may have had has long dissipated; all the text reveals is a loving brother with nothing but the best of intentions. Yet the rabbinic tradition – which identifies Esau/Edom with Israel's Roman antagonists – refuses to accept the text at face value. The Rabbis tell us that Esau remained as evil as ever (that is, as evil as the Rabbis had understood him to be). When the Torah tells us that Esau kissed his brother, the midrashists [BR 78:9] engage in a bit of Hebrew word play and read the verb to mean "bite" (*nashak* [to kiss] sounding very similar to *nashakh* [to bite]); Jacob, they tell us, is saved from injury only because God performs a miracle and transforms Jacob's neck into marble, thus rendering Esau's bite harmless. Indeed, when the two brothers weep, the Midrash reports that Jacob is weeping upon meeting his brother and Esau is crying over his broken teeth. Thus, as was the case at the beginning of the twin brothers' story – where the Rabbis transformed a boorish and impulsive Esau into a violent and malevolent evildoer – here as well a story that to an unbiased reader plainly shows Esau in a positive light is transformed to make him the epitome of evil and Israel's eternal enemy. There simply is no justice for Esau.[9]

9.   To be fair, there is some rabbinic support for Esau. In the midrash cited above one Rabbi suggests that Esau's heart really did melt at seeing his brother again, so his kiss and tears were genuine. And, as mentioned above, the Rabbis praised Esau for showing respect for his father. Furthermore, the Talmud suggests that one of

As for Jacob's dishonesty in promising his brother that he would follow him to Seir when he clearly had no intention of doing so, since a lot of the dialogue between the brothers seems very formal and stilted, perhaps both were aware that certain things had to be said even if there was no intention of carrying them out. That is to say, perhaps both Esau's offer and Jacob's acceptance were no more than an example of good manners. Alternatively, with all the goodwill in the world, Jacob may have been afraid that prolonged contact with Esau would compromise his family's spirituality, so he had to renege on this promise. While the latter makes some sense, it is belied by Jacob's settling in Shechem and, as we shall soon see, his apparent willingness (under extreme duress) to intermarry with the locals.

Dinah's Rape and the Question of Intermarriage

The Torah expresses great concern over the possibility of intermarriage. As early as Abraham's worries about finding an appropriate wife for Isaac and the unhappiness Isaac and Rebecca had with Esau's decision to marry a local Hittite woman, the text expresses a clear preference for endogamy. Marrying within the clan was paramount, and conversion was not looked upon as an acceptable alternative in the cases of Isaac, Jacob, or Esau. Ultimately, in the Torah's legislative sections we will find intermarriage with the Canaanites outrightly forbidden lest the Israelite males follow after the deities worshipped by their pagan spouses (*Shemot* 34:15–16; *Devarim* 7:3–6). Indicating that this is not an issue of racial purity, the Torah explicitly allows intermarriage with Egyptians, Moabites, and Ammonites (whose parents presumably converted) after suitable waiting periods (*Devarim* 23:4–9).[10]

---

the reasons for the Babylonian destruction of the Temple was Esau's tears at losing Isaac's blessing.

10. Complicating matters, it is interesting to note that a number of very important personages in *Tanakh* – Moses, Judah, Joseph and possibly David (Bathsheba was married to Uriah the Hittite, so she might not have been an Israelite) – married non-Israelite women without the text expressing the slightest bit of concern.

Here, in *Bereshit*, a book that with rare exception is limited to narrative, this concern expresses itself in stories. The story of Dinah's rape and its tragic consequences is (with the notable exception of the Akedah) the most troublesome of these homiletic tales.

As noted above, after leaving Esau, Jacob settles in the city of Shechem. The text tells us that his daughter Dinah went out to visit with the local women. The patriarchal rabbinic tradition (BR 80:1) looks askance at this behavior, blaming Dinah for what happened; for if she had stayed at home where she belonged, she would not have been noticed and the tragic sequence of events about to unfold would not have transpired. That point of view is not acceptable to today's reader, nor should it be. In fact, the Rabbis' outlook seems somewhat anomalous in light of the matriarchs' behavior. Both Rebecca and Rachel worked outside their fathers' homes, fetching water from the well or shepherding the flocks. In the course of their work, they clearly interacted with the local men (and even with strangers, Eliezer and Jacob being cases in point). In biblical times, women may not have been among the movers and shakers – at least, not most of them – but clearly (at least in Haran where Rebecca and Rachel lived, and in Midian, where Moses met his wife and sisters-in-law at the well) women left their homes and interacted with the local inhabitants. So the rabbinic slur on Dinah is unacceptable and incorrect.

In any event, Dinah goes out and is noticed by the local chieftain's son (who is named Shechem, just like his town). He proceeds to rape her but nonetheless is taken with the young woman, speaks to her tenderly, and asks his father to request her hand in marriage. I am not enough of a Hebrew scholar to tell from the text whether it is clear that the sex act between Shechem and Dinah was forced. The text clearly states that he "took her and lay with her and *ye'aneha*" (34:2). Whether the final word implies that he "lay with her by force", as one translation has it, or that he "afflicted her" or "defiled her" in addition to lying with her (without raping her), he clearly did not act like a gentleman. Nachmanides (34:34), for one, cites other biblical uses of this verb (*ye'aneha*) to conclude that Dinah was indeed raped. However, given the fact that Jacob was willing to consider accepting Shechem as a son-in-law and that the word for rape (*oness*) is never used, I would argue that perhaps Dinah was not raped, just seduced. In any event, the Torah makes two things clear: (1) Shechem is now in love with Dinah and wants to marry her; and (2) Jacob's sons (or at least two of them) view the act as one of defilement, an outrage which cannot be passed over lightly.

Jacob finds out about the incident and does nothing until his sons (who were out in the field with the flocks) come home. If Dinah had been raped, one would expect Jacob to have immediately demanded redress from Shechem's father. He never does so. Rather, the chieftain (whose name is Hamor) arrives and tells Jacob and his sons that his son would like to marry Dinah. He puts the proposition to Jacob virtually in treaty terms. If Jacob will permit his daughter to marry Hamor's son, Hamor will reciprocate and let the local women marry Jacob's sons and provide an opportunity for Jacob's clan to obtain significant land in the area. Making a personal appeal, Shechem goes so far as to tell Jacob and his sons that he will pay any price they ask in order to be able to marry Dinah.

Given Jacob's family history of endogamy, one would have thought that he faced an insoluble dilemma. On the one hand, Jacob will be breaking faith with his family tradition if he allows the marriage;[11] on the other hand, he risks offending the local inhabitants of the place he has chosen to settle if he does not. Hamor and Shechem are apparently not willing to take "no" for an answer, as Shechem is smitten with Dinah. As for Jacob's purported dilemma, the text makes no mention of it. As we shall see later, Judah's marriage to a Canaanite named Shua also goes unremarked. I discuss these intermarriages of Jacob's children later

11. It is of course possible that there was never any concern about a daughter marrying out. Indeed, Abraham, Isaac, and Rebecca only expressed concern about their sons.

at the end of this section and in the section on Judah and Tamar.[12] As for Shechem, his love for Dinah makes him (and his entire city) an easy target for her vengeful brothers.

The principal culprits are Leah's second and third sons, Simeon and Levi. They tell Shechem and his father that they cannot permit their sister to marry an uncircumcised man. So they demand that all of the males in Shechem undergo circumcision, after which Shechem will be permitted to marry Dinah and Jacob's clan will intermarry with the people of Shechem. This proposition raises two interesting questions. Firstly, Jacob's position as head of the family seems to have been usurped by his sons, for without consulting him they suggest the idea of mass circumcision. (It is reminiscent of the negotiations between Eliezer and Betuel for the hand of Rebecca where Laban, her brother, usurped her father's position.)[13] Perhaps, the Torah makes no comment on this because it is happy to avoid attributing any responsibility for the ensuing massacre to Jacob. Secondly, and more importantly, after Shechem's disgraceful behavior, Dinah disappears from the text. We are told nothing about her feelings. Does she share Shechem's passion for her? Does she want to leave the family and join the local population of Canaan? Is she sufficiently angry about Shechem's actions to want her brothers to avenge it? She should have been the central figure in this story, but, instead, the entire discussion is about the reactions of her brothers and, to a lesser extent, of Jacob to the incident. It is as if Dinah is solely an

---

12. Suffice it to say that perhaps Judah's intermarriage was not so problematic because the woman in such a marriage followed the husband into his clan (a *de facto* conversion). However, if this were truly so then Isaac and Jacob could have also intermarried. Furthermore, that does not explain why Dinah could intermarry. If she did so, she would be lost to the Israelite clan.
13. Rashi (24:50) declares that Laban was a wicked person because he rushed in to speak before his father. Here Rashi does not condemn the brothers in a similar manner. Apparently, Laban is again damned by his reputation, while the brothers, for some reason, are let off the hook.

object and thus a person whose feelings should be of no concern to the reader.[14]

Hamor and Shechem readily agree to the brothers' suggestion;[15] and while they and all their male companions are recovering from the mass circumcision, Simeon and Levi slaughter every one of them. Following this, the other brothers (like scavengers) descend on the town and take the women, children, cattle, and other possessions as booty. The extent to which Simeon and Levi go to reclaim their family's honor parallels the horrific honor killings in today's Islamic world.[16] As Simeon and Levi put it when admonished by their father for their actions, "Should our sister be treated as a whore?" While this sentiment seems to be expressed on Dinah's behalf, one gets the clear impression that what is at stake is the brothers' self-image and their embarrassment at the way one of *their* women was treated. Indeed, the Torah states: "he [Shechem] had committed an outrage in Israel by lying with Jacob's daughter – a thing not to be done" (34:7).

What is Jacob's reaction to the massacre? Wouldn't one expect the spiritual heir of Abraham and Isaac to be outraged? Jacob's rebuke of Simeon and Levi surprisingly runs as follows: "You have brought trouble on me, making me odious among the inhabitants of the land, the Canaanites and the Perizzites; my men are few in number, so that if they unite against me and attack me, I and my house will be destroyed" (34:30). Jacob is indeed unhappy, but not because his sons just wiped out all the males in Shechem. Pure and simple, he is worried about his own safety. He chastises his sons for having made him a pariah among the Canaanites and Perizzites who might unite against him and destroy the family. While

---

14. In Anita Diamant's *The Red Tent* (St. Martin's Press, 1997), a modern, feminist retelling of this Bible story, Dinah does become the central character.

15. While I view the men of Shechem as victims in this unhappy episode, it should be noted that the text does reveal a certain underlying greed motivating them. In his effort to persuade the males of Shechem to undergo circumcision, Hamor points out that after the two clans intermarry and the Israelite clan settles among them "their cattle and substance and all their beasts will be ours" (34:23).

16. Although of course they do not kill Dinah, at least as far as we know.

Jacob, at least tacitly, approves of the deal to intermarry with the city of Shechem, the text offers no hint that he (or the rest of his sons) was complicit in this mass murder. Yet he expresses concern only for his and his family's safety. We must await Jacob's death-bed blessing of the twelve tribes to find any outrage at this act of mass murder: "Simeon and Levi are a pair...Let not my person be included in their assembly. For when angry they slay men... cursed be their anger so fierce" (49:5–7).[17]

While it is the mass murder perpetrated by Simeon and Levi that is the most disturbing aspect of the Dinah story, there is another question that troubles me. What is the point of the story? As Dinah's disappearance from the narrative makes clear, the story is not really about the rape of Dinah. The notion that this tale is supposed to teach us how to react to the rape of one of our own is undermined by the ambiguity created by Jacob's silence. Scholars have claimed – given the extensive discussion of intermarriage injected into the plot by Hamor's proposal and the brothers' response – that the story is about the lengths to which one must go to prevent intermarriage. However, I find this explanation unpersuasive. Having reached a critical population mass (eleven sons and a daughter) and having returned to the land of Canaan (where there are no suitable spouses), the Israelite clan cannot possibly remain entirely endogamous. So a story utterly damning intermarriage makes no sense. Indeed, removing the stain of Dinah's rape by marrying a circumcised male who then becomes part of the clan (and having the rest of his city "convert") seems to be an excellent solution to the local problem of regaining family honor after Dinah's defilement and to the general question of whom Jacob's sons and daughter are to marry. Given that Simeon

17. Modern biblical critics, given a number of problematic elements in the story, have argued that it was actually created later and interpolated into the earlier narrative about Jacob's family in order to explain (among other things) Jacob's deathbed rebuke. Indeed, given the harshness of this rebuke, if a story was missing to explain it, it would have to have been added; see J. Kugel, *The Bible as It Was* (Harvard UP, 1997), 164–175.

and Levi make this solution impossible (perhaps because they are against intermarriage, although family honor seems paramount), I am not clear what lesson regarding intermarriage we are to derive from the story – especially since we will soon witness Judah's intermarriage with the Canaanite woman, Shua, and even more surprisingly Simeon's marriage to another unnamed Canaanite woman.[18]

An Epiphany for Israel

At this point God again speaks to Jacob/Israel. God tells him to leave Shechem and journey to Bethel. On the spot where God first appeared to him when he fled from his brother, Jacob must build an altar. This would appear to be a fulfillment of Jacob's vow after his ladder dream, "if I return safe to my father's house – the LORD shall be my God. And this stone, which I have set up as a pillar shall be God's abode" (28:21–22); but I find it strange that God Himself has to prompt Jacob to return to Bethel and fulfill his vow.

In preparation for this trip, Jacob instructs his "household and all who are with him" (35:2) to get rid of their idols. While Rachel is not mentioned by name, if she still has the household idols she stole from Laban this would suggest that she had been worshipping them until now. Otherwise, she would have disposed of them already. I suppose that Jacob's belief in God's providence – reinforced by his wrestling match with the Divine – has not necessarily rubbed off on everyone else. Jacob proceeds to bury all of these idolatrous relics under the terebinth near Shechem and leaves for Bethel. Explaining why the peoples of the land had not attacked Jacob yet (in reprisal for the massacre

---

18. While Jacob does bring home with him a large entourage of people from Haran, since these were slaves or servants perhaps Jacob's sons would not have found them suitable. Alternatively, since only Judah (38:22) and Simeon (46:10) are eventually reported to have married Canaanite women, perhaps the other sons found wives in this entourage. That Simeon should have intermarried may put a whole new spin on the massacre of Shechem!

of Shechem), the Torah states that "a terror from God fell on the cities round about, so that they did not pursue the sons of Jacob" (35:5). The journey to Bethel apparently serves two purposes: it allows Jacob to fulfill his vow and removes him from harm's way in the region around Shechem.

When he arrives at Bethel, Jacob receives yet another divine visitation. This one has three separate components: God confirms the name change from Jacob to Israel: "You shall be called Jacob no more, but Israel shall be your name" (35:10); God reaffirms that Jacob will have many descendants; and God reaffirms that Jacob and his progeny will receive the land promised to Abraham and Isaac. The epiphany ends with God saying nothing at all about what happened in Shechem; nor does He warn Jacob of the personal tragedy about to strike.[19]

Rachel's Death, Reuben's Unmentionable Act, and Esau's Progeny

With Rachel pregnant with a second child, the family travels from Bethel toward Efrat. Before reaching Efrat, Rachel goes into childbirth. In the course of giving birth to a second son – Jacob's twelfth – she dies and is buried at the side of the road. Thus the love affair between Jacob and Rachel comes to an unhappy and untimely end. Before her death, Rachel named the newborn Ben-oni (that is, son of my suffering); but Jacob changes the baby's name to Benjamin (son of my right hand). As a general rule, the task of naming children has fallen to the mother. It appears that Jacob did not want a daily reminder of Rachel's untimely death and took it upon himself to give the child a more positive name.[20]

---

19. From the perspective of modern biblical critics this blessing makes a lot of sense because it provides another account of Jacob's name change, and a more appropriate one at that: one, where Jacob, like Abraham, has his name changed explicitly by God. That there is no mention of the slaughter at Shechem also makes sense to biblical critics because they argue that the story was only interpolated later.
20. Rachel's grave is marked today at a spot inside the city limits of Bethlehem, and it has become a special place of prayer for barren women.

At this point in the narrative, the text – in an aside (virtually an afterthought) – notes that Reuben, Jacob's oldest son, "went and lay with Bilhah his father's concubine" (35:22) and that Israel "found out" (ibid.) about it. This appears to be an effort on the part of the firstborn son to exert authority over the clan, indeed, to usurp his father's position.[21] Perhaps, Reuben saw Rachel's death as the beginning of his father's decline. Jacob, adopting what is fast becoming a familiar stance, says nothing. So far, his three oldest sons (Reuben, Simeon, and Levi) have committed unthinkable acts that have in some manner usurped Jacob's power, and yet Jacob has remained silent. As with Simeon and Levi, Jacob waits until his deathbed blessing to hold Reuben accountable for his actions: "you shall excel no longer; for when you mounted your father's bed, you brought disgrace – my couch he mounted" (49:4). Reuben, in effect, forfeits the right of the firstborn because of his actions.[22]

The rest of this parasha consists of an extended history of Esau's family. One would think that a nation descended from Esau who was so reviled by the rabbinic tradition would not receive so long and detailed a history in the Torah. But this merely underscores the fact that the Written Torah, unlike the Rabbis who expounded it, does not view Esau as a paradigm of evil but rather as a family member who, while not the carrier of the Abrahamic spiritual tradition, nonetheless is worthy of note if not praise. I should point out that the Rabbis, in the course of explaining the divine origin of every word in the five books of Moses, stress that there is no difference in importance between the passage containing the Ten Commandments spoken by God at Mount Sinai and

---

21. The same idea occurs to Absalom (*II Sam.* 16:22) in his ill-fated revolt against David and to Adonijah (*I Kings* 2:13–25) at the beginning of Solomon's reign.
22. Modern biblical scholars suggest that this incident was created later and interpolated here and in Jacob's blessing to explain the historical disappearance of the tribe of Reuben. Jacob's silence is a result of the interpolator not wishing to add more than was necessary, not a reflection of how Jacob felt. See Kugel, *How to Read the Bible*, 193–194.

passages such as these which document the genealogical record in excruciatingly minute detail (in this case, information about Esau's progeny). I make no such claim. It seems clear to me that there are parts of the Torah which embody eternal moral truths and other parts that are, at best, pseudo-historical in nature – a position I am able to take in light of my belief that not every word found in the five books of Moses was dictated verbatim by God.

VAYESHEV

Settling Down at Last

Jacob's story is now virtually complete, and the text turns to the novella that comprises the rest of *Bereshit* – the story of Joseph and his brothers. This segment climaxes with Jacob's entire family migrating to Egypt, thus setting the stage for the Israelites' enslavement and ultimate redemption. Before commencing our discussion of the Joseph saga we should note that it begins with the statement that Jacob "settled in the land where his father had sojourned" (37:1). This marks a cadence in Jacob's saga; his travels and travails appear to be over and he is where he should be – in the land promised to Abraham, Isaac, and himself by God. If God had not told Abraham that his progeny would be enslaved "in a land not their [own]" (15:13), and that God would eventually redeem them to make them into a great nation, one might expect this to have been the end of the story. Jacob has returned to the Promised Land and settled there; his children and their progeny should live in Eretz Yisrael happily ever after. That, of course, was not to be. The family had to end up enslaved in Egypt, and the Joseph story is God's way of getting it there.

Joseph – the Favored Son and the Dreamer Par Excellence

As the story begins, we find Jacob's eleventh son, seventeen-year-old Joseph, assisting the sons of Bilhah and Zilpah. Setting the context immediately, the Torah tells us that Jacob "loved Joseph best of all his sons, for he was the child of his old age" (37:3). While strictly speaking that is not true (for Benjamin, Rachel's second child, was born after Joseph and should have been so denoted) the verse clearly means that Jacob doted on Joseph, Rachel's first-born. In any event, Jacob's preference for Joseph is manifested by the gift of a fancy coat or tunic.[1] The other brothers – at least the ten older ones, who are half brothers – resent this favoritism. In fact, the text tells us that "they hated him so" much that they were unable to "speak a friendly word to him" (37:4). One might think that Jacob, having himself experienced the mischief that parental favoritism and strife among brothers can cause, would have been sensitive to this dynamic and restrained himself from favoring Rachel's son. But human nature being what it is, Jacob does not learn from his own experience and dotes on Joseph. Perhaps, he even thinks that this is the way normal families work.

Once again, sibling rivalry is about to raise its ugly head and propel the story forward. It seems as if the entire book of *Bereshit* thus far has consisted of a series of sibling rivalries: Cain and Abel, Noah's three sons (resulting in the cursing of Canaan), Isaac and Ishmael, Esau and Jacob, and Leah and Rachel. From a divine perspective, one might well conclude that this complex set of family dynamics has only one objective, compelling Jacob's family to descend to Egypt, so that God may eventually fulfill his promise to Abraham by redeeming his descendants, founding the nation of Israel, giving it the Torah, and taking it to the Promised Land. Without the enslavement in Egypt, the promise

---

1. There is no scholarly consensus regarding how the Hebrew should be translated. Some say that the coat was ornamented and others that it was multicolored. What is important is that it was unique – which means that Jacob will recognize it as Joseph's – and that it enraged the other brothers.

made long ago to Abraham cannot be fulfilled, so the story must go on. I am reminded of Rabbi Akiba's fundamental paradox in *Pirkei Avot* 3:19 that all is foreseen by the omniscient deity and yet there is free will.

So we find Joseph in his teenage years, doted on by his father and resented by his half-brothers. To put it bluntly, we discover that Joseph is a spoiled brat. The Torah tells us that he reports his brothers' misbehavior to his father; he is a black-letter tattletale.[2] As if this were not enough, he then announces to his father and brothers that he has had two dreams, the clear purport of both being that he is destined to rule over all of them.[3] Even if we accept the text's implication that the dreams were prophetic, sent by God as a forecast of events to come, Joseph's seemingly naïve recounting of them to people who will no doubt be offended (if not worse) reflects an appalling lack of maturity. The text is somewhat ambiguous, but Jacob may have been aware of the brothers' reaction to the dreams and, hence, of their feelings towards Joseph: "So his brothers were wrought up at him, and his father kept the matter in mind" (37:11). What "matter" was Jacob keeping in mind? Was he only pondering the dreams or the dreams and the brothers'

---

2. The Torah, perhaps sparing the brothers embarrassment, does not detail this behavior. Of course, the Rabbis of the Midrash (BR 84:7) fill in the blanks explaining that the brothers were either violating Noahide law by eating limbs from live animals or violating the family taboo by gawking at the local girls in the hopes of marrying one of them. Another opinion curiously discerns an alliance between Joseph and the concubines' children with Joseph reporting on Leah's sons for acting disrespectfully toward their half brothers.

3. In an interesting response, an incredulous and angry Jacob asks Joseph whether he and Joseph's mother and brothers are ultimately to bow down before him. Either Jacob is questioning the veracity of the dream because Rachel, who is long dead, cannot bow down to Joseph, or perhaps the text is not set in chronological order and the dreams took place before Rachel's death. In that case, Jacob's incredulity has to do with the audacious dreams themselves. The midrashists account for the apparent difficulty of Rachel's being dead in two ways: (1) this demonstrates that not all dreams (even those sent by God) are completely accurate (*Berakhot* 55b; of course, Jacob seems to think they are); and (2) the reference to Joseph's mother is to the maid Bilhah who, according to the Midrash, took on the role of Joseph's mother after Rachel's death (BR 84:11).

reaction to them? Either way, he does not permit the brothers' feelings to dissuade him from his favorable treatment of Joseph.

That dreams play an important role in Joseph's sale into bondage in Egypt is significant, for it is Joseph's ability to interpret Pharaoh's dreams that will lead to the saga's happy denouement. Yet there is no suggestion at this point that Joseph is a talented dream interpreter or even that he understands these dreams (although it would not take a Freud to interpret them). To the contrary, he gives no response to his father's outburst when Jacob asks angrily whether the lad expects that his parents and brothers will bow down to him. The dreams' true significance at this point lies in their enraging the brothers and in the very fact that Joseph dreamt dreams that ironically come true years later in Egypt.

Joseph's Sale into Slavery

While Jacob seems to understand the brothers' anger directed at Joseph, he takes no steps to protect him. On the contrary he sends him directly into the danger zone. Jacob instructs Joseph to go to Shechem (where the brothers are pasturing the flocks) and find out how they and the animals are doing. Is Jacob in effect asking Joseph to do what he has done in the past – spy on the brothers and report any misdeeds back to his father? It is hard to avoid such a conclusion, which speaks ill of Jacob and underscores his blind spot when it comes to his older sons' true feelings about their younger brother. Furthermore, allowing the brothers to take their sheep to Shechem of all places (and then asking Joseph to follow them there) is somewhat bizarre. The family fled that area in order to avoid the wrath of the local Canaanites and Perizzites after Simeon and Levi had massacred the city's men and the other sons had looted it of its women and children. Has the passage of time eliminated whatever fear Jacob had of possible reprisals? One can only wonder.[4]

4. Modern biblical scholars who believe that the Dinah story was (made up and) interpolated later would have no problem with this, as they believe that Shechem

In any event, Joseph heads for Shechem and discovers that the brothers are no longer there but have moved on to Dothan. Joseph learns this from an unidentified man who says he overheard the brothers discussing the planned move. This man plays a crucial role in the saga, indeed, in Jewish history; for if he had not told our hero where his brothers had gone, Joseph would have returned to his father rather than ending up in Egypt, where Divine Providence requires him to be. Some have suggested that the man was indeed an angel (BR 84:14) or even God himself, reminding us of the "man" who wrestled with Jacob on the banks of the Jabbok and was later revealed to be of divine origin. It certainly is consonant with the Torah's worldview that events – certainly significant ones – never just happen but are all part of the divine scheme of things. Once again in the Joseph story (and for the first time in the Torah), we have the sense that free will notwithstanding, God's will cannot be denied.

The brothers see Joseph coming. Before he even arrives, they have a plan: they will kill him and tell Jacob that a wild beast devoured him. Before they set the plan in motion, Reuben, the eldest brother, steps in to save Joseph's life. Rather than shed blood, he argues, the brothers should cast Joseph into a pit and let nature take its course. The Torah explicitly tells us that Reuben "intend[ed] to save him from them and restore him to his father" (37:22). While Reuben has taken center stage in the narrative before, this is his first courageous act. His two prior appearances do not reveal any such heroic tendencies. He gathered mandrakes for his mother to make her more sexually attractive to Jacob – an admirable act but not a heroic one; and he violated fundamental family values by sleeping with Bilhah, his father's concubine. Here, however, he takes the high moral road and tries to save Joseph from his brothers' wrath. I wonder whether the ringleaders in the plot to kill Joseph were Simeon and Levi, the brothers who committed

---

was still standing and Jacob's sons had done nothing. The interpolator of the story simply forgot or decided not to delete this mention of Shechem.

the massacre at Shechem.[5] The text does not say. But we know that Reuben was against the idea, as presumably was Judah who, we shall soon see, convinces the other brothers to take Joseph out of the pit where he might have been injured or killed by a wild animal. While Joseph seems to have had a better relationship with Bilhah and Zilpah's sons as he "tended the flocks…as a helper to the sons of his father's wives Bilhah and Zilpah" (37:2), the fact that he also reported on their misdeeds would not have strengthened their relationship. This notwithstanding, having received his help those brothers might find it difficult to plot against him. The idea that Simeon and Levi (who we know had violent natures) were at the heart of the anti-Joseph conspiracy thus seems right to me – especially since, of all the brothers, Joseph decides to keep Simeon as a hostage when they visit Egypt for the first time (42:24).[6]

When Joseph arrives, the brothers strip him of his special tunic and cast him into the pit, which the text takes care to tell us is empty – "there was no water in it" (37:24). The Midrash (BR 84:16), damning the brothers, deduces that, while the pit had no water in it, it was filled with snakes and scorpions. If so it would have required a miracle for Joseph to remain alive. I prefer to suggest that the pit's dryness meant that animals were less likely to come there for water and hurt Joseph. Perhaps Reuben (and Judah) chose the pit so as to further protect Joseph's life. In any event, having deposited Joseph in the pit, the brothers callously sit down to have lunch. At this point, Reuben must have left the other brothers;[7] for given his shock at finding out that Joseph was

5. Even if one sides with the modern biblical scholars who claim the massacre never happened, Jacob's deathbed blessing clearly indicates that Simeon and Levi were violent individuals with fierce tempers.

6. The Midrash (BR 84:16) also identifies Simeon as the chief culprit, noting that when Joseph "takes" Simeon hostage in Egypt, the Torah uses the same verb as when Joseph is "taken" here and thrown into the pit. Incidentally, the term used to describe the prison where Joseph was held in Egypt is "pit", so if Joseph kept Simeon in jail, he quite literally revenged himself upon Simeon measure for measure for throwing him in the "pit".

7. The Midrash (BR 84:19; Rashi 37:29), jumping on the opportunity to rehabilitate

sold, clearly he was not around when the other brothers looked up and saw a caravan of merchants heading for Egypt.[8] It is Judah who takes the lead and forestalls his brothers' murderous intentions by suggesting that, rather than kill the boy, they sell him to the traders. The brothers agree and he is sold for the sum of twenty pieces of silver.[9]

When Reuben returns to the pit to rescue Joseph, he is gone. Making the obvious assumption, Reuben assumes that Joseph has been dragged off and killed by wild animals, and he rends his clothes – as a sign of mourning. He runs to the brothers and says to them (37:30): "The boy is gone! Now what am I to do?" The text does not tell us if and when the other brothers told Reuben about Joseph's sale. Presumably, someone told him at some point. But the next thing we know the brothers slaughter a young goat and dip Joseph's tunic in it. They then return to Hebron and show the bloody garment to Jacob, asking him if he recognizes it. Such a disingenuous question must have given rise in Jacob's mind to some suspicion about his sons, but all we are told is that he does indeed recognize the tunic as Joseph's and concludes that he was killed by a wild beast. Jacob goes into a period of deep mourning. The text tells us that his sons and daughters[10] unsuccessfully

Reuben's character, suggest that he was not at the meal because he was fasting and wearing sackcloth to atone for his sin of lying with Bilhah. Ironically, his lack of backbone in failing to stand up to his brothers leads to his failure in saving Joseph.

8. Whether these merchants were Ishmaelites (as they are described here when the brothers first see them) or Midianite traders (as they are described later in the text when the brothers sell Joseph) hardly matters, except to provide what may be further evidence of an amalgamation by a redactor of two earlier Joseph stories. The classical commentators strive mightily to make sense of the contradictory texts; see *Nachmanides* 38:25 for a summary of three approaches.

9. That the price is mentioned and is in silver suggests that this story may have served as a paradigm for Judas' betrayal of Jesus where he too is paid in silver (Matthew 26:14).

10. The only daughter previously mentioned is Dinah. This suggests that there were other daughters not important enough to be named for posterity – unless the reference is to daughters-in-law. Either way, the Midrash (BR 84:21), intent on preventing any hint of intermarriage with the local population, explains that each of

sought to comfort him. Meanwhile, the merchants arrive in Egypt and sell Joseph as a slave to Potiphar, who is some sort of officer in Pharaoh's court.

That both Reuben and Judah figure as heroes in the story of Joseph's sale may indicate that there were originally two versions of the story: one originating in the Kingdom of Israel praising Reuben, and one originating in the Kingdom of Judah praising the eponymous father of the tribe. This would also explain why Reuben is never explicitly told that Joseph was sold. In the northern version, Reuben saved Joseph's life and did not need to be told anything, and in the Judean one, Judah saved Joseph's life and Reuben was there when he did it. To be sure, I am aware of no scholarship which would support this intuition, and it is true that the tribe of Reuben settled in the south of the country, and not the north, and disappeared early in Israelite history; however, I think that the text as we have it plainly suggests that there were two versions of the tale, one featuring Judah as the hero and the other Reuben.

Judah, Shua, Tamar, Er, and Onan and the Question of Intermarriage

Smack dab in the middle of the Joseph saga, just as our hero arrives in Egypt, the biblical account suddenly shifts gears and recounts an apparently unrelated incident in the life of Judah. The Rabbis (BR 85:1–2) spill a great deal of ink trying to link the two accounts homiletically. Rashi (38:1), choosing one approach, suggests that the brothers demoted Judah after seeing their father's grief, claiming that he could have and should have convinced them not to sell Joseph. Judah in response moves away from the family. Another midrash [BR 85:1] beautifully creates a thematic link be-

---

Jacob's sons was born with a twin sister (as Cain and Abel were) and each brother married one of his half sisters, so that these women were both Jacob's daughters and daughters-in-law. Given such a claim, Joseph's disappearance must have left one sister without a half brother to marry. (This midrashic approach does not take into account the fact that both Judah and Simeon married local women.)

tween the incidents by emphasizing God's eternal providence: "the brothers were engaged in the sale of Joseph [and its aftermath], Joseph was engaged in mourning [for his fate], Reuben was engaged in mourning [for his sins], Judah was engaged in finding a wife for himself, and the Holy One Blessed Be He was engaged in creating the light of the messianic king [Judah's son Perez, who is born to Judah in this story, being the Messiah's progenitor]".[11] Homiletics aside, it is unclear just why this Judah story interrupts the Joseph saga. Perhaps the redactor wished to balance the extensive saga of Joseph, the progenitor of the Kingdom of Israel,[12] with one about the progenitor of the Kingdom of Judah. If so he chose a story that hardly paints Judah in glowing terms.[13]

Perhaps, as James Kugel argues, the redactor had no other appropriate place to insert this interesting story. Placing it before the Joseph saga begins would have been wrong in terms of Judah's age (since he becomes a father and "grandfather" in this story) and placing it after the Joseph saga would have made no sense since at that point the family is already in Egypt. So given a fully formulated Joseph novella, the interpolator had to choose the best location he could, a break in the narrative between Joseph's sale and his adventures in Egypt.[14] Other scholars have argued that this was a fortuitous choice (indeed, perhaps the best choice) because there are a number of similar literary motifs in both stories

11. Note that this midrash picks up on a theme central to the Joseph saga: God is always behind the scenes guiding events.
12. Indeed, throughout the Prophets, the Kingdom of Israel is often referred to as Ephraim, the name of Joseph's younger son.
13. Assuming that such an attempt to achieve balance explains the insertion of the Judah story here, it is still unclear whether the redactor's point of view is pro-Judah or anti-Judah. Judah certainly does not come across as utterly blameless here, although, as we shall see, he is quick to shoulder responsibility for his conduct. Moreover, the story does close with a description of what becomes the ancestral lineage of King David. But even there I find an anti-Judah bias in light of the legitimacy questions that arise – as discussed below.
14. This material is part of J. Kugel's *How to Read the Bible*, but is found only online at *www.jameskugel.com* as Appendix I, "Apologetics and Biblical Criticism Lite," 25–29.

(Joseph and Judah "go down", articles of attire are used for deception, Judah and Jacob fear losing their youngest sons, Judah and Joseph undergo sexual trials). So, in their opinion, Judah's story very successfully acts as a foil for the Joseph saga.[15]

Be that as it may, this episode is also a self-contained unit. As the story begins, Judah leaves the rest of the family to dwell in an area inhabited by Hirah, who is said to be an Adullamite, apparently one of the Canaanite peoples. In the space of thirty verses, the Torah recounts what happened there and then returns to the Joseph story. Neither before nor after this chapter does the Torah ever mention that Judah left the family conclave, and indeed there is no particular reason to think that this episode happened right after Joseph's sale and not at some other point in time. The tradition teaches (*Sifre Beha'alotcha* 64; *Pesachim* 6b; Nachmanides, *Bamidbar* 9:9) that the Torah does not always report events in chronological order, and this may be an example of that phenomenon.

As for what occurred, Judah, defying family tradition, marries a local Canaanite woman named Shua (and then later is tricked into having relations with his daughter-in-law, Tamar). Neither Judah nor the text exhibits any apprehension concerning such a marriage. Despite Abraham's concern that Isaac marry a woman from Haran and Isaac's unhappiness with Esau's local wife, there is no mention here of any discomfort on Jacob's part. This may not mean anything. Since Jacob is never mentioned in this chapter, it stands to reason that he had no knowledge of what Judah did during his sojourn away from the family. Furthermore, given Jacob's penchant for saying nothing, his silence need not indicate acquiescence. What is more significant is that Judah has no apprehension concerning the marriage. While those traditionalists who wish to claim that Jacob's children certainly did not marry local Canaanite women have argued that within Jacob's camp there

---

15. See among others, Robert Alter, *The Art of Biblical Narrative* (New York: Basic Books, 1981), 6–10.

were either half sisters (BR 84:21) or other non-Canaanite women of a lower social status available to them, as Dinah's story indicates intermarrying with the local population was another solution to finding wives for Jacob's sons. That only Judah and Simeon (46:10) are explicitly named as doing so may or may not indicate that this was the norm among Jacob's children. The problems presented by such intermarriage – possibly straying after the pagan spouses' false gods and including the Canaanites within the rubric of the Abrahamic covenant to inherit the land – were discussed above in the discussion of Abraham's marriage to Keturah.

Unlike the men of Shechem who were asked to undergo circumcision, there is no suggestion in the text that Judah's wife performed any sort of conversion to the religion of his family. Indeed, one can search *Bereshit* from beginning to end and fail to find any such concept. What appears to happen in the event of marriage is that the woman simply enters her husband's clan and adopts his religious and national identity.[16] This was presumably true of Hagar, the Egyptian, and of Rebecca, Leah, Rachel, Bilhah, and Zilpah, who all came from Haran and were absorbed into the religion of Abraham. The unyielding Jewish aversion to intermarriage (that is to marrying anyone who is not Jewish) and the insistence on non-Jews becoming Jewish through a conversion process that requires the convert to accept the strictures of the religion seems to be a later development.[17] Indeed, the only issue at hand in *Bereshit* (and even in the seminal verse in *Shemot* 34:15–16) is the stricture against marrying Canaanites, and this seems to have weakened, at least somewhat, in the generation of Jacob's sons.

Shua presents Judah with three sons. Judah proceeds to arrange a marriage for the oldest, selecting a woman named Tamar. We are not told anything about her origins. Her betrothed, Er, somehow displeases God and dies. It is interesting that the text

---

16. This might explain Jacob's lack of daughters. Is it possible that they married out, were lost to their people, and accordingly were omitted from the text?

17. Or, at least, it is not mentioned in the text. An accompanying oral tradition might have incorporated it.

tells us that God was displeased with Er and took his life. What he may have done to warrant such a drastic punishment is not revealed to us. Perhaps the text assumes that any time someone dies a premature death, it reflects God's displeasure with him – an assumption that does not sit well these days in light of the Holocaust.[18]

Judah informs the next son in line, Onan, that he is obliged to marry his brother's childless widow in order to provide offspring on his behalf. This practice is known as levirate marriage and is codified in the Torah's legal section in *Devarim* 25:5–10. Indeed, among the Orthodox the rule is still technically operative, even though the Rabbis do not permit the brother to go through with it – insisting, instead, that he perform *chalitzah*, the Torah's pre-scribed ceremony for eliminating the levirate obligation.[19] One can well understand the idea underlying the notion of levirate marriage, although it does seem to contradict the spirit of the To-rah's outright prohibition of sexual relations between a man and his brother's wife (*Vayikra* 18:16).[20] As early as the Mishnaic period (c. 200 CE), concern over impure motivations on the brother's part led to a debate over whether performing a levirate marriage or doing chalitzah was preferable. As one Rabbi declared in the Tal-mud (*Yevamot* 39b), marrying one's (dead) brother's wife for her

---

18. While the Holocaust is difficult if not impossible to comprehend, it seems to me that this idea was just as difficult to accept in eras when infant mortality, death in childbirth, death from bacterial infection etc. were rampant. Of course, the Holo-caust raises issues other than theodicy – particularly the question of God's covenant with Israel.

19. Following the promulgation of a ban on polygamy by Rabbeinu Gershom (d. 1040), the practice of levirate marriage waned among Ashkenazi Jews. As a rule, among the *Rishonim* (early medieval authorities), the Spanish school, the Rif, and Mai-monides upheld the custom, while the Northern school and R. Tam preferred ch-alitzah (*Shulchan Arukh, Even ha'Ezer*, 165:1). As I understand it, some Sephardim still practice levirate marriage and do not require chalitzah, although they of course permit it in accordance with Torah law.

20. The halachic literature on this point is vast. If for some reason the levirate mar-riage is not obligatory, then the surviving brother who desires to perform it risks violating a law carrying the death penalty.

beauty was tantamount to sexual impropriety. One thing seems certain: the practice seems much more concerned with the position of the husband and his family than with the woman's feelings. A modern sensibility would be shocked by the notion that a recently widowed woman should accept as a husband her late spouse's brother so that her dear departed may posthumously be given an heir. Indeed, while the issue is beyond the scope of our discussion here, according to the Halacha, the woman does have the right to refuse a levirate marriage and opt for chalitzah (according to most opinions in most situations, without being penalized in any way).[21]

In any event, Onan is not happy with the idea. According to the text, this is because he realizes that any offspring of a union with Tamar would count as his deceased brother's child and not his. The problem is a straightforward one. Onan would have to support the child, but the baby would be reckoned as Er's and would inherit his double portion of Judah's estate, leaving Onan with a net loss. So, according to the text, Onan lets his seed spill on the ground.

This plainly means that he went so far as to commence sexual relations with Tamar but withdrew before ejaculation in order to avoid impregnating her. Such behavior, from a later rabbinic perspective, would lead to a gross violation of the prohibition against sleeping with one's brother's wife, for that prohibition is waived only to allow for the levirate process designed to produce an heir. By sleeping with Tamar and not completing the process, Onan has violated a law carrying the death penalty (*karet*). God doesn't approve of this conduct; and Onan dies as a result. Many readers construe this aspect of the story as teaching that "onanism", that is, coitus interruptus, and by analogy male masturbation, which also involves "spilling seed on the ground," is sinful and should not be permitted. Indeed, some go even farther and read the story of Onan as teaching that any form of contraception is prohibited

21. See *Shulchan Arukh, Even ha'Ezer*, 165: 1.

and that the only proper purpose of sexual intercourse – at least while the participants are of childbearing age – is procreation.[22]

This approach is clearly alien to the Jewish tradition, which does not frown on pleasurable sex or on the discriminating use of contraception.[23] While the *Tanakh* certainly views alien women as potential temptresses, I find no suggestion that there is anything wrong in a married couple's enjoying each other sexually – as Isaac and Rebecca are explicitly stated to have done. Indeed, while *Proverbs 7* advises men to stay away from "alien women", *Proverbs* 31:10–31, extols the virtues of a capable wife. While the commandment to be fruitful and multiply must be taken seriously, Halacha treats the mitzvah as being fulfilled when a man has at least one son and one daughter.[24] But the married couple is still, in the text's words, "of one flesh", which surely suggests that they may continue to have sex whether or not more children are in the offing. The use of the Onan story to support a policy prohibiting contraception was at one time a political commonplace in America. Fortunately that day appears to be behind us; I do not think that even the current right-leaning Supreme Court is ready to overrule *Griswold v. Connecticut*[25] and permit the states of the American Union to prohibit the sale of contraceptive devices.[26]

22. For a comprehensive and insightful analysis of this story and its societal and halachic implications, see David M. Feldman's "The 'Act of Er and Onan'" in *Marital Relations, Birth Control, and Abortion in Jewish Law* (New York: Schocken Books, 1974) 144–165. As for the legitimacy of non-procreative sex, Feldman notes that it is a given in rabbinic law which hardly needs to be demonstrated (id., 67).

23. Indeed, when Sarah questions the likelihood that she will bear a child at a very advanced age, she asks rhetorically whether she will still be able to take pleasure with her husband. The reference to sexual pleasure is anything but pejorative; in addition, see Feldman cited in the previous footnote, particularly the chapter entitled "The Legitimacy of Sexual Pleasure" (pages 81–105) and his extensive discussion of the legitimate use of contraception.

24. As pointed out above in discussing Adam and Eve, it is somewhat surprising that the tradition understands the commandment to procreate to be incumbent only on the man even though he obviously cannot fulfill it by himself.

25. 381 U.S. 479 (1965).

26. I do not know whether the Catholic Church's continued ban on contraception – which is a tragedy for those overpopulated countries under the Church's sphere

But this politicization of the Bible does underscore the problems that arise when religious texts are misread and misguidedly transformed into political positions.

Judah has a third son, Shelah. But having seen what happened to the first two when they got involved with Tamar, Judah is reluctant to impose the levirate obligation on him. So he disingenuously tells Tamar to remain a widow until Shelah grows up and can marry her. Tamar follows Judah's instructions and returns to her father's house to wait. But Judah has no intention of permitting his remaining son to marry this woman. Time passes and, as the text is careful to tell us, Judah's wife dies. After an appropriate mourning period, he heads for Timnah, where his sheep are being sheared. Tamar is told that her father-in-law is coming. Plotting her revenge against Judah for having kept her a widow all these years (or perhaps in an effort to have the child from Judah's family to which she is legally entitled), she dresses in harlot's garb, covers her face, and takes her position next to the road to Timnah. Judah shows up and immediately solicits sex from the woman who he thinks is a prostitute. She asks him what he is willing to pay, and he promises to send her a kid from his flock. Apparently not trusting him to do so, Tamar (whom, of course, Judah does not recognize) asks for security to back up his promise to pay; and, at her request, Judah gives her his seal and his staff as pledges. They proceed to have sex and, as luck (or Divine Providence) would have it, she becomes pregnant.

When Judah sends the promised kid with a messenger, the prostitute is nowhere to be found. Nor does anyone the messenger asks know anything about a prostitute working that particular area. Judah decides to forget the whole thing and let the harlot keep the seal and the staff. Meanwhile, the pregnant Tamar has been accused of adultery. As a matter of law, she is betrothed to Shelah, even though Judah will not allow the young man to marry

of influence – is premised on the Onan story. But as Feldman points out, the story is foundational to Church doctrine in this matter (id., 145–148).

189

her. As far as the population is concerned, she has obviously committed adultery, and Judah (either as the patriarch or acting on Shelah's behalf) condemns her to be burnt to death. She sends a message to Judah stating that the man to whom the seal and staff belong has impregnated her. Judah recognizes the pledges and publicly admits that he is in the wrong, not because he had relations with her when he thought she was a prostitute but because he should have given her Shelah as a husband and failed to do so. Tamar is spared execution and gives birth to twins, the elder of whom is Perez, the ancestor of King David and, ultimately, the Messiah.

The text does not tell us whether after this incident and the twins' birth Shelah becomes Tamar's husband. But in *1 Chronicles* 4:21 we learn that Shelah son of Judah had a son named Er. Does the fact that Shelah's son was indeed named after his deceased brother (as would be the case if a levirate marriage between Shelah and Tamar had taken place) mean that there was in fact such a marriage? Curiously, neither of the children born of Judah and Tamar's union is named for Er, so clearly Judah did not fulfill the levirate function by sleeping with Tamar. Furthermore, the Torah text explicitly states that Judah "was not intimate with her [Tamar] again" (24:26); so perhaps Shelah did marry her and father a child for his brother.

What is the point of this convoluted story? Judah comes across as a man of honor, willing to publicly admit his sins, even though he consorts with prostitutes. Tamar is portrayed as a self-assured woman willing and able to take matters into her own hands when she is mistreated. The Judah story acts as a foil, if we accept the opinions of certain literary critics, to the Joseph one. We are made privy to some interesting information about the lineage of King David, a man who is one of the two principal heroes in *Tanakh*.

What strikes me most is that, according to this story, under Torah law David must be deemed the offspring of a *mamzer* – the descendant of an individual born as a consequence of an adulterous relationship.[27] Perez and his descendant David should have been halachic pariahs, unable, as a matter of law, to marry any woman not herself a member of this outcast group. This conclusion seems to me to be inescapable. Under the levirate rules, Tamar is legally bound to Shelah when Perez (David's ancestor) is conceived; that, of course, is the reason that she is condemned to death when she becomes pregnant. This circumstance renders the Judah-Tamar relationship adulterous and any offspring conceived through it a mamzer. Perhaps what we really have here is a text devised by a writer in the Kingdom of Israel designed to cast aspersions on the Davidic line of the Kingdom of Judah. Why else would the story find its way into the Torah? Indeed, a comparison of Joseph's actions and Judah's in their respective stories certainly supports the notion that the Kingdom of Judah's eponymous progenitor was nowhere near as righteous as the Kingdom of Israel's (read, Ephraim's) was.[28]

Joseph in Egypt – Into the Depths

Having completed the self-contained unit about Judah's adventures, the text returns to Joseph's tale. Connecting the stories is the theme of actual or potential illicit sex and the motif of recognition (Judah's of Tamar and the brothers' of Joseph). Potiphar, who bought Joseph as a slave, soon discovers his talents and appoints him as his household's major domo. This stroke of good fortune is expressly credited to the fact that God is with Joseph rendering all of his efforts successful. This is not surprising; though it is interesting that God never appears directly to Joseph as he did with his father, grandfather, and great-grandfather. Apparently

27. The law had not yet been revealed in Perez' time, but it had been by David's.
28. Traditionally, adopting a weakness as a strength, apologists for David have argued that it is the seeming flaws in his lineage that emphasize his greatness. Even though he was descended from the illicit union of Judah and Tamar and from Ruth, the Moabite convert, he was still chosen to be king of Israel. Like Judah, David, when his sins are exposed (particularly, his engineering of Uriah's death and his sleeping with Uriah's wife), immediately repents of his actions.

Joseph and, indeed, all those of his generation are not on the spiritual level of the earlier patriarchs. The Joseph story, while plainly suggesting that all of the critical events are somehow God's doing and part of a divine plan, nonetheless appears on its surface to be totally earthbound. God may in fact be running the show, but the events proceed on a purely human track. Potiphar's household thrives under Joseph's stewardship. Indeed, like Laban before him who benefited from Jacob's presence, Potiphar's house is blessed "for Joseph's sake" (39:5), thus indicating that Joseph has received the family blessing "I will bless those who bless you" (12:3). But a smoldering conflagration is about to explode. Mrs. Potiphar finds Joseph – who the text expressly tells us is "well built and handsome" (39:6) – sexually attractive and makes improper advances.

We are told very little about Potiphar's wife. For example, we don't know whether she too was well built and handsome or whether Joseph was attracted to her. But she is cast in the stereotypical role of the dangerous, sexually attractive, alien woman; and, significantly, she is accustomed to getting what she wants. She asks Joseph to have sex with her, and he rejects her offer. In saying no to his boss's wife, Joseph gives her a little sermon, pointing out how it would be an offense both to Potiphar (who has been very good to him) and to God for him to engage in an adulterous act. This speech is open to conflicting interpretations. On the one hand, it can be read to reflect Joseph's having matured from the spoiled brat we saw in the earlier confrontations with his brothers. Even in Egypt, far away from home, he is maintaining his moral standards. On the other hand, it can be read as reflecting the kind of self-righteousness an egocentric youngster might be inclined to exhibit to his social superiors. It does seem clear that the text intends us to adopt the former reading, which reveals Joseph at this stage of his life as a tzaddik in waiting.

Mrs. Potiphar does not take Joseph's "no" for an answer. On a day when no one else is around, she propositions him again. Trying to force the matter, she grasps his garment and he flees, leaving his garment in her hand. Just as a garment (the coat of many colors) played a critical role in Joseph's sale into bondage, a garment plays a central role here. But how is it that Joseph's garment is left in Mrs. Potiphar's hand? True she had grasped it, but was he in the process of succumbing when he suddenly thought better of the idea? Or did she rip it from him as he tried to escape? While I do not believe the text wants us to conclude that Joseph was in the least tempted by this latest of Mrs. Potiphar's offers, the language does permit such a reading.[29] At this point we do get a glimpse of the nasty character of Potiphar's wife. Rejected yet again, this time she lashes out to punish Joseph. She cries rape, using the garment in her hand as proof. Potiphar believes his wife – or, at the least, finds it expedient to say he does – and has Joseph hauled off to prison.

One might well ask why Potiphar, who has been so impressed with Joseph's honesty and ability, would believe his wife's story. Indeed, according to the text, Potiphar knows that God is with Joseph (39:3) and surely he must be aware of his wife's character. What is more, if some uppity servant had indeed attempted to rape Potiphar's wife, you would expect him to be tried and executed rather than merely sent to prison. I get the sense that Potiphar is severely conflicted and tries to cut the baby in half. He cannot publicly accuse his wife of lying, and because she has accused Joseph so publicly (and has physical evidence) he cannot ignore her claim. However, he has an intuition that Joseph may well be innocent; this stops him from seeking a more severe punishment. So Joseph ends up in prison; and that is exactly where God wants him to be, as future events demonstrate.

Joseph in Prison: The Dreamer as Dream Interpreter

Joseph arrives in prison and almost immediately is put in charge of "everything that was done there" (39:22). In virtually the same

---

29. There is a midrash (BR 87:7) that seizes on the peculiarity of this text to opine that Joseph was indeed about to succumb to the woman's wiles when he saw his father's face in a vision which brought him back to his moral senses.

language used to describe his status in Potiphar's household, the text tells us: "God was with him, and whatever he did God made successful" (39:23). That Joseph's sojourn in prison is part of the divine plan is made abundantly clear. God helps Joseph in Potiphar's house and helps him in prison, but leaves him to his own devices when it comes to dealing with Mrs. Potiphar. Whether Mrs. Potiphar's advances were a test or not,[30] clearly God's lack of intervention suggests that Joseph was supposed to end up in jail.

Two new prisoners arrive: Pharaoh's cupbearer and baker, both having somehow offended the monarch. Each of them has a strange dream. When Joseph asks them why they look downcast they tell him that they had dreams, and "there is no one to interpret them" (40:8). Dreams, of course, are no novelty to Joseph. It was his dreams of mastery over his family that got him into so much trouble with his brothers. But in the earlier dream episode, it was the brothers and Jacob who did the interpreting; there is no suggestion there that Joseph had any unique ability to interpret dreams.[31] Here, when his fellow prisoners mention they had dreams, Joseph replies: "Surely God can interpret! Tell me [your dreams]" (40:8). This is an astonishing statement. God has never spoken to Joseph; at least the text reports no such epiphany. Yet he has total confidence that God – the source of dreams and thus the master of their interpretation – will reveal the hidden meaning to him. Despite all of the hardships he has undergone, Joseph has not been humbled or lost confidence in his ability. This is either a sign of continued immaturity or, perhaps, more accurately, a praiseworthy symptom of his utter faith that God will move his career forward even in the face of total adversity. In either event, Joseph volunteers to interpret the dreams; and he does so.

The substance of the dreams does not appear to me to be of

---

30. The Midrash (BR 87:4) certainly thinks they were and even compares these tests to those of Abraham and Jacob.

31. As mentioned above, it would not have taken a Freud to interpret Joseph's dreams, so presumably Joseph understood them and the impact they would have on his family.

enormous importance. What is significant is the underlying assumption that God occasionally uses dreams to give the dreamer a glimpse of what the future holds in store for him. That assumption is not stated explicitly by the text at this point.[32] But the dreams' import is plain: the cupbearer will be spared and return to his job in court, while the baker will be executed. When he reports the good news to the cupbearer, Joseph asks him to remember him and mention his unjust imprisonment to Pharaoh, so that he may be released. Like his father before him, who devised stratagems for appeasing Esau, Joseph also tries to ensure his own success by petitioning the cupbearer and not relying exclusively on God.[33] Joseph's interpretations turn out to be accurate. The baker is executed and the cupbearer returned to his post; but as the verse states, "the cupbearer did not think of Joseph; he forgot him" (40:23). One might add in the context of Joseph's story, the cupbearer forgot Joseph, but God did not.

---

32. Although when Joseph had his dreams, clearly everyone assumed that they might predict the future. And when Pharaoh also has prophetic dreams, Joseph explicitly tells him that they have been sent by God to predict the future (41:25).
33. Ironically, while the Rabbis praised Jacob's actions, they berate Joseph for not having complete faith in God (*Rashi*, 40:23). Perhaps, this stems from the overwhelming sense that God is with Joseph every single step of the way.

MIKETZ

Joseph at Pharaoh's Court and His (Inter)marriage

While Joseph remains languishing in prison for two years, nothing significant happens. Then Pharaoh in one night has two dreams. They leave him agitated, and he calls on his magicians to interpret them. This is the first appearance in the Torah of the Egyptian court magicians who will play so important a role in the Exodus story. Had they been able to explain the dreams to Pharaoh's satisfaction, Joseph would have remained in jail, so it is no surprise to readers of the Bible that they fail to explain the dreams' meanings. The cupbearer recalls Joseph's feat of dream interpretation two years earlier and recommends him to Pharaoh.

Memory is a central theme throughout the Torah, from God's remembering Noah and those with him in the ark to God's remembering his covenant with Abraham, Isaac, and Jacob leading to the redemption of the Israelites from Egyptian slavery. Indeed, the Israelites, once freed, are commanded to "remember" several events: the Shabbat, God's taking them out of Egypt, and the cruel attack of the Amalekites.[1] The cupbearer's memory, in an interest-

---

1.   After *Shacharit* (Morning Prayers), some Jews even recite the Six Remembrances.

197

ing negative inversion of the norm, is the vehicle through which Israel is eventually enslaved.

Pharaoh, anxious to understand his dreams, sends for Joseph. The text tells us that Joseph's hair is cut and he is given new clothes – apparently to make him presentable before Pharaoh. This marks the beginning of what can be termed Joseph's acculturation into Egyptian society, for until now he has always been referred to as the "Hebrew slave" (39:17) or "Hebrew youth" (41:12). Pharaoh says to Joseph: "I have heard it said of you that for you to hear a dream is to tell its meaning" (41:15). Joseph replies, as he did years before to the cupbearer and the baker, that it is God, not he, who interprets dreams. After hearing the dreams, Joseph explains that God has sent them to inform Pharaoh about what is about to happen: Egypt will bask in seven years of plentiful harvests to be followed by seven years of famine. Both dreams carry the same meaning, but the fact that Pharaoh dreamt both means that "the matter has been determined by God, and that God will soon carry it out" (41:32). So far so good. Joseph has explained the dreams, apparently to Pharaoh's satisfaction. But he has not finished. Even after years of prison and the shock of being whisked suddenly before the most powerful monarch in the ancient world, Joseph has the courage – or, perhaps more correctly, the *chutzpah* – to tell Pharaoh what he must do: appoint a "man of discernment and wisdom and set him over the land of Egypt" (41:33); furthermore, let him appoint overseers to supervise the collection and storage of the bountiful produce during the seven good years, so that this man can then ration it out during the ensuing famine.

Given the confidence Joseph has shown up to this point, one cannot avoid thinking that he has himself in mind for the job. And that, of course, is just what Pharaoh is also thinking, thus capping the Bible's first "Rags to Riches" story[2] with Joseph's appointment as Egypt's grand vizier, second in authority only to Pharaoh himself. Pharaoh justifies this appointment (of a foreigner

---

2. The story presages David's ultimate rise from poor shepherd to King of Israel.

who is not even a member of the court) by declaring that since Joseph is imbued with God's spirit, none could be more discerning or wiser than he. It is most surprising to find Pharaoh – who was considered a living deity in Egypt's pantheon – recognizing the God of Israel, whose most significant attribute is his oneness. The statement appears to me to be yet another reflection of the fervent monotheism of the text's author who imparts his own religious belief to foreigners unlikely to share it.[3]

Joseph's rise to power at the Egyptian court presents us with the model for what becomes a recurring pattern both in *Tanakh* and much later in medieval and modern Jewish history – the court Jew who rises to political power without abandoning his Judaism.[4] Later parallels include Esther and Daniel in *Tanakh* and numerous powerful Jews in Spain prior to their expulsion (among them the famous Bible commentator Abarbanel) and bankers such as the Rothschilds in pre- and post-Napoleonic Europe. With this appointment, Joseph's acculturation is almost complete. He is dressed in robes of fine linen, given Pharaoh's own signet ring to wear, and has a gold chain of office draped around his neck. No longer is he the Hebrew Joseph of the many-colored coat, but Zaphenath-paneah, a member of the Egyptian court decked out in Egyptian finery.[5] He is sent for a victory lap in the chariot of Pharaoh's second-in-command and given an Egyptian wife, Asenat, who we are told is the daughter of Potiphera, priest of On.[6]

Joseph's marriage outside the Israelite family makes him the

---

3. Alternatively, perhaps the author merely localized Pharaoh's remarks for his Israelite audience's sake, transforming his original reference to an Egyptian deity into the God of Israel.

4. As we shall see, Joseph himself may not fit the model. Unless we look to the Midrash to fill in the gaps, there is little suggestion in the Torah text that Joseph sought to maintain any meaningful Jewish identity until his father arrived in Egypt. To be sure, he never denies that he is a Hebrew, but that seems to be about as far as it goes.

5. This sets a precedent for the name changes of Daniel and his companions in post-exilic Babylon.

6. Because the name Potiphera is very close to that of Potiphar, the Rabbis (BR 85:2) speculate that Joseph's wife was the daughter of his former master. Unless Potiphar

first of the patriarchs (aside from Judah and Simeon, neither of whom may deserve the title)[7] to marry without regard for the family's endogamous tradition.[8] Significantly, he marries the daughter of an alien priest – as will Moses a few generations later. The Rabbis of the Midrash, needless to say, are not happy with this match and construct an entire conversion scenario including, believe it or not, a halachic *ketubah* (Jewish religious marriage contract) for Joseph and Asenat.[9] Obviously concerned that the conversion they posit might not be enough to render the couple's sons Jewish under the halachic rules mandating matrilineal descent, the Rabbis (*Pirkei de-Rabbi Eliezer* 37) even go so far as to suggest that Asenat was Joseph's niece, her mother being Jacob's daughter Dinah, who was Joseph's half sister. How Dinah would have arrived in Egypt with her daughter in the first place is hard to fathom and, indeed, contrary to other midrashim which have her married to Job (BR 57:4; Jerusalem Talmud, *Bava Batra* 15:2). Furthermore, the masoretic reading of the text in *Bereshit* 46:15 includes Dinah in Jacob's retinue when he heads south to Egypt. How Asenat could have reached Egypt on her own and been adopted by Potiphar (who the Midrash posits is Potiphera, priest of On), is even more difficult to fathom.

The matrilineal descent issue, which so troubled the Rabbis, does not appear to pose a problem for the Torah text. The Torah *is* certainly worried about intermarriage. As pointed out above in the

---

had more than one wife, that would mean that Joseph became Mrs. Potiphar's son-in-law, which would be most ironic.

7.   We usually think of the patriarchs as limited to the three founding fathers: Abraham, Isaac, and Jacob. But it seems to me that Joseph should be considered a patriarch of the following generation in light of his importance in the story of Israel's ultimate rise to nationhood and his fatherhood of Manasseh and, more importantly, Ephraim who is the progenitor of the most important tribe in the Kingdom of Israel. Indeed, by adopting Joseph's two sons, Jacob gives Joseph the double portion of the firstborn. This by definition might make him the next patriarch. Judah, as the progenitor of the Kingdom of Judah, might also be considered a patriarch, but Simeon certainly not.

8.   The propriety of Abraham's marriage to Keturah was discussed above.

9.   See Louis Ginzberg, *The Legends of the Jews*. Vol. 2 (Soncino Press, 1948) 136.

context of Judah's marriage to a Canaanite woman, intermarriage flies in the face of the Torah's prohibitions in later books of unions with alien women likely to bring idol worship into the household (*Shemot* 34:15–16). But I find no suggestion in the Torah that the offspring of such marriages – including, for example, Joseph's sons, Judah's sons and Moses' sons – raised any Jewish identity problems. As mentioned above in discussing Judah's marriage, accepted custom during the time of the Bible appears to have been that the wife is absorbed into the husband's clan without having to undergo anything akin to a religious conversion, and the children of this union are as Jewish (or Israelite, if you will) as their fathers. Once the Rabbis of the Mishnaic period determined that religious (that is, tribal) identity should follow the mother rather than the father, it became necessary for them to rationalize all the intermarriages of important biblical figures by positing anachronistic conversions for Asenat,[10] Zipporah, and Ruth in order to render their offspring truly Jewish.

That matrilineal descent does not have identifiable roots in the Written Torah[11] does not mean that Reform Judaism is correct in eliminating it and recognizing as Jewish the unconverted children of intermarriages between a Jewish husband and a non-Jewish wife.[12] The Jewish world has accepted matrilineal descent

---

10. That is, of course, if the reader does not accept the speculation that her mother was indeed Dinah, in which event no conversion would be necessary.

11. Needless to say, for those who accept the Oral Torah as God-given, this is not a problem at all. I have no problem with the suggestion that the Oral Torah fills in the lacunae in the Written Torah. However, I have difficulty accepting the Oral Torah when it openly contradicts the written text itself. But I should note that, contra my position, according to David Weiss Halivni, there are a number of clear instances in which the Rabbis understood the oral law to be in direct contradiction to the Written Torah. See Halivni, *Revelation Restored* (SCM Press, 2001) 34–35.

12. As I understand the current Reform position, such children are not automatically Jewish. It is necessary for the parents to raise the children as Jews. One path routinely followed by the Conservative movement is a halachic conversion in infancy (including immersion in a *mikveh* [ritual bath] before a *beit din* [religious court]) with the parents committing to raise the child as Jewish and permitting the child, when he or she reaches maturity, to affirm the conversion or reject it.

for such a longtime that one cannot expect Conservative Judaism to go along with patrilineal descent (that the Orthodox will not accept it is axiomatic), and the resulting disunity is indeed troublesome. Yet, it is not so catastrophic as some make it out to be. For conversion is always available in order to avoid future intermarriage problems, that is assuming that the rabbinate is reasonable when it comes to refraining from placing obstacles before honest converts who want to be Jewish, want to raise a Jewish family, but may not yet be ready to commit to a totally observant lifestyle. Unfortunately, this is a sticking point because, as I understand it, most Orthodox (and many Conservative) rabbis will refuse to convert such an individual.

Joseph and the Brothers Confront Each Other Again

As Pharaoh's dreams had predicted, Egypt enjoys seven years of bountiful harvests; and Joseph sees to it that enormous quantities of grain are stored for use during the years of famine to come. Meanwhile, during the years of plenty Joseph and Asenat have two sons. The names Joseph chooses for them are significant.[13] The older is called Manasseh, a name which derives from a Hebrew root meaning forget. The text tells us that this name is meant to convey Joseph's emotion that "God has made me forget completely my hardship and my parental home" (41:51). While the name is in Hebrew and not Egyptian, which surely implies that Joseph has not in fact forgotten his origins, the fact remains that he thanks God for letting him forget his father and his brothers. While it is commendable for Joseph to forget the brothers who acted so badly in selling him into slavery, one would expect that a Torah hero would not be thankful for having forgotten the father who had

---

13. It is also interesting to note that it is Joseph, the father, who names the children, not the mother (as has been customary with almost all the births we have seen so far; the only exceptions have been Isaac and Ishmael whose names were chosen by God [or His angel] and Benjamin, who Jacob renamed). Curiously, Moses (who was reared in Pharaoh's court) also names his children (*Shemot* 2:22), so perhaps this is an Egyptian custom.

lavished so much love and attention on him.[14] Joseph's second son is named Ephraim denoting Joseph's gratitude to God for making him fertile in the land of his affliction. To be sure, the beginning of Joseph's Egyptian visit was full of affliction – at least after his run-in with Mrs. Potiphar. But in light of his current circumstance, it is strange to see the country's prime minister referring to his adopted homeland as a land of affliction. In other words, Joseph's sons' names reflect a deep-seated conflict within him. On the one hand, he declares himself happy to have forgotten his parental home; this would seem to imply that he is content with his life in Egypt. But, on the other hand, he still considers Egypt a hostile place notwithstanding his exalted position. Indeed, Joseph appears to be a lonely figure – successful but disenfranchised from both his parental home and his adopted homeland.

The seven plentiful years come to an end and the famine commences, as Pharaoh's dreams had predicted. Due to Joseph's grain storage program, Egypt is the only country in the region that has bread; and Joseph, in charge of grain distribution, becomes food master to the ancient world. This, of course, includes Canaan. So barely skipping a beat the text leaves Egypt and returns to Jacob and his family who are suffering the effects of the famine in Canaan. Short on food, Jacob tells his sons to go to Egypt to purchase grain "that we may live and not die" (42:2). However, he does not allow Benjamin (who he believes is Rachel's only surviving child) to go with his brothers, lest "he meet with disaster" (42:4). Even at this late stage in his life, Jacob is playing favorites, treating Benjamin (who is no infant any longer) as a precious treasure who cannot be risked. This favoritism ultimately plays out as a critical ingredient in the melodrama that Joseph sets in motion when he sees his brothers.

One would have expected that Pharaoh's second-in-command, the head of a gigantic bureaucracy, would not be personally in charge of dispensing the grain as Joseph does to his brothers.

---

14. Joseph's failure to inquire about his father's fate will be discussed below.

Indeed, the Midrash (BR 91:6), recognizing this difficulty, details
the system Joseph had in place to ensure that his brothers would
be recognized as they entered the country and sent to get grain at
a particular storage facility where he would be waiting. The story
is indeed far more dramatic if the brothers seek food directly from
Joseph himself, and that is what happens. Joseph recognizes them
at once, but they have no idea that the haughty Egyptian prince
they confront is really their lost brother. This is not surprising for
aside from aging no fewer than twenty years,[15] Joseph is dressed
in princely robes and speaking in Egyptian. Furthermore, the
brothers are presumably scared out of their wits by this royal audience. Joseph does nothing to calm their nerves when he asks
them where they come from and proceeds to accuse them of es-
pionage. Their response is interesting. After a blanket denial that
they are spies, the brothers (we are not told which one is doing
the talking on behalf of the group) explain that they are sons of
the same father, that there used to be twelve of them but that one
"is no more" (42:13) and one is back home with his father. Joseph
senses an opportunity to see Benjamin (his only full brother),
and, I believe, to test his brothers' character, so (to make a long
story short) he tells them that to prove they are telling the truth
they must return home and bring back their younger brother. In
the meantime, he will keep one brother as a hostage in Egypt.

The brothers have to decide whether to accept Joseph's proposition, and their discussion reveals deep-seated guilt feelings
about how they had treated him. In Joseph's presence (speaking
in Hebrew which they assume he cannot understand)[16] they say

15. Joseph, having entered Pharaoh's service at the age of thirty (41:46) – right before
the plentiful years began– is no less than thirty-seven years old. Assuming that
Joseph was seventeen when he was sold, his brothers would not have seen him in
at least twenty years.
16. The text tells us that the brothers' confidence that they would not be understood
was bolstered by the fact that Joseph was using an interpreter. The midrashists (BR
91:8), continuing their effort to show that Joseph had not abandoned his Jewishness,
speculate that the interpreter was none other than Joseph's older son Manasseh
who, they speculate, had been taught the family language by his father.

to one another: "Alas, we are being punished on account of our brother, because we looked on at his anguish, yet paid no heed as he pleaded with us" (42:21). They believe they are being punished for the way they treated Joseph. Reuben, the oldest, betrays his flawed character by launching into a short "I told you so" speech, in effect reproving them for not having listened to him when he urged them not to harm the boy. Since all Reuben had said was "Shed no blood! Cast him into that pit out in the wilderness, but do not touch him yourselves" (37:22), Reuben's speech in Egypt is not entirely accurate. He had merely told them not to kill Joseph with their own hands but did not attempt to dissuade them from doing Joseph any harm (no matter what his unspoken plans for saving Joseph might have been). Reuben's attempt to rewrite the past in order to aggrandize himself (and thus remain blameless for what happened) shows him to be vain and self-centered.

Joseph is so touched by his brothers' apparent regret that he turns aside and weeps. But he is still not ready to reveal himself. Rather, he has Simeon seized as a hostage and sends the others back to Canaan to get Benjamin.[17] Complicating matters, and, perhaps, testing them further, Joseph does not send them home empty-handed. He orders that their sacks be filled with grain and that their money be secretly returned. I wonder what those Egyptians who knew of these orders thought of Joseph's act of generosity to men he had publicly labeled as spies. We would expect them to think that something strange was going on, but the text reveals no such thoughts on the part of any Egyptians.

The Brothers and Jacob Back in Canaan

The text tells us that on the way back to Canaan one of the brothers opens his sack to get feed for his donkey and discovers that his money has been returned. He expresses his astonishment to his brothers, who, in turn, express their fear that God has it in

---

17. As the Midrash notes (BR 84:16), the selection of Simeon as the hostage suggests that it was he who organized the earlier attempt on Joseph's life.

for them: "What is this that God has done to us?" (42:28). But no one thinks about going back to Egypt to return the money; nor does anyone express the fear that, if they return with Benjamin to redeem Simeon, they will be accused of theft. Indeed, none of the other brothers opens his sack to see if more money had been returned. They just go on their way the next morning as if nothing strange had happened. I do not understand why the text includes this brief vignette; it does not seem to move the plot forward, particularly since, when the brothers get home, they all open their sacks and find the money they had paid. Perhaps these two versions of the finding of the money-bags are the remnants of two separate accounts that have been joined together by the text's redactor. Alternatively, perhaps each account has something slightly different to teach us, but I do not yet know what it is.

Jacob's reaction to his sons' description of what happened in Egypt is remarkably self-centered. Coming awfully close to the truth, he complains (42:36): "It is always me that you bereave: Joseph is no more and Simeon is no more, and now you would take away Benjamin. These things always happen to me!" To quote a popular song, Jacob's refrain is "Everything happens to me!" He sounds a little bit like Charlie Brown. This is not what one would expect from the spiritual forefather of God's holy people. Very little concern for Simeon is expressed; and Jacob does not even seem genuinely concerned about Benjamin's welfare. Jacob only expresses concern for one person, himself.[18] It seems as if as he became older, Jacob lost the vigor of his youth and with it his worldliness and, indeed, some aspect of his essential humanity. It is hard to imagine the Jacob who persistently won his many battles with Laban expressing such self-pity. Perhaps the Torah is

18. Jacob's attitude of self-pity is also revealed later in the story when he meets Pharaoh and in response to Pharaoh's query states that "'Few and hard have been the years of my life, nor do they come up to the life spans of my fathers during their sojourns'" (47:9). His apparent bitterness almost seems excessive given that he has just been reunited with his favorite son, Joseph.

telling us that people do change as they get older, but not always for the better.[19]

Appreciating that the only way to get Simeon released is to return to Egypt with Benjamin in tow, Reuben, the first born, steps forward and assures his father that if Benjamin does not return, Jacob can kill Reuben's two sons. That Reuben could think that a threat to two of Jacob's grandsons would assuage his fears about harm coming to Benjamin is astonishing. It demonstrates yet again the firstborn son's immaturity and unfitness to lead the next generation. Jacob, needless to say, rejects the suggestion, moaning that with Joseph already dead, if Benjamin should also die, he (that is, Jacob) would go "down to Sheol in grief" (43:38).

The phrase "going down to Sheol", which appears to be synonymous with dying, does not seem to describe a fully conceptualized underworld – like the modern Christian and Moslem conceptions of Heaven and Hell or the ancient Egyptians' detailed picture of the realm of the dead – where the surviving soul resides after the body's death. Indeed, an unvarnished reading of the Torah suggests that death is final; the Torah takes no pains to elaborate upon what the dead do after dying. Death is quite simply the indescribable and undescribed state that humans enter when they die. Rabbinic Judaism, of course, posits not only an afterlife – *Olam Haba* or the World to Come – but also the ultimate physical resurrection of the dead.[20] But I find very little eschatology in

---

19. Indeed, while Jacob does seem to have changed, his bitter, accusatory remarks hurled at Laban when they parted (31: 38–42), foreshadow this bitter retrospective on events – almost as if in the thick of things he is a man of action, but afterwards he becomes bitter.

20. The finality of death in the Torah text is a controversial issue. The Talmud (*Sanhedrin* 90a) categorically states that anyone who does not believe that the ultimate resurrection of the dead has been set forth in the Written Torah forfeits his share in the World to Come. Rashi (*ad locum*) emphasizes that even if an individual believes in the resurrection of the dead, but does not believe that it is set forth in the Torah, he forfeits his share in the World to Come. The prooftexts cited by the Talmud seem farfetched and leave me unpersuaded. For a comprehensive discussion of biblical and rabbinic doctrines of death, resurrection, and immortality, see Neil Gillman, *The Death of Death* (Jewish Lights, 2000).

the Torah text itself. To be sure, we are told that Enoch, who had walked with God, was taken by God and was no more – which some have read as suggesting a heavenly ascension rather than earthly death. But the words permit the conclusion that God's "taking" Enoch is merely a metaphor (like "going down to Sheol") for death. In any event, Enoch is unique in the Torah.[21] Nowhere else is there any mention of a person's surviving death – either in this world or the next. This is in stark contrast with Greek mythology, for instance, where heroes enter and leave Hades for a variety of purposes.

The Brothers Return to Egypt: The Final Test

The severity of the famine finally forces Jacob to permit the brothers to return to Egypt. At first he tries one last time to avoid sending Benjamin with them, chastising the brothers for having told Joseph that they had another brother. When Judah finally steps up and takes responsibility for Benjamin's safety, Jacob permits them to depart. Significantly, Judah does not grandstand as Reuben had done; he merely tells his father that he will be responsible and Jacob relents. Having made this painful decision, Jacob bounces back to form displaying a great deal of maturity and wisdom. He sends gifts for Joseph – "some balm and some honey, gum, ladanum, pistachio nuts, and almonds" (43:11)[22] – and insists that the brothers bring twice as much money as they need, so that they can repay the money they found in their sacks if necessary. Finally, he invokes God's blessing on the enterprise and concludes: "As for me, if I am to be bereaved, I shall be bereaved" (43:14). His renewed trust in Divine Providence or, at least, his taking action coupled with a stoic acceptance of his fate, reflects a Jacob we

---

21. If we read the Enoch story as referring to a heavenly ascension, it is a predecessor of Elijah's being taken bodily to Heaven in the biblical book of Kings.
22. It is somewhat strange that the residents of Canaan (who do not have grain for bread and must go to Egypt for food) nonetheless have rare delicacies to send as gifts. Perhaps the text is trying to create a parallel with the gifts Jacob sent Esau in an effort to mollify his anger.

know from his younger years. As with Esau, he sends propitiatory gifts, prays, and prepares to accept the inevitable.

When the brothers arrive in Egypt, Joseph prepares a meal for them in his house. While the text focuses on Joseph and the brothers, I wonder how this looked to Joseph's Egyptian retinue. When they had last seen the brothers, Joseph had accused them of being spies, and now they are being invited to dinner.[23] Are the Egyptian servants aware that something unusual is going on?

The brothers see the invitation as a threat. Remembering that they had left Egypt with both the grain and the money they had paid for it, the brothers surmise that they are being lured into the house to allow the Egyptians to attack them more easily. In an effort to avoid such an attack, they tell Joseph's house steward the whole story. Surprisingly, the Egyptian replies that their (that is, the brothers') god must have put the money in their sacks. Are we to believe that Joseph has been proselytizing his Egyptian servants? It is more likely that, as classic polytheists, the Egyptians recognize that the visitors must have gods of their own with some power to affect their fortunes. Following their conversation with the house steward, Simeon is returned, the brothers are given water to bathe their feet, and they wait for Joseph to appear.

When he arrives, Joseph asks the brothers how their father is. It has been almost twenty years since Joseph has seen his father and at least seven[24] since he became Egypt's prime minister. Yet there is no indication that Joseph has made any effort at all to find out about his doting father, either before the brothers' first arrival or thereafter. It certainly would not have been very difficult for a person in Joseph's position to send someone to discover Jacob's whereabouts and the state of his health. This appears to be another example of the internal conflict raging in Joseph. While he

---

23. That Joseph prepares a meal for the brothers reveals the text's beautiful symmetry. For right after the brothers had put Joseph in the pit, they sat down to lunch.

24. This would assume that we are in only the first of the seven lean years. It may even be a year later, since we know that there were five years of famine remaining when Joseph finally reveals himself to his brothers.

surely has not forgotten who he is, perhaps he is not happy being reminded of it. The question we must ponder is why this is so?[25]

Upon seeing Benjamin, Joseph is so overcome with emotion that he has to leave the room. When he returns, the meal is served. Joseph, the Egyptians, and the brothers dine in three separate groups, since the Egyptians find it abhorrent to have a Hebrew eat with them (44:32). Joseph's existential loneliness is starkly revealed as he can dine neither with the Egyptians nor with his true family. This eating arrangement also underscores an interesting irony in the story. Joseph's unwillingness to share a meal with his brothers might appear to be discourteous from their point of view, but Mishnaic Judaism imposes similar restrictions on observant Jews, prohibiting their dining with non-Jews. Indeed, according to the New Testament (Luke 15), Jesus' willingness to eat with inappropriate people results in serious approbation from the Pharisees. In seating the brothers, Joseph has them seated in order of their age. Furthermore, he provides Benjamin (his only full brother) with a much larger portion of food than anyone else. The Torah

25. Nachmanides (42:9) answers the question of why Joseph did not contact his father by positing that everything Joseph did was guided by his attempt to make the dreams of his youth come true. Contra my claims above, Nachmanides maintains that Joseph understood his dreams and even went so far as not contacting his father when he became grand vizier so that his entire family would eventually bow to him as he had dreamt. On some level he must have felt bad about this, hence the internal conflict. Rabbi Yoel Bin-Nun, a contemporary Israeli scholar, offers a different explanation. He makes the surprising suggestion that all these years Joseph had been under the mistaken impression that his father had sent him into harm's way on purpose. After all, Jacob had not responded to Joseph's dreams enthusiastically, and he must have known how the brothers felt about Joseph; so Joseph concluded that his brothers were not acting of their own accord. His father had ordered his banishment. Bin-Nun's coup de grace is that Joseph finally breaks down and reveals himself to his brothers just after Judah describes his father's reaction to Joseph's disappearance. Until then, Bin-Nun argues, Joseph had not known how Jacob felt. An English translation of this article, which originally appeared in Hebrew in *Megadim* 1:1, can be conveniently found under the title "A Tragic Misunderstanding: Why Did Joseph Not Send Word to His Father?" (trans. Dov Lappin) at the website of Yeshivat Hakibbutz Hadati – Ein Tzurim. The current URL is *http://www.ykd.co.il/english/shiurim/ravyoel_tragic_misunder.htm*.

tells us that the brothers are astonished at how Joseph could know their relative ages.

After the meal, Joseph instructs his servants to fill each of the brothers' sacks with grain and money and to place Joseph's silver goblet in Benjamin's sack. This is obviously an arrangement designed to subject the brothers to a final test of character. When Benjamin is discovered to have the goblet and is accused of theft – which is, of course, what Joseph is planning and what ultimately happens – will the brothers abandon him as they had previously abandoned Rachel's other son, Joseph? Or will they honor their family bonds (and, of course, the pledge they had made to Jacob) and refuse to part from Benjamin?

While returning to Canaan the brothers are accosted on the road by Joseph's servants. They deny everything, and echoing Jacob when a similar claim of theft was made by Laban, declare that "Whichever of your servants it is found with shall die; the rest of us, moreover, shall become slaves to my lord" (44:9). To their horror, the cup is discovered in Benjamin's sack.[26] They are brought back to confront Joseph. At this point it is Judah (the brother who had taken responsibility for Benjamin when Jacob was persuaded to allow him to be brought to Egypt) who takes charge of the family. He tells Joseph that if there is liability for theft of the goblet, it is shared by all of them. But Joseph, testing them to the end, rejects such communal responsibility and announces that only the thief himself (that is, Benjamin) shall be held liable and will have to remain in Egypt as Joseph's slave. Ironically he adds, "the rest of you go back in peace to your father" (44:17). Joseph is really turning the screws. At this critical juncture, the parasha ends.

---

26. It is interesting that Joseph's men identify the cup as the one Joseph used for divination. Of course, divination is forbidden in the Torah, and this would appear to be another layer of disguise designed to make the brothers believe that the Egyptian vizier is, indeed, an Egyptian. Joseph even says to his brothers when they are brought back before him (44:15): "'What is this deed you have done? Do you not know that a man like me practices divination?'"

VAYIGASH

Judah's Oration

This parasha begins with the Torah's first extended speech – a plea by Judah that Joseph show compassion for Benjamin and for his aged father back in Canaan. While we have already witnessed various brief speeches – Abraham's plea for Sodom (in dialogue form) and Jacob's harangue against Laban are examples – this is the first time the Torah provides a verbatim transcript of what in modern legal parlance would be called an oral argument. Judah, having guaranteed Benjamin's safety, uses every ounce of his rhetorical powers to persuade Joseph into letting the youngest brother go free.

Knowing what we know, Judah's speech is a brilliant synthesis of rhetorical skill and psychological manipulation. Judah plays on Joseph's inherent love for his brother and his father. He explains how he was able to persuade Jacob to let Benjamin go to Egypt; that Benjamin is the only surviving offspring of Jacob's favorite wife; that Benjamin's full brother was killed by wild beasts (even though Judah knows full well that this story is not true);[1]

---

1.   As also noted by Rabbi Yoel Bin-Nun above, this appears to be the first time that

213

and that Jacob would surely die if Benjamin were kept captive in Egypt. Finally, Judah offers to stay as a slave in Benjamin's stead.

But if we place ourselves in the grand vizier's position, the brilliance of Judah's oration pales. For all Judah knows, Joseph is an Egyptian prince with no affection for either Benjamin or Jacob. Why would Judah think that his invocation of fatherly concern would have any effect on the Egyptian prime minister? Maybe he senses that Joseph has a unique empathy for others. Or maybe Judah did not choose these words at all; perhaps God put them in his mouth. For God is intent on evoking Joseph's feelings of brotherly love so that Jacob and his family will be brought down to Egypt. Whatever the explanation, Judah's speech is exquisitely crafted and has the desired effect.

It seems clear that the author of the Joseph story has carefully designed the plot to exalt Judah above his brothers. Judah takes charge in rescuing Joseph from the pit; and it is Judah who takes ultimate responsibility for Benjamin, both in convincing Jacob to let him go to Egypt and in persuading Joseph to let him go free. The Judah depicted here is a genuine hero, a suitable role for the eponymous founder of the tribe from which the Davidic monarchic line (and ultimately the Messiah) springs. While Judah has demonstrated similar strength of character earlier in accepting responsibility for his dealings with Tamar, the character portrayed here appears to be even nobler. This suggests that the author of at least one strand of the Joseph novella was associated with the Kingdom of Judah.

Joseph Relents At Last

Joseph can no longer control himself. As soon as Judah asks rhetorically how he can return to his father without Benjamin and declares, "Let me not be witness to the woe that would overtake

---

Joseph learns precisely what his brothers had told Jacob about his disappearance. I wonder whether having told the same lie for so many years, Judah, on some level, has begun to believe it himself.

my father!" (44:34), Joseph cracks. He orders everyone but the brothers to leave the room and starts to cry – with sobs so loud "the Egyptians could hear, and so the news reached Pharaoh's palace" (45:2). Joseph tells the brothers who he is and asks after Jacob's health. The brothers are dumbfounded, shocked into speechlessness. Joseph tells them to approach him and repeats his dramatic revelation again: "I am your brother Joseph" (45:4).[2] Joseph then tells his incredulous brothers that they should not reproach themselves for having sold him into slavery in Egypt because the whole affair was God's doing: "Now, do not be distressed or reproach yourselves because you sold me hither; it was to save life that God sent me ahead of you…. So, it was not you who sent me here, but God" (45:5–8).

Aside from Melchizedek's brief attribution of Abraham's military victory in rescuing Lot to El Elyon (14:20), this is the Torah's first explicit exposition of one of its main themes: everything that happens to human beings on earth (and, in particular, to the Jewish people) is part of a divine plan.[3] Joseph believes that he was sold into slavery in Egypt so that he would be in a position to save not only the Egyptians but his family in Canaan as well from the ravages of famine: "it was to save life that God sent me ahead of you …to ensure your survival on earth, and to save your lives in an extraordinary deliverance" (45:5–7). We, as readers of the Torah, know that the divine plan is even more far-reaching. God's ultimate redemption of Israel from slavery, the revelation

---

2. When Pope John XXIII (Giuseppe – that is, Joseph – Roncalli) met with the Chief Rabbi of Rome and other leaders of the Italian Jewish community, he came down from his papal throne and said "I am your brother Joseph." I have always thought this to be one of the most moving and significant events of the twentieth century in Jewish-Christian relations.

3. God's intervention in human history has, of course, been clear from the very beginning when He banished Adam and Eve from the Garden of Eden, sent the flood, and destroyed the Tower of Babel. The difference between those stories and this one is that in those cases God explicitly takes charge, while here the story seems to be devoid of divine interference. Only after the fact do we learn that God is managing everything from behind the scenes.

of the Torah at Mount Sinai, and the birth of the Jewish nation all require that Jacob's family come to Egypt – an event made possible by the combination of Joseph's sale into slavery, his success in Egypt, and the ensuing years of abundant harvests and devastating Middle Eastern famine.

The Torah's stress on Divine Providence as the moving force in human history leads to a fundamental paradox, for the other pillar on which Judaism is based is humankind's free will. Judaism asserts that human beings have the ability to choose between good and evil and that their choices have consequences. In the context of the Joseph story, this means that the brothers, in deciding to treat Joseph as they did, made a choice; they could have acted otherwise.[4] Of course, had they done so, God's plans would have been foiled, and His declaration to Abraham that his descendants would be enslaved in a foreign land would not have come true – at least not in the way God had, apparently, foreseen. Thus the Joseph story limns Rabbi Akiba's paradox (*Pirkei Avot* 3:19) in bold relief: the omniscient deity foresees all, yet there is free will to act. The simplest resolution to this dilemma is to posit that free will exists, but the omniscient deity knows in advance exactly what choices will be made. In some mysterious way, His foreknowledge on one plane does not affect our free will on another.

Such a resolution of Akiba's paradox is all fine and good when people act positively; however, when people like Joseph's brothers act badly, the question of theodicy raises it head. For, problematically, if we posit that God is aware of humankind's evil intentions, or that they are even part of the divine plan, this renders God complicit in or even responsible for the evil human beings do. For instance, philosophically speaking one would have to ac-

---

4. Indeed Israel's exile after the destruction of the Temple in 586 BCE is explicitly presented by the *Tanakh* as a result of the Jewish people's choice to forsake God. Had the Jewish people not made that fatal choice, the exile would not have occurred. Even today Jews utter the prayer "But because of our sins, we have been exiled from our land…We cannot ascend to appear and to prostrate ourselves before You" (Mussaf for the Pilgrim Festivals).

knowledge that the Nazi Holocaust and the Darfur genocide (to name but two horrific examples of man's inhumanity to man) were not just a result of free will gone awry.[5] Rather, God either chose not to prevent them or they were part of His plan. This paints a very unpleasant image of our omnipotent and omniscient God.[6] In short, read from this perspective, the Joseph story raises the theological problem of theodicy every bit as much as the book of *Job* does.

Having publicly forgiven his brothers and attempted to ease their angst, Joseph sends them back to Canaan with instructions to bring Jacob and the rest of the clan to Egypt where they will reside in Goshen (apparently an area appropriate for shepherding, since Joseph clearly expects them to bring their flocks with them). Joseph explains that there are still five years of famine left and promises that he will take care of the family. Joseph is apparently concerned that Jacob will not agree to come, for he repeatedly tells the brothers to assure their father that he is in Egypt and that he is in charge. Perhaps he is afraid that Jacob will not agree to leave the Promised Land unless this is clearly God's will. Joseph's miraculous climb to power should prove this to Jacob.

Underscoring his authority, Joseph issues this invitation to his family without getting Pharaoh's approval; clearly he is con-

5. David Weiss Halivni, an Orthodox Talmud scholar and an Auschwitz survivor, attempts to resolve this paradox by adopting a concept derived from Lurianic Kabbalah. He asserts that God is continuously expanding and contracting and that His presence in the world swings like a pendulum closer to humankind and then farther away. For Halivni, it was during a period when God's presence was at a faraway apogee that the evil perpetrated by the Nazis was able to occur. See Halivni, *Breaking the Tablets: Jewish Theology After the Shoah* (Roman and Littlefield, 2007).

6. The simplest way of solving this problem is to posit that God is either not omnipotent or not omniscient, but the *Tanakh* clearly rejects this possibility. Other scholars have argued that in order for God to truly let free will operate, He must allow evil to happen as well. We have no objection to God's allowing human beings to freely do good (and reward them for this), so it is disingenuous – though understandable – for us to complain when He allows human beings to commit evil (and punishes them for it).

fident in his authority and certain that the ruler of Egypt will not object. And, indeed, Pharaoh does not. When he learns that Joseph's brothers are in Egypt, Pharaoh is pleased and instructs Joseph to send for his father, promising to give the Israelites the best of the land. In fact, he provides the brothers with wagons for the move. Joseph gives all the brothers provisions for the journey and new clothes, but he showers Benjamin with additional wealth and several changes of clothing. This blatant favoritism echoes Jacob's favoring Joseph – the tragic mistake that set the entire chain of events into motion. Perhaps this is Joseph's final test to see whether the brothers' jealousy – at the heart of their relationship with Rachel's sons– has finally been erased. Joseph also sends gifts for his father and food for Jacob's return trip. Before the brothers leave, Joseph instructs them not to be "quarrelsome on the way" (45:24) – a strange instruction indeed. Rashi (45:24) tells us that Joseph tried to remind the brothers not to blame each other for what had taken place years earlier. Indeed, such a resurfacing of their repressed emotions would certainly not be unexpected. Even though Joseph has already explained that everything happened as God planned it, he is evidently worried that the brothers will still blame each other. Indeed, he has already witnessed Reuben's "I told you so" speech.

Jacob Descends to Egypt

Jacob reacts with disbelief to the news that Joseph is alive and a mighty figure in Egypt. It is only when he sees the wagons full of provisions that he believes what his sons are telling him. The patriarch's intense desire to see Joseph again motivates him to make the trip. When the caravan arrives in Beersheva, Jacob offers a sacrifice and has another epiphany. In God's last reported direct appearance to a human until Moses' confrontation with divinity at the burning bush, God tells Jacob that he should not be afraid to go to Egypt because he will found a great nation there. God further reassures Jacob that he will be with him and will bring him (that is, his descendants, the Israelites) back to the Promised

Land. One can question whether the precise terms of this prophecy come true. The slaves that Moses leads out of Egypt are not yet a nation; they become one at Sinai. But on the whole, God's reassurance is a sound one and accomplishes its task. The text tells us in the next verse that Jacob leaves Beersheva. Yet again Jacob is leaving the Promised Land and setting out from Beersheva. This clearly echoes the earlier text (in *Vayetze*) that describes the first time Jacob left Canaan. Perhaps the Torah is using this device to frame Jacob's saga, which is marked by his wandering from place to place.

As Jacob leaves Canaan, the Torah takes the opportunity to list the members of his growing family. This includes "his sons and grandsons, his daughters and granddaughters" (46:7). Since the only daughter previously mentioned was the ill-fated Dinah, the text seems to be suggesting that Jacob had at least one more daughter. We are not expressly told whether this child was Leah's, Zilpah's, or Bilhah's, nor are we given her name.[7] The Midrash (BR 94:9) explains that Yocheved, the daughter of Levi and mother of Moses, was born as the caravan entered Egypt. This is supported by the verse in *Bamidbar* 26:59 that explicitly states that she was born in Egypt. The Talmud (*Sotah* 12a), smoothing over the contradiction regarding her place of birth, declares she was conceived outside of Egypt and born in Egypt. So she is not listed by name, but she was part of the family that went to Egypt.

The text declares that "the total of Jacob's household who came to Egypt was seventy persons" (46:27). This does not include Jacob, his wives, or "the wives of Jacob's sons" (46:26). It only includes Jacob's progeny: his sons, his grandsons, Dinah, and, apparently, Yocheved, for without her we only reach a total of sixty-nine.[8] Curiously, this list seems to contradict the midrashic

---

7.   We know that Rachel had only the two children, Joseph and Benjamin, before her death. Presumably if she had given birth to another child, even a girl, we would have been told.

8.   There is a slight discrepancy in the number of offspring accounted for by Leah and her children. The text enumerates thirty-four individuals, including Dinah. None-

tradition mentioned above that Jacob's sons married their half sisters; for if this were so, they should also have been included in the list of Jacob's descendants. This discrepancy forces Rashi (46:26) to suggest that the half sisters died in Canaan; however, Nachmanides (46:15) argues that the fact that the verse explicitly excludes the brothers' wives from the list proves that they must have been Jacob's daughters, for otherwise they would have been excluded by virtue of their not being Jacob's descendants. According to Nachmanides, the half sisters remain anonymous for the same undisclosed reason as before. The list of the seventy family members who came to Egypt at Joseph's invitation presages the list of Jacob's sons that opens the next book of the Pentateuch and serves as a sort of bridge to the Torah's second volume, even though the first book is not quite over.

When the caravan arrives in Goshen, Joseph is there to meet them, Jacob having sent Judah ahead to summon him. Joseph greets his father, and Jacob after much joyful weeping gives us another glimpse of his rather bitter mindset: "Now I can die, having seen for myself that you are alive" (46:30). While this may have been a conventional way of declaring how happy he was, Jacob again seems to focus on the negative. Why not say, "Now I can live a full and rich life surrounded by all my children and grandchildren"?

Signaling the difficulty of the clan's move to Egypt, Joseph tells his family that "all shepherds are abhorrent to Egyptians"

---

theless, the verse clearly states that Leah's offspring totaled thirty-three. Clearly, we can subtract Er and Onan from the sum total (since although they were listed, they are dead) dropping the total (including Dinah) to thirty-two. However, this still contradicts the sum total of thirty-three mentioned in the verse. The midrashists solve this puzzle by positing (as noted in the text above) that Yocheved, Moses' mother, was born just as her parents were entering Egypt. Problematically, this would mean that Yocheved was certainly long past her childbearing years (perhaps, she was even hundreds of years old) when she gave birth to Moses, who was eighty years old when he led the Israelites out of Egypt. The text makes no mention of Moses' miraculous conception and birth, so this is unlikely. Nachmanides (46:15) discusses this problematic midrash at length.

(46:34) and advises his brothers to tell Pharaoh that the family has bred livestock for generations. This is what they tell Pharaoh when they meet. I do not quite understand how this solves the problem. Are livestock breeders different than shepherds? Does the profession's having been in the family for generations ennoble it? Either way, the family has taken up residence in a land where its profession and, by extension, the clan itself, are looked down upon, a potential recipe for disaster. In any event, the statement apparently satisfies Pharaoh, who invites the brothers to stay in Goshen and even invites them to be in charge of his royal livestock.[9]

At this point, Joseph brings his father into Pharaoh's presence. Pharaoh asks Jacob his age and he replies that he is "one hundred and thirty. [He adds that] Few and hard have been the years of my life, nor do they come up to the life of my fathers during their sojourns" (47:9). Jacob/Israel, now in advanced old age, has been transformed from a trickster into a kvetch – two of the numerous stereotypes the world has fastened on Jews throughout the centuries. Interestingly, Jacob makes no mention of God during his interview with Pharaoh; however, given his negative take on his life, perhaps this is for the best.

Joseph the Provider

The text now gives us a detailed description of the manner in which Joseph goes about the business of managing Egypt's food supply during the remaining five years of the famine. In a nutshell, since he possesses the only grain stores in Egypt or Canaan, he takes advantage of the opportunity to enrich Pharaoh and to nationalize Egypt's agriculture. At first he collects "all the money that was to be found in the land of Egypt and in the land of Canaan" (47:14). Then, when the Egyptian people run out of money, Joseph accepts their other assets, particularly livestock, as payment.

---

9. Chillingly, for anyone who has read the next book of the Bible, the area of Goshen in which the clan settles is Ramses. Not that far into the future, the Israelite slaves will build a storehouse city for Pharaoh in Ramses.

When these are depleted as well, he allows the Egyptians to deed their farmland and themselves to Pharaoh, generously allowing them to keep four-fifths of their crop yield and give only one-fifth to Pharaoh. In a few short years, Pharaoh owns all the farmland in Egypt and the people are his serfs. Only the priests are left with property of their own.[10]

Joseph's family, however, is not subjected to this ignominy. Joseph does not require Jacob's clan to give the government their property in exchange for food. The result is that the Israelites acquire substantial property in Goshen and are fertile to boot, increasing greatly. Thus the Torah plants the seeds of what will ultimately become the Israelites' downfall. Joseph's generosity provides the Egyptians – not that far into the future – with an excuse to enslave the people who, they say, are increasing at a rate that threatens their hosts. This of course is all part of God's plan; however, on the earthly plane we see an early example of xenophobia, jealousy, and fear fuelling hatred of the Jews.

---

10. The text also reports that Joseph engaged in a massive population transfer, although it explains neither how this was done nor the reason for it. Perhaps Joseph feared that once the famine was over people would feel entitled to regain their ancestral lands. By moving them off their lands, he ensured that they would not be as attached to the new land they were farming as Pharaoh's serfs.

VAYECHI

Jacob on his Deathbed – Joseph and his Sons

The final parasha of *Bereshit* returns our focus from Joseph to Jacob. The Torah tells us that the patriarch lived seventeen years in Egypt and reached the age of one hundred and forty-seven. In a typically biblical manner (echoing Isaac's blessing scene, although Isaac is not on his deathbed) Jacob recognizes that he is about to die and asks Joseph to visit him. He makes Joseph promise that he will bury him in the cave of Machpelah in Hebron where Abraham, Sarah, Isaac, Rebecca, and Leah are interred. Jacob, not satisfied with Joseph's agreement, makes him take a solemn oath to carry out his promise.[1] At the end of this episode, "Israel bowed at the head of the bed" (47:31).

This is a strange scene. Why should Jacob require his beloved favorite son – who, it should be remembered, happens to be second-in-command of the greatest political power in the ancient world – to take an oath to comply with his father's dying wish? Wouldn't he expect Joseph to do what any decent child would do

---

1. Like Eliezer who swore by placing his hand under Abraham's thigh, Joseph does the same with Jacob.

223

in the circumstances? The Torah seems to be emphasizing the importance of Jacob's burial in the Holy Land. For the patriarch who carries the tribal covenantal promise that his descendants will inherit the Promised Land, goodwill and respect for parents is not enough. Perhaps Jacob is afraid that notwithstanding Joseph's devotion, something may prevent him from going to Canaan. The Talmud (*Sotah* 36b) suggests that without an oath Pharaoh might have prevented Joseph from making the trip, lest he decide to remain in the Holy Land. But I discern a more disturbing undercurrent in Jacob's demand for an oath. Perhaps he perceives how torn Joseph is between being the good Israelite and the assimilated Egyptian nobleman. Jacob may well be concerned that after he is gone Joseph will no longer care about the family's divine mission. If that is the case, requiring a solemn oath could be designed to impress upon Joseph the importance that burial at Machpelah (and the whole notion of the Promised Land) has to his father. Indeed, perhaps Joseph took this lesson to heart because, when he was on his own deathbed, he made his brothers swear to take his bones up out of Egypt (50:24–25).

What are we to make of the statement that after the oath is administered Jacob "bowed at the head of the bed"? Was he bowing to Joseph? That, of course, would fulfill the prophecy set forth in Joseph's childhood dream, but it does not make much sense in the deathbed context. Joseph's role in this scene is that of a dutiful child, not that of an Egyptian prince; the patriarch would hardly follow such an interaction with an act of obeisance. It makes more sense to read this sentence as reflecting Jacob's bowing to God, as if to say that after a lifetime of struggle and wavering faith in Divine Providence,[2] Jacob has finally submitted totally to the deity; he has lived his life and is ready to pass the family heritage on to

---

2. It should be recalled that on his way to Haran, in flight from Esau, Jacob promised to honor God only if God took care of him.

the next generation, led by Joseph – or, more precisely, as we shall see, by Joseph's sons and by Judah.[3]

What follows is another deathbed scene (as if the first came from a different source). Bridging the two is the curious phrase "and after these things had come to pass" (48:1), the same phrase used to introduce the Akedah. Whether the phrase is just meant to be an unremarkable segue linking the two juxtaposed events or is referring to some other events not mentioned in the text depends upon one's interpretive perspective. In this case, the phrase does not seem to hold any special import. Joseph is informed that his father is ill and brings his two sons, Manasseh and Ephraim, to see their grandfather. Jacob proceeds to give Joseph (apparently not noticing that his grandsons are there) a brief history lesson detailing his relationship with God, the promise of the Holy Land to his progeny, and the event that most affected his later life – Rachel's death on the road to Efrat (in what the text identifies as present-day Bethlehem). He formally adopts Joseph's sons as his own – "Now, your two sons, who were born to you in the land of Egypt, shall be mine" (48:5) – implying that the reason for his so doing is somehow connected with Rachel's premature death and her burial in Bethlehem. His deathbed adoption has an important consequence. The twelve tribes of Israel now become thirteen, the tribe of Joseph being replaced by those of Manasseh and Ephraim.[4] Significantly, the adoption also removes whatever stigma Manasseh and Ephraim's tribes might bear by virtue of Joseph's wife having been an Egyptian; since they are now Jacob's adopted sons, Asenat is no longer their *de jure* mother, Rachel is. And that turns out to be significant in the future, when Ephraim

3. While God, of course, is everywhere, the Rabbis (*Nedarim* 40b) learned from this verse that God is particularly present above the bed of a sick person. This reminds us of God's visiting Abraham when he was recovering from his circumcision.

4. Since the tribe of Levi has sacerdotal functions and does not receive any land after the conquest of Canaan, the Holy Land will be divided into twelve portions, with Manasseh and Ephraim each receiving one.

becomes the eponymous leading tribe in the Kingdom of Israel, a political entity often referred to as Ephraim.

Having finished his conversation with Joseph, Jacob finally notices the two young men Joseph has brought with him. Jacob asks who they are, and upon being told that they are Joseph's sons, Manasseh and Ephraim, he wishes to bless them. Like his father before him, Jacob's eyesight has weakened with age; Joseph places the two boys before him, placing Manasseh (the elder) to Jacob's right and Ephraim to his left. But Jacob crosses his hands, placing his right hand on Ephraim's head, even though he is the younger of the two. With his hands on his grandsons' heads, Jacob blesses them, invoking God's earlier blessings and promises to Abraham and Isaac. In doing so, he passes on the family's blessing and tradition to the next generation (the grandsons having, by adoption, been promoted to Joseph's generation as sons of Jacob).

It is noteworthy that, while the blessing itself is directed to Manasseh and Ephraim, the introductory text states that Jacob is blessing Joseph: "And he blessed Joseph, saying" (48:15). In a way, of course, this is most perceptive, since no one can have a greater blessing than that his children be blessed. However, the real insight contained in this "slip of the tongue" is that Joseph really is the one being blessed. After all, Jacob did not even notice Manasseh and Ephraim when they arrived or recognize them afterwards. For Jacob, the youths' sole import is that they are Joseph's sons. Indeed, in giving Joseph this blessing (and adopting his two sons), Jacob has officially declared Joseph the firstborn – the recipient of the double portion – and the inheritor of the Abrahamic covenant.

Ironically, Joseph (who has just superseded all of his older brothers) points out that Jacob has crossed his hands, for Manasseh is the older and should have Jacob's right hand placed on his head. But Jacob insists that "his younger brother shall be greater than he, and his offspring shall be plentiful enough for nations" (48:19). Jacob then announces that in the future the people of Israel will bless their children using the following words, "God make you like Ephraim and Manasseh" (48:20). That formula is used to this day to bless children on the eve of Shabbat and *Yamim Tovim* (holidays), followed by the familiar priestly blessing set forth later in the Torah. This is not a ritual that was observed by my parents when my brother and I were children; nor did my wife and I observe it. But both of my sons have adopted it for their children. It is a beautiful and moving ceremony.

If adopting Joseph's two sons was not enough of a hint, Jacob concludes his blessing by expressly giving Joseph a double portion of the family inheritance, thereby making him the eldest as a matter of law: "I assign to you one portion more than to your brothers, which I wrestled from the Amorites with my sword and bow" (48:22). I read this to mean that the sons of Leah and the two handmaidens do not really matter to Jacob; to his dying day, his true wife was Rachel and her firstborn was his firstborn as well.[5]

Jacob Blesses the Tribes of Israel

Having given the real family blessing to Joseph and his sons, Jacob then calls all his sons to his bedside for yet a third deathbed scene – this time entailing the patriarch's blessing of each of his twelve sons. These blessings are set forth in elevated, poetic verse. Jacob dramatically announces that he will tell his sons what is to become of them (that is of the tribes descended from them) in the future. However, the blessings are less a prophetic foretelling of the future and more a description of the character traits the sons (and by extension their descendants) possess. Indeed, to a large degree describing Jacob's parting words as "blessings" is somewhat of a misnomer. Given the complexity and length of Jacob's words, I limit myself to a few comments on their substance.

Reuben, the eldest, is called to task for having slept with his father's concubine and is stripped of the firstborn's rights as a re-

---

5.   We thus have two more examples here of younger sons being favored over older ones – Ephraim takes Manasseh's place as the favored grandson and Joseph takes Reuben's as firstborn of the clan. Likewise, Rachel supersedes Leah. Given Jacob's clear show of favoritism, it is no wonder that Reuben brought his mother mandrakes and took Bilhah to bed, and that Simeon spearheaded the sale of Joseph.

sult. Simeon and Levi are castigated for their excessive violence and lawlessness, an obvious reference to their massacre of the men of Shechem. Apparently, in an attempt to minimize their potential for violence, Jacob declares: "I will divide them in Jacob, scatter them in Israel" (49:7). That, of course, is an accurate description of what ultimately happens after the conquest of Canaan. Levi, as the sacerdotal tribe, receives no tribal territory, and instead is assigned special cities throughout the country; Simeon, according to some scholars, is ultimately assimilated into Judah. But I wonder whether one can fairly describe Levi's future treatment as penal. Not only do Moses (the only human being to ever speak with God face to face) and Aaron (the paradigmatic high priest) stem from that tribe, but the Levite cities scattered throughout the country and the priests and the Levites themselves run the religious life of the country. In essence, the Israelite religion becomes, in many ways, the sacrificial cult run by the Levitical priesthood. Although I am unaware of any scholarly support for this position, I wonder whether the author of this blessing was a member of an anti-priestly faction.

Judah's blessing is an interesting one. He is described as "a lion's whelp" (49:9), a metaphor that ultimately metamorphosed into the Lion of Judah, a symbol of the Davidic monarchy. Jacob curiously declares that "the scepter shall not depart from Judah... until Shiloh comes" (49:10), whatever that means.[6] Christians read the reference as Christological, suggesting that with the advent of Jesus there will no longer be any need of the Davidic monarchy. Other readings suggest that Shiloh is the name of the city in Ephraim's territory where the Ark of the Covenant resided before David brought it to Jerusalem. If so, the verse might be stating that the tribe of Judah will continue to rule until it reaches Shiloh, that is until (and after) it rules over Ephraim's territory as well.

6. This is my own translation. As I note in the text below, the New JPS translation irons out this ambiguity by translating the verse: "The scepter shall not depart from Judah...So that tribute shall come to him".

Other scholars emend the problematic word *Shiloh* to read *shai lo* (tribute to him), thus changing the verse to mean that Judah will rule and tribute will be brought to him. However it is read, the import of the blessing is clear: the Jewish monarchy will stem from Judah.

The territory of Zebulun is said to be "a haven for ships" (49:13), apparently predicting that Zebulun's descendants will be shipbuilders or sailors, living on the coast; Issachar is described as a donkey and his descendants predicted to be serfs toiling the land; Dan is a serpent and Gad shall be a raider. Naphtali is described as a deer that gives birth to lovely fawns; and Benjamin is a ravenous wolf consuming his foes. The longest and most complex of the blessings (with the possible exception of Judah's) is the one given to Joseph.[7] He is described as a wild ass under assault that with God's help withstands its attackers. God, in this blessing, is described as "the Mighty One of Jacob" and "the Shepherd, the Rock of Israel" (49:24). Jacob says of Joseph that God blesses him and that Jacob's blessing of him will surpass the blessings of Jacob's ancestors, whatever that exactly means.

I have not done justice to Jacob's blessing of his sons. The poetry has a strongly evocative ring that I fear is not captured in an English translation. Furthermore, the ambiguity occasioned by the elevated Hebrew and poetic allusions leave Jacob's blessing very much open to interpretation. Uniquely difficult to understand in the original Hebrew, much is lost in translation. However, the blessings' general intent is clear. With the conclusion of these blessings and a few final instructions about burial procedures, the last of the patriarchs draws his feet into his bed, breathes his last, and dies. Notably, his very last words seem to have been intended to emphasize the crucial importance of his burial in the cave of Machpelah in Canaan, the land of his forefathers.

---

7. While Jacob has formally adopted Manasseh and Ephraim, they are not included in the blessings given to Jacob's twelve biological sons; their father apparently receives it for them.

Joseph orders that his father's body be embalmed, a process that takes forty days. This is interesting because it reflects an Egyptian custom that Jewish law (of course, not yet formulated) strictly prohibits. After the embalming is completed, Joseph petitions Pharaoh for the right to take the body to Canaan for burial. Why Pharaoh has to be asked for permission is interesting. One would expect that such a brief and important trip would not require special permission. Perhaps Joseph felt that his duties in distributing food to the populace were such that he could not just leave without obtaining permission. Or maybe a trip abroad, by definition, required that certain protocol be followed and certain security be put in place for the second-in-command of Egypt. Indeed, as we shall see, the burial procession from Egypt to the land of Canaan was a grand undertaking.

In any event, Pharaoh approves of the trip, and Joseph heads north with a full entourage of dignitaries, his brothers, his household, and the rest of Jacob's household. At Goren ha-Atad (which is beyond the Jordan River), a formal memorial service of some kind is held, and then the brothers head for Hebron to bury the patriarch in the cave of Machpelah. Following this, the entire entourage returns to Egypt.

The Death of Joseph

With Jacob gone, the brothers' old fear that Joseph will take revenge reawakens. So they send a messenger to him, stating that Jacob himself had left instructions begging Joseph to "'Forgive... the offense and guilt of your brothers who treated you so harshly'" (50:17). Furthermore, they fling themselves before Joseph offering to be his slaves. Joseph reassures them that there is no reason to be concerned; he will continue to support them and their children. He does not see himself as a substitute for God (implying that God will mete out whatever punishment they deserve, not him), and he believes that while they intended to harm him, "God intended it for good" (50:20). So they should have no fear.

There is no evidence, aside from the brothers' testimony, that

Jacob gave any such instructions to his sons. Indeed, there is no evidence that Jacob ever found out about the brothers' crime. Presumably the brothers would not have told him, and Joseph would only have broken his heart by doing so. So probably he never found out.[8] This notwithstanding, clearly the brothers were not sure that Joseph harbored no ill will. I get the sense that they were convinced it was necessary to invoke the patriarch's authority in order to prevent Joseph's retribution. But, of course, Joseph needed no such prodding. At this stage of his life, whatever internal conflict Joseph may have had in the past about his Israelite origin, he is now fully a member of the clan, indeed, its head. Given this, it makes good sense to believe that he has buried the hatchet.

Bereshit ends with Joseph's death. He lives to the age of one hundred and ten, and enjoys the presence of not only Manasseh and Ephraim's children but of their children's children as well.[9] At least some of his brothers survive him. For, just as his father demanded of him, he makes his brothers swear that when God returns them (or, implicitly, their descendants) to the Promised Land, they will take his bones with them. That promise outlives all of Jacob's sons and is only fulfilled during the course of the Exodus years later. Joseph, like Jacob, is embalmed. However, unlike his father, he is placed in a coffin in Egypt. As the book ends, Joseph has fulfilled his dreams, but he has never managed to get home. That will be part of the tale told in the next book of *Shemot*.

---

8.   On the other hand, since Joseph was alive, he was obviously not devoured by a wild beast; Jacob might well wonder how so much blood got on Joseph's tunic.
9.   I wonder whether Joseph's sons married Israelites or Egyptians.

EPILOGUE

In the course of the book of *Bereshit*, the Torah has traced the prehistory of the world and the early history of the people of Israel – from the creation story to Jacob's descent into Egypt. Despite the interesting narrative, the fascinating personalities etched in the course of its telling, and its consistent theme favoring younger siblings over their elders, *Bereshit* is in essence an elaborate introduction to the fundamental story to be told in the book of *Shemot*. It is with the Exodus (demonstrating to the world God's power and His proclivity to intervene in human history) and the revelation at Sinai (bringing to a climax the relationship with Abraham's progeny and establishing Israel as a nation of priests with a universal mission) that the Torah reaches its apex and, indeed, its raison d'etre. Whether the Abraham, Isaac, and Jacob stories constitute history as we understand it hardly matters. Their sagas provide the reader with the "historical" predicate necessary to comprehend the Exodus and Sinai, events at the core of what is to become the Jewish idea – that God is at work on the stage of history and Israel has a unique role to play in His production.

CHAZAK